The Royal Society of Medicine
Guide to

HEALTH IN
LATER LIFE

The Royal Society of Medicine
Guide to

HEALTH IN
LATER LIFE

Robert M Youngson

BLOOMSBURY

First published in 1997

Bloomsbury Publishing Plc
38 Soho Square
London, W1V 5DF

A copy of the CIP entry for this book is available from the British Library

ISBN 0 7475 3250 8

10 9 8 7 6 5 4 3 2 1

Designed by Neysa Moss
Typeset by Hewer Text Composition Services, Edinburgh
Printed in Great Britain by Clays Ltd, St Ives plc

Contents

To Muriel and Eric –
who were the orginal inspiration for this book

Introduction

One of the most damaging conventions of contemporary Western society is the widely held notion that there is a pattern of behaviour to which people of a particular age should conform. This ageist stereotype has it that, at a certain chronological age, often arbitrarily set at 60 or 65, people become unemployable, sexually incapable, possibly demented, and should retire from everything, including life. If this stereotype is true, the Western world is going to be in a parlous state in a couple of decades or so. Fortunately, as this book amply shows, it is nonsense. Vigorous opposition to this unthinking bias is vital for the future wellbeing of our whole society, and, on a personal level, is vital for the health of the over-50 population. That opposition is one of the central features of this book.

In the year 1900, less than 1 per cent of the population of the world was over the age of 65. By 1992, 6.2 per cent were in this age group. It is estimated that by the year 2050 some 20 per cent of the total world population will be over 65. In the face of this unprecedented population shift many attitudes will have to be rethought, many prejudices abandoned and many social, economic and political dogmas overturned. The process is already underway. Employers are gradually beginning to recognize the wastefulness of discarding mature, experienced and highly trained workers at an arbitrary retiring age on the basis of questionable youth-oriented ideologies. And with the shift in the weighting of Western populations and the growing affluence of the middle classes, ever more economic power is passing into the hands of the elderly. Ageism is taking its place alongside all the other -isms that are currently being proscribed.

But fairness to the elderly is not the central issue. The real concern, which is growing more widespread with the passage of every decade, is the quality of life of those who have reached the so-called Third Age. These years should be our best, not our worst, and we now possess most of the knowledge – medical, psychological, philosophical, biographical and historical – needed to make them so for the great majority of us. This book is an attempt to bring together in a single volume all this vital knowledge.

Dr R. M. Youngson, London, 1997

chapter one

The Science of Ageing

M̲ost people think that the human lifespan is steadily increasing. In fact, this is not so. There is no indication that the natural span of human life – about 100 years – is lengthening. What is happening is that more of us are getting near to, or reaching, this normal upper age limit. Life expectancy is increasing because medical and technological advances are enabling an increasing proportion of people to avoid death before reaching the full span. Today, in Western societies, for the first time in history, most people can look forward with reasonable confidence to growing old.

What is ageing?

Experts disagree on this question. In spite of a great deal of research and the development of a completely new biological discipline known as gerontology (the scientific study of old age and the process of ageing), there are still arguments even on the fundamentals of the subject. Some take the straightforward view that ageing is no more than the totality of all the unrepaired damage to cells and tissues suffered during life. Such accumulated damage is clearly an important element in ageing, but it is not the whole story.

The idea that there is a single gene for ageing has also now been dismissed; although never a particularly plausible notion, it was widely held by biologists up to the end of the 1970s. Advances in the understanding of molecular biology have swept away such an inadequate concept. It used to be believed that ageing was programmed into the genes to eliminate old people who were simply a drain on the resources of the young. This idea, too, has been largely rejected: it does not fit modern notions of evolution.

One central factor in ageing is the number of times our body cells can divide and so reproduce themselves, so that tissue damage from wear and tear may be repaired. This process of cell replication is going on all the time in our bodies at different rates in different types of cell. Those in the reproductive organs, and those subject to most wear and tear (such as those of the skin or the lining of the bowel) require the most frequent division. This subject is covered on pp. 6–10, but it must be said here that any serious consideration of current theories of ageing must involve detailed reference to genetics. And for such consideration to be meaningful and interesting, a basic understanding of this important subject is necessary. From the standpoint of molecular biology – of what actually happens inside cells – genetics has become the major growth area of biological science and it is clear that however many causes there are of ageing, the most important are genetically determined. The same goes for the development of cancer, an age-related disease. Here is a short account of the way modern biological scientists think about genetics. Much of what follows will make little sense to most readers without this basic knowledge.

Molecular cell biology

A molecule is a collection of atoms – from two up to a million or so – stuck together in various ways and combinations and capable of existing independently. So 'molecular' simply means 'relating to a molecule or molecules'. Every living cell in the body has a central zone called the nucleus. This contains a long, thin, double helix, or twisted ladder, molecule of the substance DNA (deoxyribonucleic acid). The sides of the ladder are made of sugar and phosphate molecules and the rungs are made of pairs of simple molecules called bases. These bases are important as they form the genetic code. There are four of them – guanine (G), cytosine (C), adenine (A) and thymine (T). These four base molecules are of different lengths so there is only one way they can join in pairs to form equal-length ladder rungs. Guanine always links with cytosine, and adenine always links with thymine.

A gene is a length of DNA or, more precisely, a particular sequence of bases. The genetic code is concerned with forming proteins – large molecules consisting of long chains of simple 'building blocks' known as amino acids. There are 20 different amino acids and cells are full of them, dissolved in the cell fluid. The genetic code consists of sequences of bases taken three at a time. Each of these sets of three bases (triplets) provides a code that tells the cell to select a particular amino acid. But because there are only 20 amino acids and 64 combinations of bases taken three at a time, most of the amino acids have more than one triplet code. Thus both CTT and CTC code for the amino acid glutamic acid, and GCT and GCC code for the amino acid arginine. So a gene is a sequence of bases which, taken three at a time, specifies which amino acids to select and in what order, to form a particular protein. A change in a single amino acid, or a change in the position of a single amino acid, produces a different protein. This fact has major genetic implications.

The main building materials of the body, especially the strong structural protein collagen, are one class of proteins. Another important class – the soluble proteins known as enzymes – perform an equally vital function.

Enzymes

Enzymes are the remarkable catalysts that make it possible for thousands of different essential chemical reactions to occur in the body at normal body temperatures. There are many thousands of different enzymes, each with a specific function, and the great majority of the 100,000 or so different genes lying along the DNA molecule code for enzymes. Very little can happen in the body without enzyme activity and it is really the enzymes that determine the kind of bodies we have.

In addition to genes coding for structural proteins and for enzymes, some of the genes code for non-enzyme proteins whose function is to 'switch on' or 'switch off' other genes.

A gene mutation is any change in its sequence of bases. This can be a substitution of one base for another, or the absence or addition of a base. Obviously, the latter kind of mutation makes an enormous difference to the gene because all the bases beyond the affected point are shifted back or forward one place, thereby changing the values of all the triplets. Such a gene produces a defective enzyme – usually one that does not work. Many hereditary diseases result from inherited mutations of this kind. A mutation involving the substitution of a base results in a protein with the wrong amino acid at one point. This may be trivial or serious. For example, sickle cell anaemia – the serious genetic blood disorder that affects thousands of African people and their descendants – is the result of a mutation that causes the substitution of a single wrong amino acid for the correct one.

When cells divide, the DNA must replicate so that both daughter cells get the same DNA. This occurs by virtue of the ability of bases to link together. First, the DNA slits longitudinally down the middle of the rungs of the ladder, so that the base pairs separate. Because cell fluids contain millions of copies of the four bases, there are always plenty to link up with the exposed bases. In this way, each half of the ladder forms complete new rungs of base pairs. At the same time the sugar and phosphate ladder sides link up. The result is two new strands of DNA, one for each daughter cell.

Proteins are not formed directly on DNA. For a particular gene to produce its specific protein, the length of DNA containing the gene splits open with separation of its base pairs, in the same way as occurs for replication. An enzyme in the cell causes free bases to attach to the free ends of the half rungs. The bases link up as described above and a sugar-phosphate backbone is added, but there is one difference. The strand formed is called RNA and the cell has to know the difference between RNA and DNA. So instead of thymine, a different base called uracil is used. The new strand of RNA now separates from the DNA which closes up again. The RNA strand passes out through one of the many gaps in the membrane around the nucleus and moves into the general fluid of the cell. There it meets a body called a ribosome, one of thousands. Ribosomes move along RNA templates, reading the code and selecting and linking together the appropriate amino acids from the cell fluid to form the proteins. This remarkable process is going on all the time in most of our body cells.

Key definitions in genetics

Autosomal Relating to chromosomes other than the sex chromosomes.
Chromosome A length of DNA coiled and recoiled so densely that it can be seen with an ordinary light microscope.
Dominant Of a gene that has its effect regardless of the state of its corresponding partner on the other chromosome.
Gene Any functional and defined length of DNA containing a code for a protein, most commonly an enzyme.
Genetic code The sequence of bases lying along the DNA molecule, taken three at a time.
Heterozygous Of paired chromosomes that have different genes at corresponding points.
Homozygous Of paired chromosomes that have the same genes at corresponding points.
Mutation Any change in the genetic code, whether in its sequence or in the absence of one or more bases.
Recessive Of a gene that has no effect unless its partner also carries the mutation.
Sex chromosome One of the pair that determine gender – XX for a girl and XY for a boy.
X-linked A gene on the X chromosome.

Most of the time, the DNA molecule simply lies as a tangled mass in the cell nucleus. But just before cell division occurs it coils and recoils itself tightly to form bodies known as chromosomes. In humans, there are 46 chromosomes in each cell – two sets of 23 pairs. Two of these pairs are known as the sex chromosomes and the others as the autosomes. Females have two large chromosomes, known as X chromosomes; males have one large X and one small Y. Eggs and sperm have only one set of 23 chromosomes, so all eggs carry an X chromosome, while sperm have either an X or a Y. If an X-bearing sperm fertilizes an egg, the result is a girl (XX); if a Y-bearing sperm fertilizes an egg, the result is a boy (XY). Chromosome pairs in the sex cells swap over various arbitrary segments with each other before dividing and it is a matter of chance which of the pairs goes to which egg or sperm. This and other processes result in a considerable shuffling of the genetic material, about half of which comes from the mother and about half from the father. This is why we do not always closely resemble our parents.

The paired chromosomes are almost identical and the corresponding genes occupy the same corresponding positions. But, frequently, one of the pairs has a mutation so that we have one normal gene and one abnormal gene. The so-called heterozygous state depends on the importance of the protein for which the affected gene codes. In many cases the normal gene produces enough of the enzyme or other protein to keep the affected person healthy. In this event the mutation is said to be recessive. But if the person happens to inherit mutated genes for both positions, there is no normal gene and the effect of the mutation is apparent. This is only likely to happen in breeding between close relatives. Sometimes, however, a mutation produces such a major change in the protein formed that, regardless of the other normal gene, the result is a disease or disorder. This is called a dominant mutation.

Autosomal genes – those on the autosomes, or the non-sex chromosomes – may also be recessive or dominant. Those on the X chromosomes are called sex-linked or X-linked. Y chromosomes carry very few genes and it is doubtful if any Y-linked conditions exist. This has an important effect.

Males are XY. A sex-linked recessive condition involving only one of the gene pairs (alleles) does not affect females (XX) because the gene on the other X chromosome keeps everything in order. But if a male has a disease-producing mutation in a gene on the X chromosome, the disease or disorder will appear because the Y chromosome has no corresponding normal allele to compensate. So sex-linked recessive disorders affect males, but cannot be passed from father to son (because the father contributes only the Y chromosome to a son). They are passed from mother to son on an X chromosome. Daughters and sons have a 50–50 chance of inheriting the X with the mutation. Sons who do show the disease; daughters become carriers. The mother is usually only a carrier; females rarely suffer from sex-linked recessive conditions because to do so they would have to inherit the mutation on both alleles. This is most unlikely unless these is close inbreeding in a family carrying the gene.

Growing cells in the laboratory

It is possible to investigate in the laboratory the number of times cell replacement cycles can occur. It is not difficult to arrange suitable nutrition for cells, so that they can be made to survive and reproduce themselves outside the body. Tissue cultures of this type are now common. One of the most famous of these, the HeLa culture, which was started many years ago from some cancer cells taken from a tumour from a patient, appears to be immortal and is now serving various useful purposes, such as growing viruses, in hospitals and research laboratories all over the world. So long as the conditions of nutrition are satisfied, the cell culture will continue to grow without limit.

But the cells of the HeLa culture, and of all other such artificial cultures, are abnormal and incapable of the many important functions required of healthy cells in the body. They have far more than the normal number of chromosomes – perhaps as many as 400 – and so their genetic function is grossly abnormal. They have, for example, lost the normal processes of gene control and produce a very peculiar collection of proteins. They are all cancer cells and all they can do is grow and reproduce. Cancer cells do not show the characteristic changes in the expression of genes that occur over repeated generations of cell division in normal cells. This is one reason why they are often immortal. But there is another, extraordinary reason.

When normal cells are cultured, there is a definite limit to the number of times they can reproduce. This number has been repeatedly checked in different trials. Cells called fibroblasts from a fetus or young baby double in number between 80 and 90 times and the culture then dies. The average of 85 fibroblast population doublings is remarkably constant. But if cells taken from a middle-aged man are cultured, the number of doublings before the cells die is reduced to about 50; if taken from a person of 70, they are likely to divide only 20–30 times; if taken from a person of 100 they may not divide at all. This phenomenon is sometimes called the Hayflick effect, after the American microbiologist Leonard Hayflick who first described it.

Trials have shown that the limiting factor is not the age of the culture but the number of times the cells reproduce. Even keeping the cells in suspended animation by freezing for several years does not alter this fact. They simply resume where they left off, undergo the immutable 85 or so doublings, then die. Cells from a wide range of human donors, of ages from birth to 90 years, show a steady average decrease in the number of times they reproduce before the culture dies. There is a rare disease called progeria (premature ageing) in which, at 10 years of age, the sufferer has all the physical appearances of a person of 90. Cells from such a person show only two to ten doublings before the culture dies.

The reason for all this remained a mystery for decades, but scientists have recently discovered the basis of this apparent limitation on longevity.

Shortening chromosomes

The reason for this finite number of doublings became apparent in 1972, when James D. Watson – who with Francis Crick established the structure of DNA – noticed that when chromosomes replicated they did not do so all the way to their ends. The process of replication left a short length at each end uncopied. So older cells had shorter chromosomes than younger cells. To prevent loss of vital genetic material, the ends of chromosomes comprise seemingly unimportant 'junk' DNA that was thought to carry no genes and could, apparently, be lost without ill effect. These end segments are called telomeres, first noted as early as the 1930s by Barbara McClintock of Columbia University and Hermann J. Muller of Edinburgh University. The word telomere was derived from the Greek *telos* meaning 'end' and *meros* meaning 'part'.

With each cell division, some of this 'junk' DNA is shaved off. Eventually, the whole telomere is lost so that some of the true genetic material – the vital sequence of base triplets – is exposed and removed. When this happens, part of the blueprint for the cell is lost, and the affected cell cannot reproduce itself properly and becomes irretrievably damaged. Also, when the telomeres are lost, 'bare-ended' chromosomes sometimes stick together at the ends, thereby interfering with normal chromosome division. Cancer cells have very short telomeres but manage to preserve them: we now know how.

In 1978 Elizabeth Blackburn worked out the base sequence of the gene for the telomeres in a single-celled pond-living organism. This was the sequence TTGGGG (two thymines and four guanines) repeated many times over. Since then the sequence for the telomeres of many animals, plants and micro-organisms has been determined. In 1984 Greider and Blackburn, working at Berkeley, discovered an enzyme, telomerase, that could lengthen telomeres. At the time, this seemed of little interest and might have been buried among the mass of other research findings. But 10 years later a further advance by other scientists brought their discovery into great prominence and put telomerase on the map.

An important advance in cancer research was reported in 1994 in the journal *Science*. The paper, by N. W. Kim, M. A. Piatyszck, K. R. Prows and others, revealed that they had found that telomerase – the enzyme that can build up telomeres and so prevent the shortening of chromosomes – was present in virtually all cancers. This seemingly was how cancers achieve immortality. It is an indication of the amount of scientific interest in telomerase that various other groups of scientists found the same thing at around the same time. C. B. Harley of Geron Corporation and J. W. Shay of Texas University found telomerase in 90 of 101 tumour samples, but none in 50 samples of normal human body cells. Telomerase is present in human germ cells – the cells that produce eggs and sperm – and these maintain the length of their telomeres throughout their lifespan. General body cells, on the other hand, do not normally have telomerase. The DNA code for the protein telomerase is there as a sequence of base triplets, but it is simply not switched on. When body cells become cancerous this code turns on the functions that lead to the genetic production of the enzyme.

Recent research has shown that there are some other body cells that need telomerase to go on dividing indefinitely. These are the cells of the immune system, the scavenging macrophages and the vital lymphocytes that produce antibodies and attack viruses and other germs. This finding has major implications.

It would be wrong to suggest that telomerase is the cause of cancer. It is not the initiating factor. Many cancer cells have very short telomeres, indicating that a considerable number of cell divisions have occurred before the telomerase begins to be produced. This was first noted with ovarian cancers. Telomerase activity seems to be a late genetic event that provides cancers with one of their nastier properties – the ability to go on living. Cancer cells divide frequently. If they did not have a way of preventing their chromosomes from shortening, they would soon reach the 85 divisions and die. So without telomerase, cancers would probably be pretty harmless.

This new knowledge offers an exciting new possibility for the treatment of cancer. The gene for telomerase was cloned toward the end of 1995, and reported in *Science* by Carol W. Greider, Elizabeth H. Blackburn and colleagues, working at the Cold Spring Harbor Laboratory on Long Island, New York. They had succeeded in cloning the genes for both human and mouse telomerase. But these scientists went further. Knowing the sequence of bases in the gene for telomerase they were able to put together a length of 'antisense' RNA (see below) that binds to the enzyme's RNA and inactivates it. When this blocking RNA was added to cancer cell cultures, the cells continued to divide as usual. But, after 23 to 26 cell divisions, the cancer cells stopped dividing and died.

As we have seen, gene bases will only link together in a particular way. In RNA guanine will only bind to cytosine and thymine will only link to uracil. So it is easy to produce a length of RNA that complements exactly the RNA of telomerase. The gene for human telomerase consists of the sequence TTAGGG (thymine, thymine, adenine, guanine, guanine, guanine) repeated about 2000 times. The RNA template that this gene produces is complementary to these sequences and the antisense probe produced by Greider and her colleagues is complementary to that.

The enzyme telomerase has a number of unique characteristics, including the same reverse transcriptase activity that allows HIV (human immunodeficiency virus, the virus that causes AIDS) to convert its RNA to DNA and thus reproduce. These characteristics can be exploited in various other ways to prevent telomerase from working and so deprive cancers of their principal danger. Having sequenced telomerase, scientists now have plenty of it to work on so that a new form of anti-cancer chemotherapy, specific only to telomerase, can perhaps be developed. A cancer treatment that attacks only cancer cells and leaves normal cells unaffected would obviously be an enormous advance on current methods. All currently effective methods of treating cancer – apart from surgery – work on the basis of causing slightly more damage to cancer cells than to healthy cells.

There is, however, a caveat. Telomerase is obviously important to normal cells as well as to cancerous cells. We do not yet know enough about its general function in the body to be sure that it would be safe to attack it. There are several classes of cells in the body, including those of the immune system, those in the bone marrow that produce blood cells and those that line the intestine, which require a non-stop capacity to reproduce. We know that the immune system cells produce telomerase, and it seems likely that others also need it to prevent them from dying too early. So an attack on telomerase could be dangerous.

Telomeres and ageing

The principle of around 85 cell population doublings does seem to put a definite limit on our life expectancy. But this does not imply that, barring accidents or disease, we will all live until our cells stop dividing. In fact, more than 100 different changes in the structure and function of cells have been noted to occur, long before they lose the ability to replicate. These changes, which increase progressively as the number of cell divisions is used up, gradually impair the cell's ability to perform its proper functions. These changes produce all the well-known signs of old age and result in the death of the individual, around the age of 100 years, before the cells cease to divide.

Even so, it is now apparent that telomeres are of considerable importance in relation to ageing and survival. If cells are unable to divide, they are unable to repair damage to tissues. The single most common cause of death in Western societies is the effect of the arterial disease atherosclerosis on our arteries. The resulting narrowing or closure of arteries leads to heart attacks, strokes, dementia, gangrene and other conditions. Atherosclerosis is so important in ageing that it is dealt with fully in chapters 2 and 6. But damage to the inner linings of artery walls encourages atherosclerosis. Clearly, if this damage cannot be repaired because of the inability of cells to replicate, there is a greater risk of serious atherosclerosis. In the case of cells of the immune system, failure to replicate leads to an age-related loss of immune capacity and an increased susceptibility to infections. It seems now to be established, however, that these cells are protected from fatal telomere shortening by producing telomerase.

Scientific facts and theories of ageing

That there are many different theories of ageing does not imply that all but one are wrong. Some are so implausible that they can be dismissed at once, but the serious theories are all based on reliable scientific evidence, so the existence of many theories suggests that many different processes are involved in ageing. Here are some of the facts and views relating to the most important theories.

No consideration of ageing can safely ignore two major aspects of biology – genetics and evolution. We have already looked at some of the genetic aspects. Much of modern biology has also been illuminated by evolutionary theory, which provides strong indications of why humans function in certain ways rather than in others. It also explains why many aspects of human body function seem to be less well 'designed' than they might be. To give a simple example: age-related osteoporosis (see chapter 2) seems to have been a mistake of nature. But the period of historical time during which osteoporosis has been a major problem is only a blink of the eye compared with the millions of years during which humans were evolving. Osteoporosis only became prominent when humans began to survive for longer than about 50 years. Prior to that, evolution by natural selection had achieved a perfectly satisfactory arrangement, with bones remaining strong enough to last out the then natural lifespan. There was no need to evolve bones that would last to the age of 70 or more, as we now expect of them.

Osteoporosis is only one of many features of old age which would not normally have appeared in times when life was brutish and short. Evolution has not failed us when the conditions for which we evolved were so different from what they are today. There was no need for reading glasses when the expectation of life was 30 years and presbyopia did not set in until the age of about 45.

The evolutionary biologist George C. Williams of Michigan State University has put forward an ingenious theory of ageing. He suggests that certain genes might make survival more likely if expressed early in life but might reduce life expectancy if expressed later. Since people predominantly reproduce in the earlier part of life, genes that are damaging only later in life and cause ageing would not be eliminated. The biologist T. B. L. Kirkwood of the British Institute for Medical Research points out that, in an evolutionary and survival context, any species must share its energy between body maintenance and efficiency of reproduction. This implies that the need for the survival of the species may lead to less than full attention to bodily repair, especially later in life. The inevitable result is deterioration and death. This idea is supported by the observation that the genes that code for certain sex hormones can be considered to act in this way. Oestrogens, for instance, are necessary for reproduction and fertility in youth, but later in life can slightly increase the risk of breast cancer. Critics of this theory point out that the absence of oestrogen after the menopause is far more dangerous than its presence because of the serious effect it has in increasing the risk of heart attacks and strokes in women.

Advances in genetics have shown that, although the human genome – the whole of the genetic material of an individual – contains some 100,000 different genes, only a proportion of these are actually being expressed at any one time. Some lie seemingly dormant for years until 'turned on' by various factors. Similarly, some genes that are normally functional can be 'turned off'. Such changes in the expression of genes occur with age. Certain cells, for example, have a fixed probability at each cell division of losing the ability to express a particular gene. And long-term environmental factors can also influence the expression of genes.

Diet and ageing

It is known that rats fed on a restricted calorie diet live longer than rats allowed to eat as much as they like. The same has been shown to be true of mice, fish and flies. The interesting feature of this is that the rats whose lifespan is increased in this way have enhanced expression of certain genes in their liver cells. So it seems we can change our genetic expression by changing our eating habits.

The body is largely made of various strong structural proteins such as collagen and keratin. Even the bones are mainly constructed from protein and are only hardened by the minerals calcium and phosphorus. These proteins do not persist unchanged for the full lifetime of the individual, but are regularly broken down and replaced. Proteins differ widely in their lifespans. Some, like the enzymes, are turned over rapidly, others are stable. Even so, all proteins suffer damage with time from oxidative processes (see chapter 6). A proportion of protein molecules is also defective from the outset as a result of errors in translation of the DNA code.

Two remarkable proteins

The protein ubiquitin seeks out damaged proteins and tags them for destruction. Ubiquitin is a small molecule and proteins scheduled for dissolution are usually tagged with several ubiquitin molecules. Research has shown that human cells coming near to the end of their ability to reproduce have fewer ubiquitin tags on their proteins than normal. This suggests yet another theory of age-related cell deterioration. A defect in the production or binding of ubiquitin would allow damaged and defective proteins to accumulate instead of being replaced. It is a moot point whether this process is a cause or simply a consequence of cell ageing.

Another protein that is affected by age is fibronectin. This long, thin molecule is a kind of protein glue used by the body to move cells to their proper location, place them properly and fix them in position. Scientists studying fibronectin have found that there is a variant form of the protein found only in cells coming to the end of their reproductive life. This abnormal form is believed to be the result of a change in gene transcription. Cancer cells are very short of fibronectin, which probably accounts for their tendency to migrate and separate from their place of origin to set up new foci of cancer elsewhere in the body.

Free radicals and oxidative damage

An increasing amount of attention has been paid in recent years to the damaging effect on cells and tissues of oxidative reactions caused by free radicals. The literature on the subject has grown in the last 10 years or so and is now enormous. The principal interest, for most of us, is the possibility of combatting these damaging processes by means of antioxidant vitamins. This is clearly important in the context of ageing (see chapter 6).

Characteristics of the lively old

The American psychiatrist and gerontologist Dr Stephen Jewett studied a large number of people ranging in age from 87 to 103 who showed unusually high standards of health, liveliness and vitality. His purpose was to establish what they had in common, and so to try to discover the factors that make for a good old age. These people were of a kind seldom seen in doctors' consulting rooms or in institutions for the old. They were:

◆ adventurous
◆ mobile

- ◆ positive
- ◆ well-travelled
- ◆ deeply interested in life and good living.

Not surprisingly, a characteristic common to most of them was that they came from long-lived families. Heredity, it appears, is one of the most important factors. By 'heredity' should be understood all the genetic factors that conspire to promote good health and relative resistance to the diseases, such as heart and circulation disorders and cancer, that most commonly shorten life.

In addition, these people nearly all enjoyed healthy diets. None was faddy over food; they were venturesome and often fond of variety, but always ate moderately. Their diets were well balanced, with an emphasis on vegetables and fruit, and they did not have a high fat intake. There was no particular trend in alcohol consumption. Many of them were regular drinkers and some occasionally overdid it, but none could be described as alcoholics. Some were total abstainers. Some had smoked pipes for many years and remained confirmed pipe smokers. Most who had formerly smoked cigarettes had given them up long before.

The average intelligence was high and showed little indication of having deteriorated with age. It was as if intelligence had been maintained by strong interests. With high intelligence went good memory, and the two together were still prompting many of these people to undertake major intellectual challenges, such as learning new languages, late in life.

The great majority of these people were, or had been, married. The study was made at a time when unmarried cohabitation was much less common than it is today, so it is probable that in these cases marriage can be equated with high sex drive. There is plenty of other biographical evidence to suggest that this kind of vitality is commonly associated with strong sexual impulses. This is also brought out elsewhere in this book. And there is also a great deal of evidence that, in people of this class, sexual activity often persists well into old age. Marriage, however, constitutes far more than sex, and people with wide and active interests and mental vitality commonly seek to share their interests and their lives with others.

There was a remarkable similarity in some physical characteristics. None of the people in this group were overweight or grossly underweight and most had never had weight problems. Typically, they had reached their adult weight in their mid-20s and remained close to it thereafter. None were excessively tall or unusually short. Because they were all old and had the typical average height of their own generation, they were somewhat shorter than average young people today. They had maintained better than average muscle power and capacity for physical exertion.

None of these people wanted to hark back to the past. Although they retained detailed memories of their own lives, their real interests were in the present. This demonstrated a high degree of adaptability and willingness to conform to ever-changing social and other environments. This is a characteristic of people who maintain interest and the ability readily to form new interests. In professional occupation, there was a distinct trend toward individuality and the choice of jobs that allowed autonomy and freedom of choice and action.

A statutory retiring age was not a feature of their employment and their almost universal tendency was simply to go on working. Many had been, and often still were, self-employed. Many had been high earners but nearly all agreed that a narrow driving ambition to reach the top at the expense of all other considerations was a serious mistake.

An important and enviable characteristic of a majority of the people in this group was the ability to avoid worry. This was clearly not due to any lack of appreciation of the manifold risks in life from disease, injury, accident, financial or emotional disaster and so on. Rather it was a condition of mind that, while intelligently avoiding foolish risk, always took the positive rather than the negative path and reacted with optimism rather than pessimism. Such an outlook grows upon itself. For it greatly reduces the probability of misfortune and with it the occasions for anxiety.

Religion did not appear to play a large part in the lives of these people but nearly all of them professed to some kind of general belief. There was a notable absence of extreme views such as fundamentalism or cultism; and even those subscribing to orthodox religions were free from any hint of fanaticism. They were also, in general, tolerant of the religious positions of those of different denominations or of those without religious convictions. None was preoccupied with death.

These are all inspiring people. Perhaps their enviable lives were achieved simply as a result of good fortune and there is no way that we can benefit from their example. But to think in this way would be to fall into the kind of mistake that these people characteristically avoid. There is every reason to study the features of those lively old people and to determine to emulate them. It is the purpose of this book to help you to do exactly that.

chapter two

A Positive Approach to the Medical Aspects of Ageing

T his section is concerned with how the body changes with age and how many of these changes are the result of avoidable abuse. It is also concerned with some of the important disorders that affect older people more than young people and with what can be done to avoid and relieve them.

Contrary to popular belief, ageing starts just before puberty. After the earliest stages of infancy, mortality rates fall progressively throughout childhood until the age of about 12. Thereafter they start to rise. Deaths caused by accidents and violence apart (and the current rise in violent deaths in children does not alter the argument), mortality rates rise steadily with age throughout the whole of adult life. Ageing, as determined by the general performance or ability to function as a fully capable human being, occurs at different rates in different people, and there is a wide variation in the rate of ageing. The significance, and paradox, of this is that we cannot judge a person's true age by his or her temporal age. There ought, in fact, to be an age scale based on capacity rather than on years.

Such a scale would not be easy to organize, as so many different factors would compete for attention. It would also have to take into account the relative importance, or unimportance, of mere physical strength in the context of the modern technological world. But in societies in which an increasing proportion of the population is of advanced age, it would be a far better way of comparing individuals than the present reliance on the length of time since birth. Current patterns of assessment, which relate people to age, can give a general idea of capacity in a statistical or average way, but they say nothing about any particular individual of a particular age. There are plenty of people in their 80s whose general performance and capacity is equal to that of the average person of 40.

Increasing age is commonly associated with an increasing incidence of various diseases. Against this, however, is the positive factor that people who reach old age clearly have an inherent medical advantage over those who die in middle age. This is called selective survival and medical research has shown that it is not due simply to luck but indicates that genetic, behavioural and environmental factors are operating. Some of these are obvious. People whose parents both survived into old age are, themselves, much more likely to reach old age than those whose parents died in middle age from diseases such as heart attacks or strokes; this is a genetic effect. People who smoke cigarettes throughout their life will not attain their full lifespan; this is a behavioural effect. And people who have to spend their lives in physically hostile surroundings such as coal mines or granite-polishing yards are likely to die early from lung disorders; this is an environmental effect.

There has been a great deal of misunderstanding about the effects of ageing on mental ability. Unthinking assumptions based on inadequate evidence are the rule. Technological advances have caused many difficulties for older people and resulted in the widespread opinion, among the young, that old people cannot cope because their mental powers have declined. What both groups usually forget is that today's old people were educated in a different and much less technological culture; young people, with whom they are being compared, were educated in the present culture.

Individual comparisons

If the mental performance of old people is compared, not with that of their young contemporaries but with their own performance when young, differences are less pronounced. This is the only fair basis of comparison, and when it is used it is found that mental functioning declines less than most people suppose. Many old people who have maintained an active interest in technology and its applications, perform well above average even when compared with young people.

There is a widespread belief that new learning in old age is virtually impossible: 'You can't teach an old dog new tricks.' Recent studies have shown that old people certainly can learn if they are taught by appropriate methods that take due account of their cultural backgrounds. There is no denying that learning may be slower and that it is not likely to occur unless the people concerned wish to learn. The problem is to provide the appropriate motivation.

If this seems like 'locking the stable door after the horse has bolted', remember that it is never too late to change the ways of life that lead to some of the gross misfortunes dealt with in this chapter. Much research has shown that, while many avoidable degenerative bodily changes cannot be reversed, it is never too late to take steps to prevent further deterioration or even to improve bodily condition and performance. The body – and the mind – are wonderfully responsive to the demands made upon them.

Age and the arteries

It is strange that so little attention is paid to the arteries in the popular medical press, because the state of our arteries is by far the most important determinant of length and quality of life. This is because the proper functioning of every cell in our bodies depends on a good supply of oxygen, glucose fuel, amino acids, fatty acids and other substances, all of which are brought to the cells by the blood. If the tubes that carry blood to the cells – the arteries – are narrowed and rigid so that an adequate flow of blood is impossible, the organ or part supplied by the narrowed artery malfunctions. If the blood supply is completely cut off, the organ or part dies.

By far the most important arterial disease, causing narrowing of arteries, is atherosclerosis. Doctors used to talk of arteriosclerosis but this term is now largely abandoned because the disease has a more important feature than simply sclerosis (hardening). Atherosclerosis is by far the most important cause of death, disability and damage to the quality of life in elderly people, hence the emphasis on the condition here (see also chapter 6).

Atherosclerosis, commonly referred to as 'the number one killer of the Western world', is a degenerative disease of arteries in which fatty plaques (atheroma) develop on the inner lining so that the normal flow of blood is impeded. Atherosclerosis affects almost all of us, and its earliest signs are apparent in childhood. But the condition is in general steadily progressive with age. Although most arteries are affected, those in which the condition is most dangerous are the coronary arteries supplying the heart muscle with blood, and the carotid and vertebral arteries and their branches which supply the brain. Atherosclerosis of these two systems – the delivery of blood to the heart and to the brain – leads, respectively, to coronary thrombosis (heart attack) and stroke (apoplexy).

Fats and cholesterol are carried around in the bloodstream in the form of tiny spherical bodies known as lipoproteins. There are two types: high-density lipoproteins (HDLs) with much protein and little fat; and low-density lipoproteins (LDLs) with much cholesterol and little protein. LDLs carry cholesterol to the arteries; HDLs carry it from the tissues to the liver. So LDLs are regarded as 'bad' and HDLs as 'good'. There is a very strong correlation between high levels of LDLs and a high incidence of atherosclerosis, heart attacks and strokes. High levels of HDLs protect against these diseases. Each LDL has a small number of large molecules called apolipoproteins on its surface. Cells take up cholesterol by binding to these proteins.

Recent advances in the understanding of the processes by which athero-sclerotic plaques develop suggest that the low-density lipoproteins are activated into depositing their cholesterol in the walls of the arteries by the oxidative action of free radicals. There is growing evidence that these can be effectively combatted by regular daily doses of the antioxidant vitamins C and E in amounts considerably greater than are required to prevent vitamin deficiency. For this reason this book contains an entire section devoted to the subject of free radicals and antioxidants (see chapter 6).

We should all be trying to delay or halt the progress of atherosclerosis.

Living longer

People who wish to live long and well should:

- eat little more than is required to maintain a normal, low-end-of-range body weight
- avoid saturated fats
- take exercise to the point of breathlessness, ideally once a day
- never smoke cigarettes
- drink alcohol in moderation
- have regular blood pressure checks
- take antioxidant vitamins
- avoid undue stress.

Atherosclerosis and the heart

The heart is a strong muscular bag which tightens rhythmically (beats) to force blood into the arteries and around the body. This blood enters the heart from the veins. Because heart contractions occur more than once a second, the heart's energy requirements are considerable. It must be supplied with a considerable amount of glucose fuel and oxygen, which are only available from the blood passing through the branching system of coronary arteries. If these arteries are significantly narrowed by atherosclerosis, they are likely to be able to supply the muscle with enough blood to function adequately while the person concerned is at rest. But if the person exerts himself or herself the oxygen and fuel supply may not be enough for the work the muscle is being called upon to do. The result is the symptom known as angina pectoris (a symptom, not a disease).

Angina is a pain in the centre of the chest which is often severe and frightening and may spread up the neck and down the arms. It relates predictably to a given amount of exertion, comes on earlier in cold weather or after a heavy meal, and is relieved by resting or by drugs such as nitroglycerine, which temporarily widen the coronary arteries. The inadequacy of coronary blood supply is almost always caused by atherosclerosis of the coronary arteries. These atherosclerotic plaques cause no symptoms, nor any other indication of their presence, until they narrow the artery to less than half its normal bore so that the blood flow is insufficient to permit full exertion and angina occurs. At rest, the person concerned seems normal, but a fixed amount of exercise – say, walking for a kilometre – causes angina pectoris.

If atherosclerosis is present in the coronary arteries, there is always the risk that blood will clot on top of a patch of atheroma so that the artery is blocked altogether. This is called a coronary thrombosis, or heart attack. It is usually described by doctors as a myocardial infarction, and is the result of a complete obstruction to blood flow in one of the branches of the two coronary arteries through which the heart muscle is supplied with blood. Any substantial diminution in the fuel and oxygen supply to any part of the heart muscle interferes, not only with its ability to function, but also with its survival as a living tissue. Blood does not normally clot within the blood vessels. But the presence of a roughened plaque of fatty, degenerative, cholesterol-containing atheroma in the inner lining of the vessel often prompts it to do so. When a total blockage occurs, part of the heart muscle loses its blood supply and dies. Depending on the size of the artery blocked, this dead area may involve the full thickness of the heart wall, or only part of it. The heart cannot continue to function as a pump if more than a certain proportion of the muscle is destroyed. Blockage of a major branch, with destruction of about half of the muscle in the main (left) pumping chamber, is almost always immediately fatal. Previous smaller attacks make death more likely.

Coronary thrombosis usually causes:

◆ severe pain, or sense of pressure, in the centre of the chest
◆ the pain often spreads through to the back, up into the neck, or down each arm
◆ there is a horrifying sense that one is about to die
◆ there is often extreme restlessness
◆ the pulse is weak, difficult to feel, and often irregular
◆ sometimes the pulse is very slow.

Severe pain is usual, but not always a feature. In less major cases pain may be absent and there is evidence that up to 20 per cent of mild coronaries are not recognized as such or even as significant illness by those affected. This means that there are millions of people who, because of previous unrecognized attacks, are much more vulnerable than normal.

Half of those who die from a particular attack do so from heart stoppage (cardiac arrest) within three or four hours of the onset of the attack, so it is always urgent to get a person with a coronary thrombosis to hospital with minimum delay. Many who might have been saved have died because they did not recognize or believe that they had a life-threatening condition. A valuable emergency measure that can save many lives is to give a drug that dissolves clots in the arteries – a thrombolytic drug. A small dose of aspirin is also very helpful. A survey published in August 1994 suggests that many general practitioners are not using thrombolysis or prescribing aspirin to those at risk. Many men take a small dose of aspirin every day as a routine.

Factors which increase the risk of coronary thrombosis are, or should be, well known: smoking, lack of exercise, overeating with resultant obesity, a high-fat diet, excessive stress and parents who died of arterial disease. Only the last is beyond our individual control and there is now ample evidence that people are markedly reducing their chances of coronary thrombosis by adjusting their behaviour. Since these facts have been widely known, the incidence of coronary thrombosis has declined significantly in certain social classes. But in a study of 7,735 middle-aged men, published in 1987, the prevalence of coronary thrombosis was found to be 44 per cent higher in manual workers than in non-manual workers. This was attributed mainly to cigarette smoking, obesity and lack of exercise in leisure time.

A strategy for the prevention of coronary artery disease, based on the concordant views of experts from 19 countries, was published in *The Lancet* in 1987. The main points were directed to the eradication of smoking, reduced cholesterol intake with emphasis on unsaturated fat and high fibre content, and the promotion of exercise. The aim was to reduce obesity, lower blood cholesterol levels and reduce blood pressure. There was particular emphasis on encouraging social pressures against smoking.

Another important effect of atherosclerosis on the heart is heart block. The timing of the contraction of the chambers of the heart, necessary for the smooth directional movement of blood, is under the control of a bundle of specially conducting muscle fibres in the heart muscle called the bundle of His, after the German anatomist and histologist Wilhelm His (1831–1904), who discovered it. This bundle starts in a natural pacemaker (the sino-atrial node) in the wall of the right upper chamber (atrium) and passes into the wall between the two halves of the heart, dividing into two and running down each side of the wall to reach the lower chambers (the ventricles). The bundle of His is the only conducting link between the upper and lower chambers of the heart.

Heart block is the condition in which some part of the conducting bundle has been damaged so that the controlling impulses no longer pass from the upper to the lower chambers of the heart. Such damage usually occurs as a result of coronary thrombosis, but there are other causes, including drug toxicity, rheumatic fever, syphilis or tumour. There are different kinds of block, depending on the location of the damage. There may be right bundle branch block, left bundle branch block or complete heart block, and each characteristically dissociates the affected chamber or chambers from the parts of the heart above the block.

Heart block, in general, causes the pulse to be very slow, as the lower chamber can only beat at its intrinsically low rate. Heart block is one of the major indications for the implantation of an artificial pacemaker.

Atherosclerosis is present to some degree in almost all adults in the Western world. Its prevalence and degree are much greater in men than in premenopausal women and increases in both sexes with age. When these facts are considered, it is hardly surprising that coronary thrombosis is responsible for about half of all deaths in Western countries and is generally regarded in medical circles as the major problem in preventive medicine.

There is more about heart disease and atherosclerosis in chapter 6, where the tone is more positive, and the remarkable advances in its prevention are discussed.

How to avoid heart attacks

◆ Never smoke cigarettes.
◆ Cut down radically on your intake of dairy fat products.
◆ Get most of your calories from starchy and floury foods, such as wholemeal bread, rice, pasta and grains, and from vegetables and fruit.
◆ Limit your daily animal protein intake (because of its fat content).
◆ Exercise to the point of breathlessness at least three times a week, preferably every day.
◆ Get your blood pressure checked once a year – more often if it borderlines on being high.
◆ Keep your weight a little below the recommended average for your sex, age and frame type.
   Note: These recommendations apply equally to the avoidance of strokes.

Atherosclerosis and the brain

The brain is more dependent on a good blood supply than any other organ of the body, and its demands for oxygen and fuel are greater than those of any other organ. Deprivation of blood to the brain is disastrous. When it is simply reduced overall by a general narrowing of arteries, the effects are slow and not immediately apparent but may amount to something as serious as progressive dementia (see chapter 4). When deprivation occurs suddenly, as when an artery supplying part of the brain is closed off by blood clotting on an atherosclerotic plaque, the effects are more striking and obvious, and known as a stroke. Such a stroke may vary in severity over the whole range, from the mildest – featuring a slight, one-sided muscle weakness, a minor disturbance of vision or speech, or a temporary loss of comprehension – to the most severe, with devastating brain damage, loss of consciousness or sudden death.

Although stroke is most commonly the result of acute deprivation of blood in a part of the brain, it may also be caused by an even more dramatic event – physical damage to part of the brain by internal or external bleeding from an artery that has been weakened by arterial disease. This is called cerebral haemorrhage and it is the cause of the most serious, and most commonly fatal, kind of stroke. Bleeding into the brain is usually the result of the rupture of a small artery, damaged and weakened by atherosclerosis, which gives way under the influence of raised blood pressure. High blood pressure contributes to atherosclerosis and is the main risk factor for stroke. The bleeding can occur almost anywhere in the brain and the effect varies with the location.

The pumping action of the burst vessel forces blood into the brain tissue, which is disrupted and compressed. The effect is most obvious in those parts in which the nerve tracts concerned with movement, sensation, speech and vision are situated close together and so work together. Haemorrhage into the brain stem, where the centres for the control of the vital functions of breathing and heartbeat are situated, is the most immediately dangerous to life.

The first indication of a cerebral haemorrhage is usually a sudden severe headache. This is quickly followed by an obvious loss of function such as paralysis down one side of the body, loss of vision to one side, fixed turning of the eyes to one side and perhaps a major epileptic-type fit. Often consciousness is lost early and when the haemorrhage is large, it may never be regained – more than half of the people affected in this way die within hours or days. Those who recover consciousness always have an initial defect of function which is often severe. Smaller haemorrhages produce less damage and there may be no loss of consciousness, but simply the signs of functional injury to the nervous system.

This is almost always worst at the beginning and much of it is caused by recoverable and temporary loss of function in the tissue surrounding the damaged area. Brain swelling (oedema) occurs and this temporarily interferes with nerve conduction. Recovery also occurs, to some extent, as a result of reabsorption of the released blood. As recovery proceeds there is a slow, but usually substantial improvement and, unless further haemorrhages occur, the end result may be good. Some degree of permanent disability is, however, usual. Strokes may be caused by bleeding from a ruptured berry-like swelling, known as an aneurysm, on one of the arteries supplying the brain. This is called a subarachnoid haemorrhage.

Strokes from cerebral thrombosis are generally less severe than those from cerebral haemorrhage. They may occur in people with atherosclerosis of the carotid arteries or their branches, or in people with diseased heart valves on which small blood clots form, and then break loose to be carried up to the brain. Stroke is also commonly caused by another effect of atherosclerosis, known as embolism. Embolism is the sudden blocking of an artery by solid, semi-solid or other material brought to the site of the obstruction in the bloodstream. The object, or material, causing the embolism is called an embolus (plural emboli). It is always abnormal for any non-fluid material to be present in the circulation, and because blood proceeding through arteries encounters ever smaller branches, such material inevitably impacts and causes blockage, thereby depriving a part of the body of its essential blood supply.

Many different forms of emboli occur. Embolism is commonly caused by blood clot emboli, often arising in diseased arteries or veins. It may also be caused by crystals of cholesterol from plaques of atheroma in larger arteries; by clumps of infected material; by fat or other material in severe injuries; by air or nitrogen in diving accidents; by bone marrow and fat in fractures of large bones; and by tumour cells and other substances.

Not all emboli involve the arteries. If a large vein is infected or inflamed a clot may form in it. The chief danger in vein thrombosis is the formation of long, soft, snaky blood clots, in the deep veins of the legs, which may become very large before breaking loose into the bloodstream. Such clots pass quickly through the right side of the heart and impact in the main branches of the arteries to the lung. This is called pulmonary embolism and is a common cause of sudden, unexpected death. Similar, but smaller, emboli may form on the inner lining of the heart, often on the left side, after a coronary thrombosis. These are often carried upward to cause embolism in vital brain arteries, leading to stroke. Small cholesterol emboli, arising from atherosclerosis of the carotid arteries, commonly cause mini-strokes known as transient ischaemic attacks.

After a stroke, sustained efforts should be made to restore maximum function by as much activity as possible. A person who consistently attempts to walk after a minor stroke, for example, is much more likely to recover mobility than one who stays in bed.

Atherosclerosis and the legs
A reduced blood supply to the legs from atherosclerosis of the arteries supplying them is likely to cause pain on walking. This symptom is known

as intermittent claudication. The term comes from the Latin verb *claudicare*, meaning 'to be lame or limping' and commemorates the roman emperor Claudius whose limping gait and tendency to stop walking and grimace, as if in pain, must have closely resembled a man with atherosclerosis of the leg arteries.

Claudication is a sudden pain in the leg muscles, often in the calf, associated with temporary loss of the normal power of contraction and a consequent inability to walk. Intermittent claudication is caused by an inadequacy in the blood supply to the muscles from atherosclerosis and, just as in the case of angina pectoris, occurs after the affected person walks for a certain, often constant, distance. There is a build-up of waste products in the muscles and these pain-causing substances cannot be dispersed quickly enough. As the arterial disease process worsens, the symptoms come on earlier. Intermittent claudication is a clear indication that medical attention is required and that the state of the entire heart and blood vessel system should be investigated, as should the possibility of metabolic causes.

Recent evidence suggests that performance can be improved by deliberately 'walking through claudication'. This does not mean continuing to try to walk in spite of the pain, but resuming walking as soon as the pain has gone. People with intermittent claudication are advised to walk for an hour every day, or to walk to the point at which pain appears several times a day. Those who do so are usually able to walk a progressively greater distance before the pain comes on. The idea behind this is that exercise may lead to the opening up of smaller arteries to provide a bypass for the blockage and thereby increase the blood supply to the affected muscles. The worst possible thing such people can do is to stay in bed.

Claudication is a serious warning of the danger of losing a leg from gangrene. Gangrene is death of tissue usually resulting from the deprivation of its blood supply. Thousands of people have to have a leg amputated every year because atherosclerosis of the large arteries that should supply the legs with a large volume of blood has led to blockage. Established claudication that has not responded adequately to the 'walking treatment', which has been present for at least three months, and which seriously interferes with work or leisure activities, may be treated by arterial reconstructive surgery to provide an artificial shunt or bypass for the blockage. This is usually done as a matter of urgency if the pain is constant at rest or if there are indications of early gangrene.

Atherosclerosis and the eyes
Like other biologically highly active organs, the eyes are critically dependent on a good blood supply. Atherosclerosis affecting any of the arteries that directly or indirectly supply the eyes can be very serious. The condition known as

chronic ocular ischaemia (ischaemia means shortage of blood supply to any part) is due to narrowing of any artery along the sequence from the heart to the immediate eye artery – the ophthalmic artery.

Chronic ocular ischaemia causes a persistently painful red eye with reduced vision, signs of internal inflammation and a reduction in the normal internal fluid pressure. In an attempt to improve the blood supply, the internal blood vessels widen and become twisted. This may be seen by a doctor or ophthalmologist on normal ophthalmoscopic examination. These widened blood vessels may leak blood internally, one possible cause of the reduced vision. In addition, however, the eye's lens responds to an inadequate supply of nutrients and oxygen by becoming clouded and opaque. In other words, it develops a cataract. (Note, however, that this is not the usual cause of cataract in elderly people.)

Chronic ocular ischaemia can sometimes be relieved or reversed if an atherosclerotic obstruction to an artery, such as a carotid artery, can be removed. But such an established cataract requires routine surgery (see below).

Age and the heart

As we have seen, atherosclerosis can have a profound impact on your heart, but it is not the only age-related condition affecting the heart. Minimizing the risks of atherosclerosis will also reduce your susceptibility to both high blood pressure and heart failure.

High blood pressure
There is a very clear association between high blood pressure and premature death. Indeed, the risk of dying rises faster than the proportionate rise in blood pressure. This so-called exponential relationship provides a very good reason to be aware of the importance of high blood pressure and to do something about it.

Abnormally high blood pressure is called hypertension. The pressure in the circulation constantly varies, rising to a peak – called the systolic pressure – soon after the contraction of the main pumping chambers of the heart (ventricles), and falling steadily to a lower level – called the diastolic pressure – just before each heartbeat. Because of this dynamic situation, a person's blood pressure cannot be represented by a single figure but is given as two numbers, the systolic first and then the diastolic, such as 120/80. These numbers indicate the pressure in terms of the distance in millimetres which a column of mercury would be forced up a glass tube by the pressure. Such a column of mercury is still widely used in a sphygmomanometer, an instrument to measure blood pressure.

In addition to these two levels of pressure, physical exertion, anxiety, stress, emotional changes and other factors frequently result in changed levels of blood pressure. So single measurements are not particularly meaningful and your doctor really needs to measure your blood pressure a number of times under resting conditions, and at different times of day before he or she can be sure that you have hypertension.

Blood pressure depends on the force and volume of the heart output with each beat and on the resistance offered by the larger blood vessels. During each squeeze of the heart muscle – the heartbeat – a quantity of blood is forced into the arterial system, but only about one-third of that volume simultaneously moves out into the smallest of the blood vessels – the capillaries. This extra volume has to be accommodated. If the main arteries are healthily elastic, they will give a little with each heartbeat and the systolic pressure will not be particularly high. The recoil of the arteries then drives the remainder of the additional blood onward. Well before the pressure has fallen to zero, another beat occurs. If, however, the arteries are stiff and rigid, or abnormally narrowed from disease, the pressure with each ventricular contraction rises to a high peak. In addition, the diastolic pressure before each beat is higher.

Hypertension seldom causes symptoms until it has reached an advanced and critical stage and is causing secondary complications in the arteries, kidneys, brain, eyes or elsewhere. Uncomplicated high blood pressure does not cause dizziness, headache, fatigue, nosebleeds or facial flushing. By the time symptoms occur, the affected person is in real danger.

No one can afford to ignore raised blood pressure because sustained high pressures damage the blood vessels, causing an acceleration of the ageing processes. In particular, they promote atherosclerosis and all its attendant risks of heart attacks, strokes and damage to the heart, kidneys, eyes and often limbs. Because of the lack of symptoms, hypertension has to be looked for and every adult should have regular checks. The older you are, the more frequently you should have your blood pressure checked. Fortunately, proper and effective treatment can largely eliminate the additional risk of developing serious complications.

The treatment of hypertension involves both a change in lifestyle and, if necessary, the prescription of drugs. In the case of moderately raised blood pressure in an overweight person who does not exercise, a change in lifestyle is the first requirement.

Minimizing the risks of high blood pressure

- ◆ Eliminate smoking – even the otherwise most effective drug treatment may fail to reduce the probability of death if smoking continues.
- ◆ A change in eating habits is also important. In many cases, the change to a healthy, natural lifestyle, with regular exercise, no more food than you actually require to maintain your weight and with the emphasis on low dairy fat intake, and a reduction in salt intake, will be sufficient to get the blood pressure down to normal.
- ◆ Limit alcohol consumption to less than 21 units a week if you are a man, 14 if you are a woman.
- ◆ Regular attendance at the surgery for check-ups, usually with the practice nurse, will give you confidence and help to reduce stress levels.

The *British Medical Journal* of 23 November 1996 includes a report of a three-year controlled trial of treatment for hypertension in nearly 1000 patients aged 60 to 80. All these people were taking a drug to keep their blood pressure below 150/90. Of these patients, 585 were overweight and, as a result of advice to change their lifestyle, many managed to lose about 4 kilos (10 lb). The remarkable thing is that after 30 months follow-up, almost 40 per cent of these patients no longer required the drug to keep their blood pressure within normal limits (very few of these patients dropped out of the trial).

Three main classes of drugs are used to treat hypertension. The first, diuretics, act to produce more water and salt in the urine and to relax the small arteries, so bringing down the pressure. The second group, beta blockers, interfere with the hormone and nervous control of the heart, slowing it and causing it to beat less forcefully, so reducing the pressure. The third group, vasodilators, act on the arteries to widen them. This group contains drugs which act in different ways. They include alpha blockers, calcium antagonists and ACE inhibitors.

Doctors treating hypertension sometimes have complex decisions to make. Among others, it may be necessary to decide whether to use drugs at all. Because the patient's body may have adapted to raised blood pressure, reducing it may actually make him or her, for a time, feel worse rather than better. Until readjustment to normal pressures has occurred, there may be weakness, lack of energy, depression and a tendency to dizziness or faintness on standing up. The doctor has to take these effects into account and make sure the patient does not use them as reasons for avoiding treatment. The idea is to try to get the desired effect with the minimum possible prescription and, in this, the patient's change in lifestyle is vital. The doctor needs your cooperation to help you to live out a full lifespan in safety.

Heart failure

If the heart fails to continue to beat, we die, but that is not what happens in heart failure. The term does not mean that the heart has stopped but that, although still contracting regularly, it does so in such a weak manner that it is no longer pumping the blood around the circulation in sufficient volume to carry adequate oxygen and nutritional substances to all parts of the body.

This occurs as a result of various forms of heart disease, especially repeated small heart attacks which have progressively damaged the contracting power of the muscle by replacing a proportion of it with scar tissue. In heart failure the blood flow to the tissues and to the lungs is diminished and slowed. Blood accumulates in the large veins because of the heart's inability to pump out the returning blood fast enough. Congestion results, with engorgement of the veins and other small blood vessels, leading to obvious signs and symptoms. These may vary considerably because the failure usually affects one part of the heart more than another.

When blood returning from the body to the right side of the heart cannot be pushed on to the lungs quickly enough, the condition is called right heart failure. The result is blueness of the skin and accumulation of fluid in the tissues, causing ankle swelling, enlargement of the liver and, in severe cases, a considerable build-up of fluid in the abdomen.

Left heart failure occurs when the left side of the heart is unable to clear the blood from the lungs quickly enough, causing fluid to accumulate in the lungs. The main symptom of left heart failure is breathlessness, which may occur on mild exertion or even when the affected person is at rest. There may be attacks of sudden breathlessness during the night. As the condition worsens, the tendency to breathlessness increases. Eventually, the degree of disability becomes extreme. In both right and left heart failure activity becomes severely restricted.

Heart failure can usually be treated effectively, especially if the underlying cause of the heart damage is remediable. There are drugs, such as digitalis or its derivatives, that can be used to increase the strength and effectiveness of the heart contraction and their use often greatly improves the condition of the affected person. Fluid in the lungs and the tissues can be removed by the use of diuretic drugs, which greatly increase the urinary output so that accumulated fluid is disposed of. After effective treatment for heart failure, the patient is likely to feel greatly relieved. Abdominal fluid may also be removed by drawing it out through a needle.

Sex hormones and ageing in women

It is worth bearing in mind a more general point when considering the effect of declining levels of the sex hormones on women (and men) as they age. When our bodily systems, including the hormonal systems, were being evolved, very few people ever reached old age. The average expectation of life, even as late as the Stone Age, was less than 30 years, so the systems that evolved were appropriate to that kind of lifespan. There were no evolutionary forces determining systems that would work satisfactorily for upward of 80 years.

Once a young couple had produced children, the processes of evolution and perpetuation of the species were satisfied and it did not really matter if neither men nor women reached what we now call middle age. This consideration is particularly apposite in the case of the female sex hormones. During the fertile period – from the onset of menstruation to the menopause – women secrete large quantities of oestrogens into their bloodstreams. These hormones are feminizing and anabolic, that is, they build up body tissue including bones and muscles. After the menopause, oestrogen production stops. Males of the same age range continue to secrete sex hormones and to benefit from their anabolic effect, so women are at a serious disadvantage in this respect.

Evolution operates slowly. We have not been enjoying our current lifespan long enough for evolution to catch up with it. So at this stage women are caught in a trap. If they accept things as they are and, at the same time wish to live well beyond the menopause, they are likely to suffer at least some significant disadvantages.

The menopause

There are several female sex hormones, but for convenience they can be described under the single term oestrogen. Once oestrogen production shuts down, several things happen. The loss of the anabolic effect, and the resulting osteoporosis, is so important that a separate section is devoted to this below. But oestrogen deficiency has a number of other effects.

Although it is not scientifically proven that the symptoms that commonly accompany the menopause – hot flushes, depression, irritability, sweating, insomnia and so on – are wholly the result of oestrogen deficiency, it is widely accepted by doctors and their patients that the prescription of female sex hormones (natural oestrogens) helps to alleviate these symptoms. Few doctors deny women the advantages of such therapy in the short term. Again, the evolutionary argument is strong. If oestrogens were necessary for full health before the menopause, why should they not be necessary after it?

Another important aspect of oestrogen deficiency is its effect on the vagina. Oestrogen is needed to produce a normal vaginal lining with a high content of a sugar-like substance called glycogen. In health, certain normal vaginal bacteria act on glycogen to produce lactic acid, thereby reducing the probability of infection by more dangerous organisms. Vaginal infection caused in this way – as an indirect result of oestrogen deficiency – is now known to be a major cause of persistent urinary infections such as cystitis in post-menopausal women. The vaginal dryness that results from oestrogen deficiency is, by itself, a major disadvantage, making sexual intercourse painful or impossible. This can be rectified without even taking oestrogens by mouth, patch or implant. The vaginal changes are readily corrected by using oestrogen creams, which are widely prescribed, or an oestrogen-containing vaginal ring.

Vaginal atrophy is only part of a general atrophy of all the pelvic organs – the vulva, vagina, cervix, womb and urethra, the tube that carries urine from the bladder to the exterior. This general atrophy can cause pelvic discomfort and encourage an abnormal downward protrusion of the womb known as prolapse. Atrophy of the urethra further encourages urinary infection with frequency of urination, and urgency and discomfort on emptying the bladder, the so-called urethral syndrome.

Oestrogen creams

A report in the prestigious *New England Journal of Medicine* in September 1993 showed that a simple vaginal cream containing oestrogen, applied nightly for two weeks and then twice a week for eight months virtually eliminated urinary infection. In those who were using the cream, only lactobacilli – normal vaginal organisms – were found.

Atrophy from oestrogen deficiency applies also to the skin, the nails and the hair. Skin atrophy is due to a considerable decrease in skin collagen – the protein that gives skin its resilience and elasticity. The result is thinned, dry skin, loss of hair and brittle nails. Similar loss of collagen in the bones is the principal reason for osteoporosis.

Oestrogen deficiency can also have serious effects on a woman's sense of wellbeing. Probably the most serious psychological effect is depression, which tends to be at its worst during the period when oestrogens are tapering off over the course of the menopausal months. Suicides are common then. Depression usually settles after the periods have completely stopped. Other associated mental effects include:

◆ lassitude
◆ loss of energy and motivation

◆ loss of confidence
◆ irritability.

There are so many other possible reasons for these effects at the menopause – children leaving home, awareness of ageing, fear of loss of sexual attractiveness, a sense of reduced value from the inability to conceive – that some doctors remain unconvinced that oestrogen deficiency is the cause. None can deny, however, that when oestrogens are given, there is nearly always a remarkable improvement in a woman's state of mind and her outlook on life.

The most serious effect of oestrogen deficiency, however, has nothing to do with bones, hot flushes, pelvic, skin or psychological problems. Throughout the reproductive period of their lives women have a major health advantage over men – they enjoy a virtual immunity to coronary heart disease and strokes. This immunity is conferred by oestrogens, and once these are cut off the liability to heart attacks and other artery-related disorders increases rapidly. This, in fact, is the principal justification for ensuring that women continue to enjoy the benefits of oestrogen throughout life, in other words, have hormone replacement therapy (HRT).

It follows from all this that, in any real medical sense, the idea of the 'male menopause' is not one to be taken seriously. In fact, it is not much more than a journalistic fiction. It may be that, in a metaphorical sense, some men experience a kind of crisis from awareness of their waning virility and attractiveness. But to call this a 'male menopause' is to equate the menopause with a psychological disorder, which does women no favours.

Hormone replacement therapy (HRT)
The arguments in favour of HRT are still not accepted by all doctors, but the overwhelming majority now agree that HRT is justified. Many take the view that the effects of oestrogen deficiency are just as abnormal as those of any other disease process and that there can be no reason to withhold treatment. These doctors consider that HRT should be offered routinely to all post-menopausal women. The persisting controversy is based on statistical evidence of a slight but real increase in the risk of cancer of the breast and endometrium (the lining of the womb) when oestrogens are taken alone. Although many studies have been done, it is difficult to obtain consistent figures for the increase in the risk. In one typical study of nearly 2000 women in Kentucky who were given oestrogens after the menopause, and followed up for an average of 12 years, 49 developed breast cancer. The expected figure, for the general population, was 39, so 10 extra cases in 2000 were, apparently, caused by the treatment. The study that showed the worst effects indicated an increase to 1.6 women with breast cancer for every 1 woman not on HRT.

All the studies have, however, shown that the overall mortality, including that from breast cancer, is significantly reduced in women on HRT. (None of the studies has shown that there is an increase in the number of deaths from breast cancer following oestrogen HRT.) This is because although men have a much higher risk of serious heart disease than pre-menopausal women, heart attack (coronary thrombosis) is rare in pre-menopausal women, compared with men. This relative protection is due to oestrogens and is lost after the menopause, when the incidence of atherosclerosis rises steeply in women. Hormone replacement therapy allows this protective effect to continue, and this has been borne out in a number of trials.

Principles of hormone replacement therapy

◆ HRT restores lost levels of circulating oestrogen hormones in women after the menopause.

◆ This protects the heart against the development of coronary artery disease, reduces the risk of severe osteoporosis and relieves meno-pausal symptoms.

◆ HRT for 5 to 10 years is likely to be helpful, but indefinite usage may be preferable.

◆ In women who have had a hysterectomy, oestrogen alone may be used.

◆ In others, it is safer to take HRT in cycles of oestrogen followed by oestrogen together with a progesterone hormone (progestogen).

◆ Methods vary but, in a typical cycle, the oestrogen is taken daily, with combined oestrogen/progestogen for about 12 days of that time.

◆ Tablet or skin patch packs ensure that these are correctly administered.

◆ Such combined sequential treatment protects against cancer of the lining of the womb.

◆ HRT should be stopped immediately if you develop migraine-type headaches for the first time, or develop frequent severe headaches, unusual visual disturbances, vein tenderness (venous thrombosis), yellowing of the skin (jaundice) or a rise in blood pressure.

◆ You should discontinue HRT six weeks before any planned surgical operation or if, for any reason, you are forced to remain immobile for any abnormally long period.

◆ Consult your doctor if you have any concerns about HRT.

Before the menopause, natural oestrogens are balanced by progesterone, and interest has been focused on the value of oestrogen replacement therapy combined with progesterone. The evidence suggests that this is safer since it closely resembles the natural state. The addition of progesterone to oestrogen

HRT, apparently, eliminates any additional risk of endometrial cancer. A considerable range of preparations containing the combined formulation is available. There is, however, the disadvantage of continuing menstruation. Ironically, the women best suited to HRT are those who have had the womb surgically removed through hysterectomy. They no longer have any risk of uterine cancer and can enjoy the full benefits of oestrogen therapy without the disadvantages of progesterone. There are some preparations of progestogens (progesterone hormones) with oestrogenic properties, such as livial (Tibolene), designed to avoid menstrual-type bleeding.

HRT uses natural female sex hormones rather than synthetic oestrogens (as used in contraceptive pills). These hormones are oestrone, oestradiol or oestriol and are treated by the body in an entirely natural way, and broken down in the normal manner. In addition to vaginal creams, the hormones may be given by mouth, by skin patches or by implantation into the skin.

In addition to HRT, preparations for overcoming the disadvantages of the loss of natural sex hormones include:

◆ calcium supplements (Ostram, Sandocal 400, Ossopan 800, Ostram)
◆ calcitonin (Calsynar, Myacalcic) – a natural body hormone derived from salmon, that suppresses bone absorption and so maintains bone mass
◆ alendronate (Fosamax) – a drug that interferes with the action of the cells (osteoclasts) that break down bone
◆ anabolic steroids such as nandrolene (Deca-Durabolin) that help to build up bone mass
◆ vaginal oestrogen creams (Ortho Dienoestrol, Overstin, Premarin), pessaries (Ortho-Gynest, Tampovagan) or tablets (Vagifem)
◆ vaginal moisturizers (Replens).

There seem to be other advantages of HRT. The *Lancet* of 17 August 1996 reports an American study of 1124 elderly women in New York City who were checked annually over a five-year follow-up. About 13 per cent of these women had been taking oestrogen HRT for an average of 6.8 years. During the period of the trial 167 women developed Alzheimer's disease. None of those who had been taking HRT when the study started developed Alzheimer's disease, and the figures showed that those who did develop the disease but had previously had HRT took significantly longer to develop Alzheimer's than those who had not had HRT.

Osteoporosis
Osteoporosis is a reduction in the density of the collagen protein scaffolding of the bones and of the calcium salts deposited on the protein. Like other tissues

of the body, the bones are in a state of constant physical and chemical change, losing and gaining calcium and protein, to and from the bloodstream. These changes are controlled by various growth and sex hormones, and alteration in the amounts of these in the body affects the strength of the bones. Various diseases can cause osteoporosis but by far the most common cause is oestrogen deficiency. Other causes include:

◆ overactivity of the thyroid and parathyroid glands
◆ disorders of the adrenal glands
◆ disorders of the pituitary gland
◆ physical underactivity
◆ Cushing's syndrome
◆ acromegaly
◆ diabetes.

The bones are thickest and strongest in early adult life. Thereafter, they become gradually thinner with age, as a result of progressive loss of the protein structure and of calcium. Bones stay strong by being used. Underuse, which occurs in the bedridden or in astronauts living in zero gravity, for example, leads to osteoporosis. Even a change from an active to a sedentary life can cause osteoporosis, as do the ordinary processes of ageing, with associated loss of activity and reduced hormone levels. Women are much worse off than men in this respect because while men continue to secrete anabolic sex hormones into old age, women have an oestrogen shutdown at the menopause and begin to lose calcium in the urine, with progressive weakening of the bones. Adequate dietary calcium in youth is important in minimizing the risk, especially in women.

In most cases of osteoporosis there are no symptoms until some effect of the weakening in the bones occurs. This may be:

◆ loss of height from shrinkage of the bones of the spinal column
◆ severe curvature of the spine
◆ sudden collapse of one of the bones of the spine with severe pain and disfigurement
◆ a wrist or forearm fracture after a fall
◆ an unexpected fracture of the neck of the hip bone as a result of a quite minor stumble or fall.

About one woman in four over 75 suffers hip-bone fracture and the consequences are often serious. They may even shorten life.

These misfortunes can be largely eliminated by ensuring that women maintain a normal oestrogen level after the menopause. The most important period in this respect is the first 10 post-menopausal years. Oestrogens retard the process of bone loss, and may even increase bone bulk.

How to minimize osteoporosis

◆ Take plenty of exercise so as to stress the bones.
◆ Avoid too much lying about.
◆ Walk instead of drive whenever possible.
◆ Have a daily intake of at least 1500 mg of calcium. The main sources of calcium in food are dairy products, eggs, fish and green, leafy vege- tables. Skimmed and fat-reduced milk contain as much calcium as full milk.
◆ Maintain your body's oestrogen levels by HRT.

Cancer of the womb

The commonest womb cancer is that of its neck (cervix); this is second in incidence only to cancer of the breast. The peak incidence of cancer that is confined to the lining (epithelium) of the cervix occurs around 30 years of age, but it is usually another 20 years before this type of cancer becomes seriously invasive. This is why the Pap smear screening test is so important. If detected before invasion occurs, the condition can be completely cured.

For older women, cancer of the lining of the womb (endometrial cancer) occurs most commonly after the menopause, and has a peak incidence at the age of 61. This has different features from cervical cancer, and the first sign is usually irregular bleeding from the vagina or a blood-stained discharge. This is a critically important sign in women after the menopause and must never be ignored. Early diagnosis is essential but this will not be achieved unless post-menopausal bleeding is reported without delay. The diagnosis is made, or eliminated, by taking for microscopic examination a scraping from the inside of the womb by a simple procedure, done under anaesthesia, called dilatation and curretage (D and C).

If the condition is detected at a reasonably early stage and the womb removed (hysterectomy), the outlook is usually excellent. Surgery may be supplemented with radiotherapy.

There are certain known factors that increase the risk of endometrial cancer. These are:

◆ age
◆ not having had children

- late menopause
- obesity
- certain cysts of the ovary
- ovarian tumours that secrete oestrogen
- oestrogen hormone replacement therapy alone.

The risk of endometrial cancer is not considered, in itself, a reason to avoid HRT, but many women feel safer if they take oestrogen and progesterone together. This is something you should discuss with your doctor.

Hysterectomy

This is the operation of removal of the womb. This may be done through the vagina, or, more easily, through an incision in the front wall of the abdomen. Hysterectomy is done for a variety of reasons. These include:

- cancer of the womb
- large benign fibrous tumours (fibroids)
- severely excessive menstruation (menorrhagia)
- excessive menstrual pain.

Large numbers of women have had a hysterectomy, especially in the United States where an estimated half a million women have their wombs removed every year and where, at one time, about a quarter of all women over 50 had had the operation. In Britain, hysterectomy is performed on a lesser scale but is still a common operation.

A hysterectomy may be 'subtotal', in which the body of the womb is removed but the neck (the cervix) is left, or total, in which the upper part of the vagina is cut around and stitched closed. The latter is now the more usual procedure. A Wertheim's hysterectomy, for cancer, involves removal of the womb, Fallopian tubes and ovaries, the upper third of the vagina and all the lymph nodes in the region.

There are two possible approaches to total hysterectomy. In vaginal hysterectomy, the womb is pulled down. A cut is made around the cervix and down the front wall of the vagina to allow access to the interior so that the attachments of the womb to the side walls may be cut and the womb removed. The floor of the pelvis is then strengthened and the opening in the vagina stitched closed. This avoids a visible scar on the abdomen, but has the disadvantage that the vaginal scars are more extensive. After abdominal hysterectomy the internal scar is confined to the upper end of the vagina, which is now a blind-ended tube.

In either case, no ill effects arise as a result of the slight shortening of the vagina, as this structure is highly elastic and stretches easily. Sexual intercourse is best avoided for about six weeks after a hysterectomy, especially after a vaginal hysterectomy. Any subsequent problems with sexual intercourse are unlikely to be caused by such mechanical problems, but may arise from hormone deficiency if the ovaries have been removed.

Sex hormones and ageing in men

Sex hormone treatment for osteoporosis in men is useful only in those relatively rare cases in which bone loss is due to inadequate natural sex hormone production. But in both sexes, calcium supplements are valuable and help to strengthen the bones. Paradoxically, in men the continuing secretion of sex hormones is responsible for one of the commonest age-related medical problems – benign enlargement of the prostate gland.

Prostate gland enlargement
The prostate is a gland, comparable in size, shape, colour and consistency to a chestnut, which surrounds the first few centimetres of the urethra in men. It lies immediately under the bladder and close in front of the wall of the rectum, through which it can easily be felt and its size estimated. The prostate secretes a thin, milky, slightly alkaline fluid which helps to keep sperm active while they are waiting to be released at ejaculation. The prostate enlarges progressively from about the age of 30 onward under the influence of the male sex hormone testosterone. This enlargement is due to the production of additional cells and for this reason it is called benign prostatic hyperplasia.

About a quarter of men over 65 experience moderate to severe symptoms due to benign prostatic hyperplasia. Enlargement is liable to interfere with the outflow of urine from the bladder by narrowing the urethra, or even by expanding upward into the bladder so as to form a kind of ball-valve. There is reduction in the force of the urine stream and incomplete emptying of the bladder (residual urine), leading to increased frequency of urination with repeated necessity to get up at night. Sudden acute stoppage may occur, requiring the emergency passage of a catheter or, if this is impossible because of the degree of narrowing of the urethra, drainage of the bladder by means of a wide needle passed through the abdominal wall. Back pressure can damage bladder function and the kidneys. Fortunately, such acute emergencies are uncommon.

Millions of older men suffer considerable inconvenience and distress as a result of prostate enlargement. The major disadvantage results from the increased difficulty in emptying the bladder. There is a limit to the amount of force the muscular wall of the bladder can exert to empty itself and if the outlet is obstructed this limit is soon reached. But, as some of the urine is passed from a full bladder, the desire to urinate diminishes and the affected man, for a time, feels comfortable. He may even think that his bladder is empty. But because the bladder actually still contains a considerable quantity of urine, it quickly fills up again and the need to urinate soon returns.

Urinary frequency of this kind is a major social embarrassment and can seriously limit mobility. These effects can be even more distressing than having to get up every hour or so during the night. When matters reach this stage, treatment is long overdue, but this outcome is by no means universal. The average 50-year-old man has a 20 to 25 per cent chance of requiring treatment for prostate enlargement at some time in later life. One important observation is that up to one-third of men who begin to have prostate problems of this kind actually enjoy at least some degree of spontaneous improvement. This may be because of a reduced output of testosterone. It is also a reason for not rushing too quickly into prostate surgery. Reduced testosterone output also somewhat reduces libido.

There are various ways in which prostatic enlargement can be treated and great advances have been made in this field. The condition often has to be treated by removal of part or all of the gland. This is most commonly done through the urethra, using a special viewing and cutting instrument called a resectoscope. If the enlargement is considerable, a direct surgical approach through the lower part of the wall of the abdomen and the wall of the bladder may be necessary. The results of this operation, known as trans-urethral prostatectomy (TURP) are usually excellent. About 80 per cent of patients are improved and 74 per cent entirely happy with the result.

But surgery is not the only option. Because testosterone affects the enlargement of the gland, drugs can be used to interfere with the process. In fact, testosterone is converted into dihydrotestosterone before it can act on the gland. This conversion is performed by an enzyme called 5-alpha-reductase. The action of this enzyme can be blocked by a drug called finasteride (trade name Proscar), which many men with prostatism have found helpful. Other drugs act by reducing the production of testosterone or blocking testosterone receptors on cells. Finasteride does not change the levels of testosterone in the blood so does not affect libido or potency. Some of the other drugs may do so.

There is a lot you can do for yourself to help reduce the effects of a prostate problem. First of all, never ignore symptoms of urinary obstruction. If you are in any doubt, carry out a simple test of flow rate. With a comfortably full bladder check how long it takes to fill a 200 ml container. If it takes more than 20 seconds, you almost certainly have an obstruction. In such a case, the least action needed is to see your doctor for a proper rectal examination of the prostate. You also need a urine check.

Remember that prostate problems vary in severity from time to time. There is, for instance, a fairly common condition known as prostatitis that can cause severe obstruction, often seeming to cut off the flow altogether for a time. Prostatitis is an inflammation of the gland and, unlike benign enlargement, this causes pain. Treatment with an appropriate antibiotic or sulpha drug can cure this and restore the full force of the stream. Remember also that the bladder is in close contact with the rectum, which lies immediately behind it. In men with prostate enlargement, a full rectum, or even a rectum distended with gas, can angle the bladder forward enough to produce a kinking effect in the urethra and make urination even more difficult. A good diet high in roughage can help to relieve the effects of prostate enlargement.

To empty the urine trapped in the urethra and avoid dribbling, after finishing press upward with your fingertips just behind the scrotum and massage forward. Once the urethra is emptied, dab with a clean tissue.

It is not a good idea to try to solve the problem of too-frequent visits to the toilet by drinking smaller quantities of fluids to produce less urine. This can lead to a rise in the levels of waste products in the blood and may also encourage urinary infection. Even so, you can help yourself to some extent by limiting evening drinking. So far as urine production is concerned, the effects of a large drink of water or other fluid are not felt after about three hours. So if you take plenty to drink during the day but avoid drinking in the three hours or so before bedtime, you should be able to reduce the number of times you need to get up at night. You can apply the same principle to special occasions, such as long car journeys, visits to friends or theatre, and so on. But remember that regular washing out of the bladder is necessary to reduce the risk of infection.

There is a more radical solution to the problem of benign prostate enlargement. This is to pass a tube – a catheter – into your own bladder to let out the urine. Modern catheters are made of materials with a low coefficient of friction so that they slip in easily, although you may have to push a little to get through the narrowed part directly below the bladder. The catheter has a pointed bung to close the outer end so, once the clean end is in the bladder you can nip the tube with your fingers, direct it into the toilet bowl, pull out the bung and let go. Some men use a catheter every time they need to urinate; others do it at night before going to bed, or once a day at some other time to avoid the accumulation of residual urine.

On no account try to achieve this on your own; the method must be done under medical supervision and instruction. Many doctors dislike catheters, mainly because their hospital training showed how often catheterization led to bladder infection. But there is a basic difference between long-term (indwelling) catheterization and the kind of intermittent catheterization described here. Infection is far more common with the former than the latter. Never-theless there are one or two important points to be made. You may have difficulty in finding a doctor who will agree to cooperate, so you might have to shop around (continence nurses are likely to be more enthusiastic). The method is certainly an advance on having a permanent catheter connected to a urine bag in place.

Remember that the principal risk is infection, so high standards of cleanliness are vital. It is impracticable for a lay person to achieve hospital standards of sterility with this procedure, but your doctor or adviser will make sure you understand how to minimize the risks and how to look after the catheter. If you can keep your bladder in a normal state of regular emptying so as to avoid stretching its walls by overfilling, the blood supply to the lining will be improved and the body's natural immune mechanisms against infection will work better.

Although it is good to do as much as possible for yourself, it is a mistake to assume you can do everything. Remember that the more severe the obstruction, the more potentially serious the situation. If the symptoms of obstruction are severe, you also need a blood check to ensure that your kidneys have not been damaged by raised back pressure. Today the routine way to scan the prostate is by ultrasound. Modern, high-resolution machines can immediately show the size of your prostate and indicate whether urine is retained in your bladder after urination.

Remember also, that benign hyperplasia and prostatitis are not the only cause of prostate enlargement. The other important cause is cancer. If a close relative has (or has had) prostate cancer, you must have a complete prostate examination at regular intervals. Although digital rectal examination is man-datory, ultrasound scanning is also necessary. This method can detect twice as many prostate cancers as rectal examination alone. If there is any doubt, the urologist can take a prostate biopsy easily and painlessly. This is often done by passing a needle into the gland from the inside of the rectum and sucking out small samples of tissue.

Cancer of the prostate

Cancer of the prostate is the second most common cancer in men. Its symptoms are similar to those of simple enlargement, but on rectal examina-tion the gland is felt to be very hard and irregular. The degree of malignancy of prostate cancers varies widely and in many cases the tumour may be present for years, causing no trouble. On the other hand, it sometimes happens that at the time of diagnosis there may already be indications that the tumour has spread to other parts of the body, often to the bones.

These facts underline the importance of regular checks for prostate trouble in elderly men. Currently the best screening method for prostate cancer is regular digital rectal examination in conjunction with the prostate-specific antigen (PSA) test. This tests the levels of a tumour marker in the blood that is raised when prostate cancer is present. PSA is an enzyme that normally acts to help liquefy the seminal fluid. Its levels are raised in both benign enlargement and in cancer. The normal levels in young adults are between 0 and 4 nanograms per millilitre; an increase in prostate bulk of 1 g raises the level by about 0.3 ng/ml. The rise in the case of cancer depends on the degree of malignancy of the tumour. Levels of between 4 and 40 ng/ml occur, and the higher the level the more advanced the cancer. So far as you are concerned, the test merely involves taking a little blood. Although borderline levels tell us little, if the levels are high the test is a reliable indicator of prostate cancer. A modestly raised PSA is not an absolute indication of cancer, and prostate cancer does not necessarily indicate that immediate surgery is necessary.

There is some good news about prostate cancer. The condition is far more common than is supposed, which indicates that many prostate cancers do little or no harm. Thirty per cent of post-mortem examinations of men over 50 show that prostate cancer is present. The incidence also rises with age. For this reason, prostate cancer is often left untreated in elderly men, because the risk of progression during the normal lifetime is low.

If treatment is considered necessary, it may be done by external beam radiotherapy or surgery. Radiotherapy is painless and can give excellent results. Surgery may involve removal of the prostate, either as is done for benign enlargement (see p. 38) or by a standard open operation through an incision in the abdominal wall. Prostate cancers are encouraged by high levels of male sex hormones, and elimination of these hormones is a valuable additional measure in the treatment. This is done either by neutralizing the hormone by giving female sex hormones or by removing the testicles. If the testicles are removed, they can be replaced by plastic prostheses. Female sex hormone treatment can cause side effects such as a degree of enlargement of the breasts, which may complicate this treatment.

If the PSA level is low, the probability of extensive spread of the cancer is also low. Bone scans are usually done to check whether the cancer has spread. These are 97 per cent negative if the PSA is low.

Age and the senses

Age is often characterized by a reduction in sensory acuity, chiefly in a loss of clarity in hearing, and in short sightedness and other problems affecting the eyes. The tastebuds may be less sensitive than previously too, and the sense of smell may decline. Touch may not be affected.

Hearing

One of the stereotypes of the elderly is that they are deaf. This is not so, of course. Many quite old people retain almost fully functional hearing. But progressive loss of hearing associated with advancing age is common. It occurs often enough to warrant a title – presbyacusis, derived from the Greek word *presbus*, meaning 'an old man'.

There are good reasons for the decline in hearing with age. The upper frequency limit of hearing in childhood is at least 16,000 cycles per second (Hz), but this falls progressively with age so that few people over 70 can hear much above 5000 Hz. The loss of ability to hear high-pitched sounds, such as sibilants (hissing sounds) in speech and the highest notes in music, is due to degenerative changes in the delicate hair cells and nerve fibres in the organ of Corti, part of the cochlea in the inner ear. No one knows for certain why this occurs, but we do know that hair-cell damage can be caused by a number of different factors. They include:

♦ prolonged exposure to high noise levels
♦ brief exposure to very high noise levels such as explosions
♦ slaps or blows to the ears
♦ diminished blood supply to the inner ear from arterial disease
♦ toxic damage from drugs
♦ various viral and bacterial infections
♦ hereditary influences.

Since developments in sound reproduction technology made it easy and cheap to produce sound levels in the 1000 watt range, large numbers of young people, especially musicians, have been exposed to excessive levels of acoustic trauma. These people are now beginning to suffer deafness. Personal stereo equipment can also cause permanent hearing loss. It is too easy to turn up the volume to compensate for deafness, thereby compounding the problem. The firing of shotguns and other weapons is another common cause of acoustic trauma and deafness. Spontaneous ringing or hissing inside the head (tinnitus) is a clear warning that damage is being caused.

As a result of these often unconsidered factors, many people in their mid-50s have already suffered so much high-tone loss that normal conversation may be difficult or impossible for them. Background noise increases the problem and loud sounds often produce an unpleasant, almost painful, blasting effect called recruitment. This is one reason why people with presbyacusis often resent being shouted at. Another reason is the tendency, because of the gradual progression of the condition, not to recognize that deafness exists and to blame external factors, such as the failure of others to speak clearly enough.

Nothing can be done to restore function to hair cells that have been destroyed by any of these processes. Modern hearing aids are often, but not always, helpful.

Hearing aids

Although modern aids can do much to overcome the problems of deafness, fewer than one-third of candidates for hearing aids have them.

Hearing aids are more than simply electronic amplifiers that increase the strength of the sound. The normally functioning inner ear is exquisitely sensitive to low-intensity sound, but it also has remarkable discriminating powers that enable us to hear quiet sounds in the presence of loud ones. It has a built-in automatic volume control that adjusts the amplification, instantly, as required. But hearing aids, although sophisticated, have not yet advanced to this stage and many people find them unsatisfactory. The main reason for this is that aids increase the levels of all sounds, including background noise, which can be annoying.

Hearing aids have a tiny, highly sensitive microphone that picks up sound and turns it into electrical fluctuations or, in the more recent models, digital pulses. These are then increased in amplitude and turned back into sound at a much higher level. It is essential that there should not be any feedback from the sound output stage to the microphone. If this happens, the whole equipment turns into an oscillator that produces loud squeals. These are painful on the ear and preclude hearing anything.

This effect can be eliminated by substituting for the microphone a simple coil of wire to act as an electromagnetic pickup. Most aids have this facility and you switch to it by moving a tiny lever to the 'T' position. Most theatres, cinemas, churches, rail and bus stations and many other public places are equipped with an electromagnetic inductive loop system so that people with hearing aids can get announcements and hear dialogue without interference. The electromagnetic pickup system works only in buildings equipped for the purpose but can usually be used with the telephone. Homes can be fitted with an inductive loop so that TV and radio can be heard well.

Hearing aids may be worn behind the ear or in the ear canal. They can be fitted into the side-pieces of substantial spectacle frames. They should not be confused with cochlear implants which are used only for people with no useful hearing whatsoever and which produce, at best, a very limited standard of performance.

Most people with a hearing defect can benefit from a hearing aid but in many the deafness is so severe that amplification cannot make up the deficiency. It is not that amplification is insufficient but that in severe deafness high amplification often causes recruitment, or 'blasting' – an unpleasant and uncomfortable feeling of loudness. This limits useful amplification. Recent hearing aid designs have attempted to overcome the problem of recruitment by amplification compression. This means that quiet sounds are amplified more than loud sounds. Unfortunately, this method may result in background noise being amplified so much that it swamps the sounds we want to hear. Most back-ground noise, however, is at a lower pitch than speech, which contains many high-frequency sibilants. So the latest idea is to split sounds into low- and high-frequency components and to amplify each separately. The crossover point can be adjusted to provide the best results. And in each channel, the compression levels can also be adjusted. The result is a greatly improved system that can offer real benefits to a higher proportion of deaf people.

Hearing aids are available on the NHS and current designs are a vast improvement on those originally issued. They are not, however, as sophisti-cated as some of those available privately. Until recently, only four people out of five who obtained hearing aids were still using them six months after being supplied. The latest aids should improve this figure, but it is important not to be influenced by the hype of the hearing aid salesperson. There are self-styled hearing aid 'consultants' who actually have little or no real knowledge or qualifications. Don't consider buying an aid until you have had a full examina-tion by an ENT specialist and sought his or her advice. Some forms of deafness can be cured by such simple means as syringing out ear wax; others can be cured by surgery. In many cases deafness is caused by middle ear disease or by disease of the eustachian tubes, outer ear canals or eardrums. Many of these conditions can be effectively treated.

Vision

The commonest visual problem affecting older people is presbyopia. This is not so much a disease as the natural consequence of the continuing production of lens fibres in the eyes' lenses. As a result of the packing in of ever more lens fibres, the lenses become less elastic and thus less able to alter their shape to focus on near objects. The effect is usually noticed around the age of 45 in people with normal eyesight, but comes on earlier in long-sighted people and may never occur at all in short-sighted people (who can see close things without focusing).

Essentially, the problem is a progressive loss of accommodation – the ability to change the curvature of the lenses to increase their power for near vision, which is greatest in childhood. Because of the way the lenses continue to grow, this ability gradually weakens with age until, around the age of 65, very little focusing power remains. As a result, the nearest point at which clear vision is possible gradually moves away. You will still be able to make out print which is large enough, but the diminishing effect of perspective may make small print impossible to read.

Simple lenses of low magnification, prescribed as reading glasses, are used to compensate for presbyopia. Assuming that distance vision is normal, the first prescription will be lenses of the power of one dioptre (a lens of focal length 1 m, or 3 ft). These will need to be progressively increased in strength, every few years, over the course of about 20 years until, eventually, all the focusing is being done by the glasses. On average five or six changes of prescription are necessary over that period. If you have a basic refractive error that requires glasses, such as long sight, short sight or astigmatism, the presbyopic correction is added to the basic correction. A long-sighted (hypermetropic) person wearing + 2.00 dioptre lenses for constant use who begins to have reading difficulties at the age of 45 will probably need + 3.00 dioptre lenses for reading. A very short-sighted (myopic) person wearing glasses or contact lenses of – 10 dioptres, who begins to have reading difficulties at age 45, will probably need – 9.00 dioptre lenses for reading. So a hypermetropic person will need stronger lenses and a short-sighted person, weaker lenses. A person with two or three dioptres of myopia (short sight) will never need reading glasses.

It should seldom be necessary to change reading glasses more often than about once every four or five years, by about half a dioptre each time. The usual reading correction, at 60, for a person with normal distance vision, is about + 2.50 dioptres. Lenses of this power focus at 40 cm (16 in) – a convenient reading distance – with no accommodation. The power needed in the reading glasses is affected by the basic refraction at distance.

It is essential for older people, in particular, to appreciate the importance of adequate illumination. Many presbyopic people have been surprised to note how easily they can read out of doors on a bright sunny day. This is because presbyopic problems are caused as much by poor lighting as by internal lens inadequacies. Photographers are aware of the effect of 'stopping down' a lens system – making the aperture smaller. This always increases the depth of focus – the range of distance over which a clear image is formed. A camera with an enormous aperture lens focused on a near object may have a depth of focus of only a few centimetres; a pinhole camera focuses from a close point to infinity. The obvious way to stop down the human eye – make the pupil smaller – and increase its depth of focus, is to increase the brightness of the light entering the eye. It is no good trying to do this by shining a light directly into the eye: that would only cause dazzling. The way to do it is to ensure that maximum brightness is reflected from the book or newspaper page.

This raises another important point. In trying to increase brightness on a surface, the distance of the light source is far more important than the absolute brightness of the source. This is because light from a source spreads out. Imagine a point of light at the centre of a sphere. The light is illuminating the whole of the inside surface of the sphere. Now, if the radius of the sphere – the distance from the point to the surface – is doubled, the same light will not have twice the area to cover, but twice the area squared, that is four times the area: its brightness is reduced to a quarter. If the radius is increased tenfold, the brightness is reduced by 10 squared, that is to one-hundredth.

This so-called inverse square law is very important to presbyopic people trying to read. It means, for instance, that an electric light bulb in an anglepoise lamp set 30 cm (12 in) from the page you are reading will produce 100 times the brightness of the same bulb hanging 3 m (10 ft) away from the middle of the ceiling.

Acquired short sight in the elderly

Short sight is normally a lifelong condition, starting in childhood or adolescence. Occasionally, however, an elderly person who has been using reading glasses for years, finds that he or she can manage to read reasonably comfortably without glasses. This phenomenon is always associated with a reduction in the clarity of the distance vision, and in fact is a form of acquired short sight. The reason for this condition is a change in the light-bending power of the internal eye lenses brought about by a pre-cataractous condition known as nuclear sclerosis.

This term simply means hardening of the central parts of the lenses. The condition is usually progressive and tends to lead to ever-increasing degrees of short sight. This special form of short sight is called index myopia because the refractive index – the bending power – of the lens has increased. Index myopia can progress steadily to high degrees so that many changes of glasses may be needed for correction. It it is occurring rapidly it is probably a waste of money to buy a succession of ever-stronger glasses for distance vision or TV, but glasses can be useful for a time. Sooner or later the centres of the lenses will begin to become so opaque that neither distance nor near vision is adequate. This opacification is called cataract (see below). The essential thing to remember, however, is that if your vision was normal before this last stage developed, there is no reason why it should not be fully restored by treatment of the cataract.

Cataract

Many older people still dread cataracts, partly because of a natural revulsion at the prospect of having anything done to the eyes and partly because some may, in their youth, have heard stories of operations going wrong. There may have been some foundation for these worries many years ago, but there are certainly no grounds for them today. The surgical treatment of cataract – and there is no alternative to surgery – is one of the most successful of all operations and, given that the eye is otherwise healthy, the results are excellent. Millions of people have been restored to full vision by this essentially straightforward operation.

The term cataract arose from the fanciful notion that the appearance of whiteness, seen in the pupil in cases of dense lens opacity, was caused by a 'cataract' or waterfall descending from above. This imaginative idea is complete nonsense, but the name has stuck. Many people confuse cataract with the whiteness of the cornea – the outer window or lens of the eye – caused by scarring or inflammation. But cataract has nothing to do with the cornea.

Another popular notion is that cataract is some kind of 'skin' growing over some part of the eye. This, too, is wrong. Cataract is an opacification of the internal focusing lens of the eye (the crystalline lens) which lies behind the coloured iris. Only a small central part of the lens can normally be seen through the pupil, the circular hole in the centre of the coloured iris. Most cataracts, even those that cause quite severe loss of visual clarity, do not cause obvious whitening of the visible part of the lens. Only dense cataracts which have extended right to the front of the lens so that the lens matter immediately behind the plane of the iris is very white, produce a visibly white pupil.

Cataract is due to irreversible structural changes in the orderly arrangement of the fibres from which the lens is made. The change is due to coagulation, or denaturing, of the lens fibre protein, in much the same way as occurs in the transparent albumen of an egg when it is heated. This opacification may be limited to the periphery of the lens, in which case it causes no trouble, since this part of the lens is covered by the iris except when the pupil is widely dilated. Alternatively, the opacity may be confined to the central part of the back of the lens. In this case, the eye appears normal to an external observer and the pupil remains black, but because the central part of the lens is involved in focusing the image on the retina, such opacity causes scattering of the light rays and produces severe effects on vision. A central opacity at the front or in the middle of the lens unless it is very small, also severely affects vision. Isolated very small dense opacities, which are frequently present from birth, have little effect on vision because they do not scatter light.

Cataract never causes complete blindness in the sense of total absence of the perception of light. People with dense cataracts can still usually distinguish an open from a closed door and always see windows in daytime. But as the transparency of the lenses is gradually lost, image clarity slowly declines and perception of detail decreases until eventually it is lost. If a cataract is associated with total inability to perceive any light at all, there must be something else seriously wrong with the eye or the optic nerve. This is an important point: vision cannot be restored by cataract surgery in such a case. If the blindness is of recent onset, and the inside of the eye cannot be examined because of dense cataract, ultrasound scanning is needed to try to determine the cause.

Some degree of lens opacification is present in almost everyone over the age of about 60. Usually this is patchy and worse at the edges of the lenses so that there is little effect on vision. But the process almost always progresses steadily with age and testing of people over 75 usually shows a drop in visual acuity from lens opacity. Few people in their 80s are free from appreciable visual loss from this cause. So cataract in the elderly should be considered almost normal. These opacities come on gradually and are often inapparent to those affected until they have reached a fairly advanced stage.

Cataract usually causes a change in the perception of colours. Reds, yellows and orange are accentuated at the expense of blue but, because of the gradual nature of the change, this too may remain unnoticed. Comparison of the vision in the two eyes may show that one is a little yellower than the other. This suggests an early cataract in the eye with the yellow vision. Patients are commonly surprised at the brilliance of blues after cataract operations. The irregular opacification of the lenses, a common feature of cataract, causes some rays of light entering the eye to be scattered while some are not. This may occur at an early stage and can be very annoying. The effect is particular noticeable when the headlights of approaching cars shine in the eyes while driving at night. Many people, otherwise barely affected, find they have to avoid night driving for this reason.

It is impossible to restore transparency to a cataractous lens and unrealistic to imagine that cataract can be cured by medication. The treatment is to remove the opaque lens surgically and replace it by a tiny, featherweight plastic lens. This is increasingly being performed as a day procedure under local anaes-thesia so that there is no need to remain in hospital overnight. This is a brief account of the operation as performed by most eye surgeons today.

Before being taken to theatre the patient is given eye drops to make the pupil as wide as possible, and a sedative to relieve anxiety and promote relaxation. Many patients fall asleep spontaneously but this is not necessary. The local anaesthetic involves a few small painless injections in and through the eyelids. The anaesthetic quickly removes all sensation from the whole of the eyeball, lids and surrounding parts. It also temporarily stops the optic nerve from working so vision is blacked out. The skin of the face and lids is carefully cleaned and everything but the eye to be operated on covered with sterile towels, so the patient sees and feels nothing and is unaware of what is going on.

The operation is performed using an operating microscope and delicate instruments. A short curved incision is made in the upper part of the cornea to open the eyeball. Because the pupil is artificially enlarged by the drops, a large part of the front surface of the lens capsule is exposed. The central part of this is removed and sterile saltwater injected into the lens capsule to separate the lens from it, so that the lens can be gently squeezed out of the capsule and out of the incision. Any residual lens matter – there is always some – is removed by washing and suction, leaving an empty capsule. The lens implant is slid inside. Sometimes the surgeon works through a very short incision using a fine ultrasound probe that can emulsify the whole lens so that all lens material can be sucked out. In this case, he or she may use a recent type of lens implant made of flexible material which can be rolled up so that it can be inserted through a very small opening that is self-sealing and requires no stitches. In most cases, however, the incision must be closed. Stitch material much finer than a human hair may be used in a continuous zigzag. The knot can be pulled in below the surface so as to avoid minor discomfort after the operation. Sometimes stitches have to be removed by a minor procedure later; sometimes they are left in place.

A light pad and a plastic protective shield may be applied and the patient is taken back to the ward. The operation may also be performed under general anaesthesic but this usually requires at least one or two nights in hospital.

Macular degeneration

This is one of the most serious ocular misfortunes suffered by older people. Macular degeneration is a disorder of the retina, usually affecting elderly people and causing progressive loss of the central part of the field of vision. It is caused by defects in the insulating layer between the retina and the layer behind it – the choroid – so that leakage of fluid occurs into the retina with progressive destruction of the rods and cones and connecting nerves.

The condition affects only the central, most sensitive parts of the retina and thus produces loss of central vision. Vision to the sides remains normal but, of course, peripheral vision is less clear and useful than central vision. It is of value only for getting about safely. Established macular degeneration in both eyes means that the affected person cannot read, tell the time, recognize other people or watch TV. It is a disabling condition that justifies registration as totally blind.

Macular degeneration can affect both eyes simultaneously, but usually one eye is affected weeks or months before the other. In some cases the process can be arrested by laser treatment to seal the leak in the membrane behind the retina. This results in a permanent gap in vision, but stops further degeneration of the retina. Anyone noticing any loss or distortion of central vision or a gap in the field of vision in one eye should report this at once. It is a very good idea to check the vision of each eye separately, every now and then, by covering one eye at a time.

Glaucoma

There are several forms of glaucoma, but the kind that is especially prevalent in older people is chronic simple glaucoma. The principal feature of all the glaucomas is that the pressure of the fluid within the eyeball is too high. A certain minimum pressure is required to maintain the shape and size of the eyeball so that it can function efficiently as an optical instrument and not be easily indented by minor external force. But if the pressure is too high, it exceeds the pressure of the blood in the small arteries inside the eye and these are flattened and obstructed. Certain arteries supplying the beginning of the optic nerve are especially liable to be closed off by excess pressure, and it is this region which suffers most in glaucoma.

Long-term, minor deprivation of blood to the head of the optic nerve gradually kills off the nerve fibres from the retina, which bundle together to form the optic nerve. When this happens, segments of the retina cease to function and parts of the total field of vision are permanently lost. The disorder is particularly insidious in chronic simple glaucoma because the fibres first affected are those coming from the outer part of the retina which allow vision around to the sides and above and below. The visual system works in such a way that we are largely unaware of the quality, or even the presence, of vision in areas to which our attention is not directed. Since we can, in general, direct attention only by looking straight at something, using the central retina, defects in the peripheral visual fields readily pass unnoticed. Unless looked for, therefore, glaucomatous damage is often extensive before it is detected. Chronic simple glaucoma is a major cause of blindness and visual field loss is irremediable. If detected early, however, the pressures can be controlled and the damage stopped.

Pressure in the eye is maintained by the continuous secretion of water (aqueous humour) inside the eyeball. This has nothing to do with tears. This water can escape from the interior of the eye into the veins only by way of a filter, running all around the inside of the eye, near the root of the iris. This filter has tiny meshes that offer considerable resistance to the outflow of the water, and the normal pressure range within the eye is maintained by a fine balance between the production of the water on the one hand and its escape through the filter on the other. If the resistance offered by the filter rises for any reason, the pressure rises because even very high pressure does not stop the water from being secreted. This is what happens in chronic simple glaucoma. The process is gradual, subtle and almost entirely painless and the affected person is usually unaware that any damage is being done. The reason for the obstruction to outflow in this form of glaucoma is not fully understood but its effect is exactly as if the filter had become clogged up.

Chronic simple glaucoma runs in families and is more likely to occur in relatives of people with the disease. Only in the late stages are there obvious signs and, by that time, so much peripheral visual field has been lost that the affected person is probably constantly bumping into others on crowded pavements. Central vision is usually the last to go and one eye may be completely blind before the affected person is aware that anything is amiss.

Only about one person in 100 has glaucoma at the age of 40, but the incidence rises steeply with age so that, by 70, about one in 10 has significantly raised eye pressures and is at risk. For glaucoma to be detected before severe damage is done, it must be looked for. One of the signs is a hollowing out (cupping) of the optic nerve head, which can be detected during a routine eye examination. But the real test is to measure the internal pressure by a technique known as tonometry. If the pressure is found to be above the upper limit of normal, the visual fields are checked and arrangements made for follow-up. If glaucoma is diagnosed, eye drops are given to keep the pressures within normal limits. Occasionally, medical treatment fails and an operation may be needed.

In other, less common, forms of glaucoma, the outlet obstruction can be caused by mechanical processes or disease and the effects may be much more sudden and severe, with great pain and sudden loss of all vision. This is the case in acute congestive glaucoma or in glaucomas caused by inflammatory eye disease with adhesions.

Everyone should be aware of the possibility of glaucoma. This is one of the main reasons for routine eye checks every two or three years. These are provided free under the NHS for anyone who has a relative with glaucoma. Don't be put off with a simple test of vision; insist that the pressure in your eyes be tested. This is a painless procedure involving, at the worst, a drop of quick-acting local anaesthetic in each eye. Air-puff tonometers are commonly used for routine screening and require no anaesthetic, but a more accurate and reliable method involves momentary light physical contact with the surface of the cornea. This method requires local anaesthetic eye drops.

The optician will report raised eye pressure to your GP who will arrange for a referral to an eye specialist in hospital.

Taste and smell

Research into age-related changes in the ability to taste and smell indicates that a minor decline in taste and a somewhat greater decline in the sense of smell are usual. These changes are related to a degree of atrophy of the tastebuds on the tongue and of the nerve fibres that stimulate smell. Common experience, however, shows that as a rule these changes do little to diminish the pleasure and satisfaction to be derived from good food and wine.

The pleasures of the table are one of the many consolations of advancing age. The real problem is to prevent this pleasure from getting out of hand so that it becomes a danger to health. For some, eating and drinking become a central preoccupation, and this should be avoided. One way of so doing is to remember that such overindulgence quickly detracts from the total satisfaction. Discrimination implies moderation, and there is no better stimulus to the appetite or better promoter of delight in sensual gratification, than the odd hunger pang.

Age and the skin

What may appear to be pure 'age changes' are often more conspicuous in the skin than anywhere else. In fact, many of these changes are due not so much to age as to long exposure to sunlight, much of which is avoidable. Another established and avoidable cause of skin 'ageing' is smoking cigarettes. In one research project, after adjusting for age, sex and sun exposure, it was found that heavy smokers were nearly five times more likely to have wrinkled skin than non-smokers.

Many people assume that the skin is simply a waterproof body covering. But it is a great deal more than this. The skin is a major self-renewing and self-repairing organ, 1.5 to 2 sq m (4.5 to 6 sq ft) in area, that provides heat regulation for the body and protection from the outside world. It is sensitive to touch, pressure, pain, irritation, heat and cold and is an important sensory interface between the body and the outer world, endlessly sending environmental information to the brain. In addition to preventing undue loss of water – the interior of the body is largely composed of water – it controls loss of some small soluble molecules (known as electrolytes) and proteins.

The skin screens against light damage by absorbing light energy into the pigment melanin, and is a complete barrier against the alpha particles of radioactivity. A healthy skin resists bacterial attack, and the constant shedding of the outer horny layer of the outer layer of the skin (epidermis) also actively dislodges microorganisms. The skin synthesizes vitamin D.

Pores are the small openings in the skin through which sweat passes from tiny glands situated in all layers of the skin. Hair follicles into which the sebaceous glands producing the oily secretion sebum are also pores. In the skin of the nose, the hairs in these follicles are usually small in comparison with the sebaceous glands, so that the pore appears to be concerned solely with sebum production. Sebaceous glands in the areola of the breast, in the labia minora and in the prepuce discharge through pores which are also independent of the hair follicles.

The epidermis is the outermost layer of the skin. As the name implies, it lies beyond or outside the true skin, or dermis. The epidermis has no nerves, blood vessels or hair follicles, and acts as a rapidly replaceable surface capable of tolerating a great deal of abrasion and trauma.

The deepest layer of the epidermis is called the basal cell layer and it is this layer which grows abnormally in the common skin cancer basal cell carcinoma, or rodent ulcer. This layer contains the pigment melanin in concentrations which vary from person to person. It is this layer that is involved initially in the dangerous condition of malignant melanoma. Above the basal layer is the prickle cell layer, and it is the prickle cells which grow abnormally in common warts. The outermost cells of the epidermis are dead and are continuously shed.

The apocrine glands are sweat glands found in the hairy parts of the body, especially in the armpits and groin. They develop after puberty and produce sweat which is broken down by skin bacteria to substances responsible for unpleasant body odour. Apocrine sweat should be washed off daily.

'Age' effects

Skin elasticity and strength are affected by collagen, a protein. Diminution in the quantity and quality of collagen with age results in thinning of the skin and its increased fragility, with a severe reduction in elasticity and resultant wrinkling and sagging. These changes only affect to an important degree those areas of skin exposed to light. A comparison of the skin of the face with that of the abdomen or buttocks in an elderly person brings out this point strikingly.

The real reason for these changes is the effect of ultraviolet light on the skin. These effects are cumulative and depend on both sunlight intensity and the amount of deliberate exposure. Regular use of artificial ultraviolet light sources (such as 'sunray' lamps) compounds the problem.

Ultraviolet light (UVL) is a component of sunlight, and an electromagnetic radiation of shorter wavelength than visible light, but longer wavelength than X-rays. It is invisible to the human eye and cannot be felt as heat, as can infrared light. The spectrum of UVL is arbitrarily divided into three zones. That nearest to visible light (UVA) covers wavelengths from 380 down to 320 nanometres (billionth of a metre); UVB extends from 320 down to 290; and UVC from 290 down to one tenth of a nanometre. UVC is especially penetrating and harmful to human tissue but is strongly absorbed by the ozone layer in the earth's stratosphere. Most of the UVB content is also filtered out by this layer, but the UVC and UVB that get through do the most harm to human skin.

Ultraviolet light intensity varies with distance from the equator and with altitude. It is more intense on mountaintops and in regions with minimal cloud or low atmospheric water. Glass offers a good deal of protection to UVL. It is UVL that causes sunburning and, in excessive dosage, damages collagen in the skin, leading to excessive wrinkling and premature ageing. UVL is also a major factor in the development of the skin cancers basal cell carcinoma, malignant melanoma and squamous cell carcinoma.

Basal cell carcinoma is one of the commonest of all cancers, and one of the least dangerous. It affects the skin, mainly in areas exposed to the sun, especially the nose and around the eyes. It is a slow-growing, raised-edged swelling, with a dimple in the centre and often with small radiating blood vessels visible below the surface. Although the tumour can, if neglected, spread widely and cause extensive tissue damage, unlike other cancers it hardly ever seeds off tumour cells and spreads to remote parts of the body. The diagnosis of basal cell carcinoma is confirmed by sampling (biopsy) and the tumour can be treated by direct surgical removal, by radiation or by freezing.

Much more serious is malignant melanoma. The incidence of this tumour is rising. In Britain it now affects seven men and ten women in every 100,000. In women it is commonest on the legs; in men on the trunk. Because of their relationship to long-term exposure to sunlight, melanomas are rare in child-hood and most common in middle-aged and elderly people. About half arise from pre-existing moles and this is made more likely, in white people, by prolonged exposure to sunlight. Nearly everyone has pigmented moles but only one in a million becomes malignant. Hairy moles rarely turn into malignant melanomas. Melanomas are removed with a wide area of normal-seeming tissue around them; skin grafting may be necessary to cover the defect.

Changes to moles

Malignant change in a mole can be detected by various signs. These include:
- change in shape, especially increasing irregularity of outline
- change in size
- increased protuberance beyond the surface
- change in colour, especially sudden darkening and the development of coloured irregularities appearing as different shades of brown, grey, pink, red and blue
- itching or pain
- softening
- crumbling
- the development of new satellite moles around the original one.

Those which become nodular are the most malignant as they tend to penetrate deeply.

Once your suspicions are aroused, do not delay in reporting the condition to your doctor and asking for referral to a skin specialist.

Squamous cell carcinomas usually start in a condition known as solar keratosis – another effect of UVL – featuring raised, scaly, yellow-brown patches on a red background with tiny visible blood vessels. These patches occur only on the exposed skin and are painful and tend to bleed if attempts are made to remove them. The change from solar keratosis to a malignant condition takes a long time and is relatively uncommon. But a proportion of these patches thicken, ulcerate and begin to expand. Such a sequence must never be neglected or ignored because, unlike basal cell carcinoma, this skin cancer can spread to remote parts of the body and be fatal.

Hair

One of the most obvious signs of ageing is the loss of hair colour and, often, hair bulk. Hairs are threadlike filamentous growths of the protein keratin from the hair follicles in the skin. At the base of each follicle is a growing cell mass called the papilla. This is surrounded by the bulb of the follicle. Both contain blood vessels which carry raw materials, such as the amino acids which are necessary for the synthesis of hairs, to the follicle. The papilla also contains nerve endings. The cells of the bulb are actively reproducing and secreting the protein from which the hairs are made. Above the bulb is the sheath of the follicle, which is lubricated by fatty sebaceous material secreted into it from small adjoining sebaceous glands. Outside each hair follicle is a tiny muscle attached to its side. This is the erector pili muscle, which contracts under intense emotional stimulation causing hair to 'stand on end'.

The outer layer of the hair, the cuticle, is made of overlapping flat cells arranged like slates on a roof. Below this is the thickest layer, the cortex, consisting of cells which become horny (keratinized) as they are pushed up the sheath of the follicle. The inside of the hair is made of softer rectangular cells. Once formed, hairs are no more living than fingernails or the outer layers of the epidermis. Keratin is a non-living chemical substance. Typically, a hair follicle produces a little more than 10 mm (⅓ in) of hair in a month but hair is not produced continuously – it occurs in cycles with about one-tenth of the follicles in a resting phase at any one time. Each follicle continues to secrete hair for a cycle of three to five years and then rests for a time.

The colour of hair in the main hair areas comes from melanin, a pigment produced by cells called melanocytes. This pigment, which is a uniform colour, together with a reddish variant called phaeomelanin, produces the whole spectrum of hair colours, from black to blond, by differences in its concentration. Melanocytes secrete melanin, which is deposited in the shaft of the hair as it grows. Black hair has a high concentration of melanin; very blonde people have no melanin; red hair is caused by a predominance of phaeomelanin. When the melanocytes die and cease to reproduce, the hair turns grey or white. Existing hair cannot suddenly lose its colour overnight, except by external chemical applications. Much of the fine body hair is unpigmented.

With age, scalp hairs tend to lose their colour and become finer and more easily broken. Pubic and underarm hairs are usually slower to lose pigment, so there may be an environmental factor at work here, too. Hair greying and whitening simply mean that there are fewer pigment cells in the hairs than formerly. Greying is a special case of age-related change in that it does not always keep pace with other age changes. Some people go grey or white early, some late. There is simply no connection between this and other indications of ageing.

The commonest form of hair loss with age is hereditary and affects males. Male-pattern scalp hair loss is often associated with an exuberant overgrowth of hair elsewhere – in the ears, nose and eyebrows and on the chest and abdomen. There is a general tendency for scalp hair loss to occur with advancing age in both sexes. On average, the hair density (hairs per square cm of scalp) at the age of 50 is about 75 per cent of that at age 25. This rate of loss often continues into old age.

But age-related hair loss is not exclusively a natural phenomenon. It may be caused, in either sex, by general disease, chemotherapy or radiotherapy treatments for cancer, and treatment with thallium compounds, vitamin A or retinoids. It may occur some weeks after a severe feverish illness such as scarlet fever (toxic alopecia), or by thyroid gland underactivity and syphilis. Scarring alopecia may follow burns, skin atrophy, ulceration, fungus infection or skin tumours.

Alopecia areata is a form of patchy baldness, of unknown cause, often affecting only one or two small areas of the scalp, but sometimes affecting all the hair of the body. Abortive hair growth at the edges of the patches makes the hairs short and stubby, like exclamation marks. Alopecia areata has been attributed to heredity, stress, infection and emotional factors, but none of these is a proven cause. The most likely explanation is that it is an immune system disorder. The hair bulbs in the affected patches are infiltrated with helper 'T' cells and cases have been cured by immune therapy. Experimental production of a mild contact dermatitis has also been used to promote hair growth in people with alopecia areata.

Although hair loss is of cosmetic importance only, it may cause much distress, especially in women. In many cases, the best solution is a good wig, and it is worth bearing in mind that at several periods in human social history wigs were widely accepted as desirable enhancements to appearance. Much interest has been shown in the possible value of the drug minoxidil. This is normally used to treat high blood pressure and is applied in a solution directly to the skin. Results vary and when the treatment is stopped the new hair tends to fall out. Hair transplants from another part of the skin, or scalp reduction, may be helpful.

Nails

The nails are protective covers for the vulnerable finger and toe ends and provide useful tools for many manipulative purposes. When we feel with the fingertips, the nails exert counter-pressure.

The nail consists of a curved plate of keratin, resting on the nail bed and growing outward or from the growth zone (nail matrix). The base of each nail shows a variable-sized 'half moon'. The inturned skin edge around the nail is called the nail fold. The cuticle is the free skin edge over the half moon. In younger people, fingernails take four to five months to grow from matrix to fingertip, growing at a rate of about 1 cm (⅓ in) in three months. Toenails take about three times as long. The speed of nail growth slows somewhat with age, but not markedly. At age 90 the nails are still growing at rather more than half the rate of those in young adults.

Other nail changes are often found with increasing age. There is a tendency for nails to become more brittle and sometimes to peel. They may separate from the nail bed or become distorted and discoloured. Toenails often become markedly thicker, yellow and more opaque.

Many older people, however, have perfectly normal nails and it is questionable whether these changes are ever a natural consequence of ageing. It seems much more likely that they are the result of accumulated damage from injury and disease. Nails are susceptible to a variety of fungal infections, notably those that also cause athlete's foot and thrush, but others too. They can also be infected with herpes viruses and with scabies. Many general diseases such as psoriasis, various forms of dermatitis, alopecia areata, anaemia and other blood disorders and rheumatoid arthritis are associated with often severe nail changes. A number of prescription drugs can cause nail changes. These include:

- tetracyclines
- antimalarial drugs
- beta-blockers
- retinoids
- gold salts
- anti-cancer drugs
- phenothiazine anti-psychotic drugs.

Exposure to weedkillers such as paraquat and diquat can seriously damage the nails.

Since so many different factors can cause nail changes it is perhaps not surprising that the nails in older people are often less healthy than in the young.

Age and cancer

Cancer is an age-related problem. Although not true of all cancers, with many of them the incidence rises steadily with age. Half of all cancers become clinically evident in people over 70. Some cancers are 1000 times more likely to affect a person of 75 than they are to affect a person of 20. Ironically, the scientists who know most about this cannot agree on why ageing is associated with a rising incidence of cancer. Some notable authorities even state that there is no direct causal connection. Others hold that there is evidence to show that ageing and cancer have a common cause. Part of the problem here, of course, is that there is no consensus as to what ageing really is.

The probable reason for the association between ageing and cancer is that the causes, whatever they are, are cumulative. There are some important exceptions to this general rule. Cancer of the breast, for instance, starts appearing after puberty and increases rapidly in incidence until the meno-pause. Thereafter the incidence remains roughly constant for a few years before beginning to rise again slowly. Cancer of the cervix (neck of the womb) shows a similar pattern of incidence except that it continues to rise for a few years after the menopause before becoming stable or declining.

Cancer is a complicated subject and any account in a more general book must be simplified. Even so, it is necessary to go into some of the basics to provide worthwhile information or make any real sense. Some of what follows, therefore, will make rather gloomy reading.

What is cancer?

The word 'cancer' is a convenient term, applicable to at least 200 different conditions. Cancer can involve any tissue or organ of the body, either as a primary change in that tissue or organ, or by invasion of it from elsewhere in the body. Some cancers are so minor that they can be cured by a needle prick and 10 minutes' painless surgery. Others are so malignant that long before any signs appear, the disease may already be beyond remedy, so that it later resists every attempt at treatment. The common carcinoma of the lung, caused by cigarette smoking, is often of this type. There is, however, an important sense in which cancer is a single disease. All tumour cells, whatever their origin and type, share a common set of basic changes and follow a common pattern of abnormal behaviour. All cancer cells show very similar, or even identical, changes.

All human body tissues are composed of cells. Tissue cells operate as communities, and are restricted in their growth and reproduction by control-ling factors. Normal tissue cells remain localized in their particular organs, growing and reproducing slowly and in sufficient quantities to compensate for accidental cell death. One reason for this is known as contact inhibition. When cells are tightly packed together and unable to move, they reproduce slowly. If cell density is reduced, cell movement occurs and this is associated with an increased rate of reproduction. Liver cells, for instance, normally grow very slowly, no faster than is necessary to make up for wear and tear. But if a piece of liver is removed, the surrounding cells multiply rapidly, regenerating liver tissue until the deficiency is restored. In cancer, the restraints on reproduction are removed and cell replication is rapid and unchecked. Unlike normal cells, cancer cells also frequently move into tissue that is foreign to their type and place of origin.

Benign and malignant tumours

Not all tumours are cancers. There are two categories of tumours, and the difference between them is important. Benign tumours are not cancers at all, just lumps of cells which, while still closely resembling the tissue from which they have arisen – muscle, nerve, fat, blood vessel and so on – have begun to reproduce and multiply more rapidly than normal. Benign tumours remain intact and grow by expansion only.

The features of malignant tumours are different. Malignant tumour cells do not remain in a well-defined, circumscribed lump, insulated from surrounding tissue. They are essentially invasive, and stretch out in columns which pass into nearby tissues, crossing anatomical barriers, spreading along surfaces, seeding off into blood and lymph vessels, and usually reproducing and growing at a much faster rate than normal cells. A cancer which starts with one small group of cells has to divide many times before reaching a mass large enough to be detected. The smallest such detectable mass is of the order of 1 g ($\frac{1}{25}$ oz). Cancers are usually fatal when the tumour mass has reached 500 g to 1 kg (1 to 2lb). This size is reached after only 7 to 10 further doublings of the 1 g mass.

Mutations and cancer

Malignant tumours are collections of cells which have suffered a mutation (change) in their genetic material (DNA). Most major mutations are lethal; the affected cell dies and no further harm is done. Some mutations, however, cause cells to reproduce in a wholly disorganized and uncontrolled manner, causing a cancer. All important cell functions, especially reproduction, are under the control of DNA. Damaged DNA does not, of course, necessarily cause a cell to become cancerous; but certain kinds of DNA change will disrupt normal gene regulation, activate certain tumour-producing genes known as oncogenes and in this way induce cancer. Any factor that can damage DNA is thus potentially capable of causing cancer, and we know of a number of things – radiation, certain chemicals and viruses – that can cause these changes. Radiation and dangerous chemicals do their harm by producing free radicals, so these are clearly implicated in the stage of chemical damage to DNA (see chapter 6).

DNA damage is associated with several enzymes whose job is to repair the breaks. One of these, DNA protein kinase (DNA-PK), detects breaks in both the strands of the DNA double helix and holds the ends together so that they can be joined by the action of other enzymes. This enzyme was discovered in 1990 by Dr Steve Jackson, a molecular biologist working at the University of Berkeley, California. His research showed that when DNA-PK was missing from cells, they were extremely sensitive to any factor, such as radiation, that can break DNA. They were, consequently, likely to become cancerous.

In 1995, now at Cambridge, Jackson made another remarkable discovery. He showed that DNA-PK was chemically closely related to a defective form of a protein called ATM present in cells in a rare recessive genetic disease called ataxia telangiectasia or Louis-Bar syndrome. This disease causes abnormal spasms and movements, gross walking disabilities, redness of the eyes, ears and skin creases, a severe tendency to infection and, above all, a high liability to develop cancer. The gene mutation in both corresponding chromosomes causes faulty ATM and this terrible disease. An Israeli team succeeded in sequencing the gene for defective ATM and Jackson sequenced the gene for DNA-PK. The two were found to be almost identical.

How cancer spreads

Cancers spread in two ways. They burrow into and invade adjacent tissues and structures, becoming incorporated into them and often destroying them. But they have another, and even more dangerous, way of spreading. When an invading cancer encounters a small blood or lymph vessel, it can grow through its wall until it reaches the blood or lymph stream, and small collections of cancer cells can then be carried off by the flow of blood or lymph to be deposited in another part of the body. This is called metastasis and is the major cause of death from cancer. By this means, cancer cells from the lung or colon or prostate gland can be transported to the brain or bones or liver, to set up a new focus and continue to grow and invade in the new site. In the absence of effective treatment, metastatic cancer is almost always fatal.

Many people with cancers which are apparently confined to one site already have small inapparent metastases (micrometastases) in distant parts of the body. So even radical surgical removal of the primary tumour may not cure the cancer, which may appear in the new sites. It is for this reason that anti-cancer drugs, which affect the cancer wherever it may be throughout the body, are often given after surgery in cases in which such metastases are suspected.

Degrees of malignancy

Cancers vary enormously in the speed with which they spread locally and, consequently, in the readiness with which they form new colonies elsewhere. This tendency is called 'malignancy', so malignancy may be termed low or high. A tumour of low malignancy may take months or even years to cause trouble and may not spread distantly for a very long time, if ever. Tumours of high malignancy, by contrast, have sometimes spread widely before the victim has any idea that anything is wrong. Skilled pathologists can tell, by examining a thin slice of cancer tissue under a microscope, whether it is of high or low malignancy. In tumours of low malignancy, the cells quite closely resemble the parent tissue and form themselves into aggregates which are not greatly different in structure from the normal tissue from which they arise. Very malignant cells, on the other hand, are 'primitive' simple cells with little or no capacity to form recognizable tissues.

The effects of cancer

Cancers are, of course, destructive. Some become very large and cause local effects by their sheer physical bulk, compressing or displacing important structures. They erode and damage organs and blood vessels, block tubes, destroy vital functional tissue, form abnormal connections between organs and body cavities, promote internal bleeding and the production of abnormal quantities of fluid, and allow access to infecting organisms. In addition, cancers have general effects. These are caused by chemical substances, often proteins, released by the tumour cells and carried throughout the body by the blood-stream. Some of these substances resemble hormones and can have wide-spread and severe effects. Some tumours manufacture a wide range of these hormone-like substances. The small cell cancers of the lung, for instance, can produce hormones affecting the calcification of bone, the lining of the womb, the output of the adrenal glands leading to high blood pressure and other effects, and the function of the kidneys leading to inability to excrete enough water. Breast cancers and some lung and kidney tumours can produce hormones which raise the levels of blood calcium to dangerous degrees, causing vomiting, excessive urinary output and coma.

In addition to the hormone-like effects, tumours produce a variety of general effects, not all of which are fully understood. These include: nausea, loss of appetite, anaemia, fever, skin rashes, weakness, abnormalities of taste and severe and progressive loss of weight.

The end result is often a severely debilitated state, with gross weight loss known as cachexia, and this is often terminal. Cachexia may result from malnutrition from defective absorption of food or simply from loss of appetite and nausea which are common features of widespread cancer. In addition, tumour cells have a greater demand for amino acids – the 'building bricks' of protein – than normal cells, and may use these up at the expense of the patient's muscles, so that body wasting occurs. The cause of death in people with widespread cancer is usually a combination of several factors such as cachexia, infection, internal bleeding and compression of vital tissue – such as the brain – by a growing tumour mass. Actual destruction of essential structures is a less common cause of death.

Diet and cancer

It is now generally accepted that the incidence of many of the cancers which afflict Western societies could be reduced by modifying our diet. Much of this evidence comes from observing differences in the number of cases of various cancers in populations with different eating habits. Western diets contain a large number of different ingredients and, to the basic foodstuffs are added a legion of additional substances – condiments, flavouring agents, flavour enhancers, sweeteners, preservatives, colouring agents, emulsifiers, solvents, antioxidants, stabilizers, bulking agents, antifoaming agents and others. All of these are, of course, tested for safety but their very number, and the possibility that some might act on others with harmful effect, impose a major problem for the government agencies concerned.

At present, only a few substances known to be capable of causing cancer have been identified as possible dietary elements. Such substances are known as carcinogens. An example of these is aflatoxin, a poison produced by the common food contaminant mould *Aspergillus flavus*. Aspergillus grows readily on damp grains and nuts and is a common contaminant of peanuts. It is believed to cause many thousands of cases of primary liver cancer each year in countries in which food is stored in unsatisfactory conditions. Most cases occur in people whose livers have already been damaged by hepatitis B.

Other known cancer-causing substances include nitrosamines, produced by overcooking or smoking animal protein, but they have not yet been positively identified as a cause of cancer in humans; nitrates and nitrite preservatives, which may form nitrosamines from dietary protein; salt fish, widely eaten in the Far East, and believed to be related to the development of cancer of the back of the nose; bracken fern, which is known to cause cancer in animals, and is popular in the Japanese diet and thought to be associated with cancer of the gullet. Less certain are the suggestions that stomach cancer is caused by highly spiced food, highly acidic foods such as pickles, nitrates in water, and irritants such as the concentrated alcohol in spirits. None of these has been definitely proven.

We know that a high fat diet can cause cancer in animals. The United States National Research Council, in its 1982 report *Diet, nutrition and cancer* judged that the evidence linking dietary fat and cancer in humans was stronger than for any other dietary constituent. It recommended, on these grounds alone, that we should all reduce fat intake, both saturated and unsaturated. The evidence consists mainly of the strong link, in various countries, between the number of cases of cancer, especially of the breast and colon, and the consumption of fat. The number of cases has increased proportionately with an increase in the fat intake and has also increased in immigrants to countries with a higher fat intake than their countries of origin. Remember, however, that a high fat intake nearly always implies a low fibre intake and it is probable that the effect may be caused by low dietary fibre rather than high dietary fat. The evidence linking high-fibre diets and a low incidence of cancer and other bowel diseases is strong and generally accepted.

The role of antioxidant treatment in the prevention of cancer is dealt with in chapter 6.

Diet and cancer

◆ Cut down your dietary fat intake as far as possible.
◆ Ensure that you have a high intake of vegetables of all kinds. Serve vegetables raw or lightly steamed to preserve nutrient content.
◆ Eat at least five helpings of fruit every day.
◆ Avoid burned or heavily cooked protein – nitrosamines can, in theory at least, cause cancer.
◆ Never eat mouldy peanuts or grains.
◆ Avoid an excessive intake of highly spiced food.
◆ Moderate your alcohol intake, especially of spirits, but a glass of wine with a meal may do you good.
◆ Consider the arguments in favour of antioxidant vitamins C and E in chapter 6.

Cancer of the large intestine

The greater part of the large intestine is known as the colon. The short terminal part, lying just above the anal canal is called the rectum. Cancer of the colon or rectum is common. After the lung, the colon is the most common site of cancer affecting both men and women, and the second most common cause of death from cancer. Cancer of the colon or rectum becomes more common with increasing age and most cases occur in the 60 to 75 age group. These cancers appear to affect affluent people more often than the less well off.

Most colorectal cancers start off as harmless polyps (small tumours of mucous membrane) and grow slowly. They are usually well advanced before they produce symptoms. The first sign is often an alteration in the normal bowel habit, with constipation followed by frequent motions. Pain is not typical until cancer of the colon reaches a very advanced stage, and spreads to other nearby organs. Cancers can grow around the wall of the bowel, causing partial obstruction and sometimes altering the shape of the stools into a more ribbon-like appearance. Blood in the stools is always a danger sign, but bleeding may be microscopic and detectable only by chemical tests (occult blood). Sometimes there is colicky pain or, occasionally, even complete obstruction.

Cancer of the rectum is more common in men than in women. Here, the most frequent sign is blood in the stools. Note, however, that blood in the stools is much more likely to come from piles (haemorrhoids) than from cancer. But it is a serious, and perhaps dangerous, mistake to assume that this is where blood is coming from, especially if you have no previous indications that you have haemorrhoids.

The tests for occult blood in the stools are simple and are an effective method of screening. A positive result indicates that examination by an expert, with a viewing instrument such as a rigid tubular sigmoidoscope or a flexible, self-illuminating internal examination device (fibre optic endoscope), is necessary. Polyps can alert the examiner to the higher likelihood of current or later cancer. If a polyp is found, the whole of the inside of the colon should be inspected. If all is well, the check should be repeated about every three years.

Important points about cancer of the colon

◆ Ensure that your diet is high in fibre so that there is plenty of roughage in the stools.
◆ Be aware that cancer of the colon is unknown in peoples whose diet is high in fibrous carbohydrates (wholemeal breads, cereals and grains).
◆ If such people take up a typical Western diet, they begin to have a rising incidence of colonic cancer.
◆ Always take rectal bleeding seriously.
◆ Never assume, without good reason, that this is simply due to piles.
◆ Ensure that your regular checkups include a digital rectal examination and, preferably, a visual inspection of the rectum with a sigmoidoscope.
◆ Consider a more complete check of the interior of the colon for polyps, especially if you have a family history of polyps or cancer of the colon.

Cancer of the colon is treated by a wide surgical removal of the affected segment of the bowel, together with the associated lymph nodes. If the rectum has to be removed, a permanent colostomy – an opening to the exterior through the abdominal wall – is necessary, but higher removal permits internal joining of the cut ends. Many cases can be cured by surgery, but this depends almost entirely on the stage the cancer has reached at the time of diagnosis. If it is still confined to the internal lining of the bowel, the cure rate is 90 per cent, but if the lymph nodes are involved the outlook is much worse. The value of radiotherapy and chemotherapy in this form of cancer has not yet been fully established.

Importance of early diagnosis

This factor, commonly emphasized in the case of younger people, may be neglected in the elderly. It is, however, as important in them. Early diagnosis markedly increases the possibility of a cure, reduces the damage to the quality of life by the cancer, increases the length of the disease-free period following initial treatment and reduces mortality.

How to minimize the risk of cancer

There are certain danger signs that should be known by everybody.
They are:
◆ any unusual change in the bowel habit
◆ black stools
◆ blood in the stools
◆ vomiting blood
◆ new breast lump
◆ unexplained loss of weight
◆ failure of a sore to heal in a month
◆ unexplained hoarseness
◆ difficulty swallowing
◆ coughing blood
◆ blood in the urine
◆ change in a coloured skin spot
◆ yellowing of the skin (jaundice)
◆ persistent cough and unremitting headache
Look out for these signs and never under any circumstances ignore them. Remember that, with cancer in particular, the earlier it is caught the more likely it is that it can be cured. Report any suspicions to your doctor without delay.

One of the characteristics of the ageist stereotype is that older people are less in need of screening and health-promotion programmes than younger people. But older people need these initiatives more, not less, than younger people since cancers in the elderly often have a longer latency period and symptoms that emerge more gradually than in younger people. Also, older people often find it more difficult to recognize these early symptoms and the symptoms may sometimes be masked by other physical disorders.

Some research has shown that there is a tendency for certain cancers, such as those of the breast, womb, bladder and ovary, to be diagnosed at a later stage in older than in younger people. Malignant melanomas are also often diagnosed at a later and more dangerous stage. (The evidence on this is somewhat conflicting, and it seems probable that different results may reflect different standards of medical care or medical awareness of patients in different areas or social groups.) It seems clear that elderly patients are, themselves, often responsible for delays in diagnosis. Many older people are reluctant to report symptoms or to undergo examination, especially for routine screening purposes. Many delay for the worst possible reason – fear of being told that they have cancer.

Cancer and pain

One of the most dreaded aspects of cancer is pain. There have, however, been notable advances in the understanding of this subject in recent years and there is now no reason why people who develop severe cancers of the types that cause pain should not be kept pain-free throughout their illness.

Pain is a sensation which nearly everyone finds unpleasant. It is usually, but not necessarily, localized and felt in the area of the body in which its cause occurs. Pain is caused by strong stimulation of sensory nerve endings by an event or process that is damaging, or is liable to damage, body tissues of any kind. Unless it is very persistent (chronic), pain commonly serves as a warning of danger and leads to action that should end it.

Pain causes distress and anxiety and sometimes fear, and the psychological and physical changes associated with it may be similar to those you experience during anger and aggression. The significance you attach to the pain depends more on the degree and quality of these secondary effects than on the actual intensity of the pain itself. The psychological reaction to pain is often modified by past experience. If pain is separated from its mental reaction, as happens when you are given drugs like morphine, it may still be felt but you may no longer consider it unpleasant and may even be indifferent to it. The distress caused by pain depends also, to a large extent, on your awareness of the cause. If pain is known to be caused by cancer you are likely to react more strongly to it than you would if the same pain were the result of an accident. Pain associated with fear is always much worse than pain without fear. This is why the relief of cancer pain must always involve more than simply the relief of the pain itself. It must be directed also to measures to dispel fear.

Although the nerves carrying pain impulses terminate in the brain, and give rise to neurological activity there, the pain is usually felt in the region in which the nerve endings are situated. Nerve impulses passing to the brain may be blocked by local anaesthetics, by electrical stimulation applied through the skin, by acupuncture, and by the inhibitory action of other nerve fibres coming down from the brain. The latter are believed to release blocking substances called endorphins and enkephalins. Morphine, and other similar drugs, are believed to relieve pain by acting on nerve receptor sites in a manner similar to that of endorphins. Pain control can also be effected by hormones, since removal of the pituitary or adrenal glands increases sensitivity to pain. The hormones involved have not been positively identified, but are believed to be endorphins.

Pain impulses travelling up the spinal cord pass through neurological 'gates'. These impulses can be blocked by signals coming from elsewhere. This provides an explanation for some of the physical methods of pain control. Many of these methods are effective, and include rubbing the skin with a soft cloth, electrical stimulation of the skin (TENS) using a variety of machines, acupuncture or acupressure, massage or cold sprays to the skin.

Experts on pain control emphasize that pain should be treated by the simplest and safest available means, but that attempts should always be made to relieve it once the cause is clearly known. Prolonged pain is demoralizing and debilitating and should be controlled as early as possible. Neglected pain becomes more difficult to control. Pain-controlling drugs work best if they are used as soon as the pain reappears, and they should not be withheld until pain becomes unbearable. Different forms of pain control, used in combination, are more effective than any methods used in isolation. Authoritative reassurance by a doctor, when appropriate, increases the effectiveness of pain-control measures.

Local anaesthetic injections can control pain, but the effect is brief and this is not a practicable method. They may, however, be useful as a preliminary trial before resorting, in extreme cases, to permanent nerve destruction by alcohol injection or by surgical severance. In general, surgical methods of pain control should be avoided. They inevitably involve unpleasant permanent loss of sensation and, even when the pain fibres are cut in the spinal cord, do not necessarily succeed in controlling the pain.

Pain control has become a speciality in its own right and many pain clinics now exist for the sole purpose of providing the best possible relief. If you suffer from long-term (chronic) pain, you should enquire whether you could be referred to such a clinic.

Morphine and pain

The principal agent for controlling severe cancer pain is morphine. But many cancer victims have, in the past, been denied the remarkable psychological and physical benefits of this drug because of fear of inducing addiction. We now know that addiction is very uncommon in people who are given morphine for persistent pain. Morphine is effective taken by mouth and can be given in controlled-release formulation that can last for up to 12 hours. If, for any reason, it cannot be taken by mouth it can be given by injection. The effect is the same, but the duration of action is limited to about four hours.

There are some side effects of this drug. It can, initially, cause nausea but this can easily be controlled and passes off in about a week. Morphine is also liable to cause constipation but this, too, is easily managed. Some patients find that morphine makes them drowsy. In this case, various alternative drugs with similar properties to morphine may be given instead.

Cancer and quality of life

Since most elderly people acknowledge that they have a limited lifespan, the two most important things about developing cancer are whether it will seriously shorten life and whether it will adversely affect the quality of life. Many cancers have so little effect on longevity that doctors often leave them untreated. This may or may not be a good thing and patients are entitled to question the basis for decisions of this kind by doctors. Age alone is certainly no reason. Nor is an arbitrary decision made by the doctor – especially on the basis of age – about the patient's fitness for general anaesthesia.

It is true that some cancers are very slow to progress and that post-mortem examinations of very old people often disclose unexpected cancers. A high proportion of old men, for instance, die with unsuspected cancers of the prostate gland. But no doctor can give more than a general assessment of the likelihood that a particular cancer will remain slowly progressive, so it is impossible to be sure whether or not a given cancer will shorten life.

Most growing cancers, if untreated, adversely affect the quality of life sooner or later. They may do so by their physical, psychological or social effects, and these effects can often be reduced by treatment, even if the treatment is not expected to cure the condition completely. Such treatment may involve palliative, rather than radical, surgery or the use of drugs or other means. At the same time, it must be remembered that cancer treatments can in themselves adversely affect the quality of life – at least for a time. This is deemed acceptable in younger people in the interests of possible cure or of substantially prolonging life. But in older people, it is often put forward as a reason for withholding treatment. But research has shown that there are fewer reported side effects from cancer chemotherapy in the 70–83 year age group than in younger people. This may simply be because older people have learned how to live with the effects and problems of illness.

Difficult decisions need to be taken, but these decisions ought not to be made solely by doctors. The patient is most centrally concerned and he or she is entitled to participate centrally in the decision making. Decisions should be informed, so the patient requires knowledge to allow him or her to ask the right questions.

Age and mobility

One of the most serious age-related problems affecting mobility, especially in women, is osteoporosis (see pp. 33–5). But there are other conditions that affect both men and women. In addition, factors that at first sight appear unrelated, such as a growing tendency to instability in many people, can have profound effects on future mobility if, for example, you become so unstable that you fall and suffer a broken bone.

Osteoarthritis

The most obviously age-related joint problem is osteoarthritis, a degenerative disorder involving damage to the cartilaginous bearing surfaces (the articular cartilage) and sometimes widening or remodelling of the ends of the bones in the joint. Osteoarthritis is the commonest form of arthritis and it is only recently that research into twins, carried out at St Thomas' Hospital London, has shown that the condition has a genetic basis. In addition to this, however, osteoarthritis is commonly associated with injury or deformities of the skeleton which disturb the normal mechanics of the joints and the relationships of the joint surfaces. There are also occupational factors, which may involve joints rarely affected in the general population. Ballet dancers and footballers, for instance, may develop osteoarthritis of the ankles. Obesity is an important aggravating factor. Although the term 'arthritis' implies inflammation of joints, this condition – unlike rheumatoid arthritis – involves little inflammation. Bony spurs often develop at the margins of the affected joints.

Osteoarthritis is age related and many people of 30 show early osteoarthritic changes. By age 65, about 80 per cent of people have some evidence of the disorder, but no more than a quarter of these have symptoms. Osteoarthritis most commonly involves the spine, the knee joints and the hip joints. Certain joints in the hands may also be affected. In the elderly, women tend to be more severely affected than men, especially in the knees and hands. The incidence of hip joint involvement is about the same in both sexes. The disease causes immense suffering and disability in older people and has enormous economic implications.

Symptoms usually come on gradually, with pain which at first is intermittent and then becomes more frequent. Joint movement becomes progressively more limited, at first because of pain and muscle spasm, but later because the joint capsule becomes thickened and less flexible. Movement may cause audible creaking, and swelling results from quite minor injury. The pain of osteoarthritis does not originate in the worn or damaged articular cartilage. Such cartilage has no nerve endings and the grinding together of roughened surfaces is painless. The pain comes from the adjacent bone and from the ligaments and capsules of the affected joints. It is worse when the joint concerned is under load; this is one reason why osteoarthritis of the knees is so affected by obesity. In very severe cases, however, pain may even occur when the affected person is lying in bed.

In addition to pain, sufferers from osteoarthritis are troubled by stiffness and tightness of joints, so that the normal range of movement is severely limited. This stiffness tends to be worse after resting. This can cause disability, which is commonly increased by muscle weakness secondary to the joint movement limitation. Muscles remain strong only by use and if their exercise is prevented because the joints are not moving, they will quickly weaken. So people with osteoarthritis commonly have great difficulty in walking freely and in climbing stairs. Every effort must be made to maintain muscle power in spite of the difficulties. Osteoarthritis of the spine tends to cause curvature and other deformities, as well as pain.

Short of joint replacement, there is no specific remedy for osteoarthritis, but much can be done to relieve its symptoms. It is important to avoid undue stress or injury to the joints, so loss of excess weight is very helpful. Rubber heels can reduce jarring and a walking stick can be valuable. Knee splints can help, and walking may be aided by shoes with rocker soles or by adjusting the heel height to compensate for any inequality in leg length. A change of occupation, however difficult this may be, may prove necessary. In many cases, injection of corticosteroids into the affected joint can markedly reduce pain and disability.

It is natural for people with a painful condition of this kind to want to fall back on drugs for the relief of pain. There is certainly no harm in the occasional use of painkillers such as aspirin, paracetamol or one of the non-steroidal anti-inflammatory drugs (NSAIDs). But none of these drugs is particularly effective in osteoarthritis and their long-term use can cause undesirable side effects, such as stomach or duodenal ulcers. If NSAIDs are found to be effective in controlling pain and drugs such as indomethacin (Indocid), ibuprofen (Brufen Retard), tenoxicam (Mobiflex), propionic acid (Lederfen), ketoprofen

(Alrheumat) or fenoprofen (Fenopron) are being taken a long-term basis, remember that there is a cumulative incidence of about 20 per cent of stomach ulcers and about 13 per cent of duodenal ulcers. Drugs may be taken to protect the stomach, by decreasing the rate of acid production.

Severe symptoms, poorly controlled by drugs, are an indication for surgery. Hip joint and knee joint replacement surgery has helped hundreds of thousands of osteoarthritis sufferers. These are, of course, major procedures not undertaken lightly. But the results, for those severely affected, can be extremely beneficial. Modern anaesthetic techniques have made such surgery safe for many people who would formerly have been considered high-risk subjects, such as the elderly. There are several other surgical procedures that can help people with osteoarthritis.

Instability and the risk of falls

The effects and prevention of falls are dealt with in Chapter 3. More than half of all falls are caused by factors external to yourself, such as slippery surfaces and trip hazards. Here the internal causes of falls are highlighted. These include:

- vertigo
- sudden loss of consciousness, especially due to an inadequate supply of blood to the brain (vertebrobasilar insufficiency)
- visual impairment
- the effects of drugs
- heart problems
- neurological disabilities such as decreased sensation, decreased awareness of the position of the limbs or defects of the balancing mechanisms
- dementia
- muscle or bone disabilities
- a drop in blood pressure on standing up (postural hypotension)
- abnormalities of gait

Multiple disabilities greatly increase the risk of falls.

Vertigo is the illusion that the world is spinning around, or sometimes that the world is stable but you are spinning. The effect may be slight and barely noticeable, or so severe that you fall instantly to the ground as if thrown down. Mild vertigo is common and such cases are seldom due to underlying disease, or require any treatment. Vertigo in older people has several possible causes. These include:

- overbreathing (hyperventilation) brought on by anxiety, alcohol or drugs
- a disorder of the balancing mechanisms in the inner ears, such as Ménière's syndrome or labyrinthitis

◆ a disorder of the neurological mechanism of balance in the cerebellum or its connections, resulting from vertebrobasilar insufficiency.

Prescription drugs often contribute to instability and may lead to falls. The most important drugs in this context are narcotics used for pain relief, sleeping pills, sedatives and tranquillizers. These all reduce alertness and slow protective reactions. Some drugs interfere with posture control and this can also cause falls. These include drugs for high blood pressure, antidepressant drugs, and some drugs for mental disorders, heart problems and diuretics.

Ménière's syndrome is an episodic disorder consisting of a combination of dizziness (vertigo), nausea, variable hearing loss, a sense of fullness in the head and ringing in the ears (tinnitus). During the episodes of vertigo the deafness and tinnitus temporarily increase. These improve after the episodes are over but there is a tendency for hearing to decline progressively. Episodes are highly variable and some people have long periods of freedom. The disorder often starts on one side, but tends later to affect both ears. The prevalence of the disease peaks in middle age but it can also affect elderly people. One-third of Ménière's sufferers are also prone to migraine.

The syndrome is caused by an increase in the amount and pressure of the fluid within the inner ear. This causes distention, with damage to the delicate balancing and hearing structures, which may eventually be destroyed. Each episode may cause further damage. The reason for the increase in fluid is often inapparent but, in some cases tests can reveal the cause. Most cases are managed by medical treatment to control the vertigo and nausea. In some cases surgery is advised. Removal of the balancing mechanism on one side (labyrinthectomy) relieves the vertigo, but produces total deafness on that side.

Vertebrobasilar insufficiency is a serious situation in which the supply of arterial blood through the arteries running up through the bones of the neck (the vertebral arteries) to supply the lower part of the brain, is diminished by narrowing. Such narrowing is almost always caused by atherosclerosis. People with vertebrobasilar insufficiency tend to suffer episodes of severe vertigo due to interference with the nerves concerned with balance. They get:

◆ double vision due to disturbance of the nerves to the eye muscles
◆ weakness or paralysis on one side of the body due to interference with the major motor nerves passing down through the brain stem
◆ speech difficulties
◆ in severe cases, loss of consciousness.

These episodes may be transient and occur at times when, for various reasons, the already prejudiced blood supply is further reduced. They are, however, a clear indication of the risk of stroke and should never be ignored.

Whatever the cause, falls are often serious for older people. Injuries may be severe, even from seemingly minor falls, and the resultant immobilization can, in itself, have serious consequences. Falls, too, commonly lead to loss of confidence and physical courage with resulting decrease in activity. And activity is vital in achieving a good old age.

The dangers of bed rest

Prolonged bed rest causes many undesirable physiological changes that seriously reduce fitness and mobility, especially in old people. These include:

♦ a decrease in the blood volume and in the blood output of the heart per beat
♦ a reduction in the oxygen-carrying capacity of the blood
♦ wasting away (atrophy) of the unused muscles and consequent loss of strength
♦ inability to stand upright.

In addition to the physiological changes, prolonged bed rest leads to various actual medical conditions. Bones decalcify and lose bulk (osteoporosis) and become more liable to fracture; pressure (bed) sores may develop; and there is an increased tendency for clotting to occur in the large veins of the legs (deep vein thrombosis). The latter is especially common after surgical operations in the elderly. Vein thrombosis commonly leads to the formation, within the veins, of a loose, gelatinous and ever-lengthening snake-like blood clot which, initially attached at one end, may break loose and be carried up to the heart; from there it is pumped to the lungs to cause a highly dangerous obstruction to one of the main arteries (pulmonary embolism). This is often fatal.

As a result of these advances in knowledge, ideas have changed in recent decades about the importance of bed rest for the sick. Clearly it is a comfort for the acutely ill, the fevered or the weak to rest in a well-made bed, but it is now seen as a mistake for all those suffering from any disease whatsoever to be automatically confined to bed.

It is now accepted by all doctors that bed rest often does more harm than good. Prolonged rest is, in itself, harmful and will take at least as long to recover from as the period spent in bed. Elderly people confined to bed may never recover their former vitality. The body, at any age, is responsive to the physical demands made upon it, and its capacity for work, within limits, adapts to these demands. Enforced bed rest, unless clinically necessary, therefore is usually damaging and often leads to a notable decline in fitness.

Age and incontinence

There are two broad types of incontinence, both of which are more common in elderly people than the young. Urinary incontinence is the involuntary and undesired passing of urine, while faecal incontinence is the inability to retain faeces in the rectum. Neither is an automatic adjunct of increased age; both should be considered treatable.

Urinary incontinence

A universal tendency to urinary incontinence is often regarded as a feature of old age. But the fact is that occasional episodes of incontinence are common in people of all ages and, for anatomical reasons, especially in women. Up to half of all women have experienced it. It affects about 12 per cent of middle-aged women and about 16 per cent of women over 75 – not a great deal of difference in incidence, indicating that this embarrassing and distressing complaint is not specific to age. No one wants to admit to urinary incontinence – so thousands of women of all ages suffer in silence. Only about a third get medical care or help from the social services. It is important to remember, however, that incontinence is a pathological condition that can usually be put right.

Older people are affected slightly more often than young people mainly because of a tendency for the circular sphincter muscles around the urine outlet tube (the urethra) to weaken with age. In addition, older women are more likely to have strained the muscles of the floor of the pelvis in childbirth. Infection of the urinary tract, also common in older people, is another contributory cause. Urinary problems in elderly women are often due to oestrogen deficiency (see p. 30).

Living with incontinence

Incontinence should never be tolerated and should always be considered curable. It is much too damaging to the quality of life to be simply accepted as a necessary feature of the later years. Untreated incontinence may lead to the need for indwelling tubes (urinary catheters) and these can lead to urinary tract infections, worsening of pressure sores, rashes, trips and falls, fractures and groin and lower limb skin infection. The social consequences may be even more serious and include embarrassment, isolation, depression, and even the need for a move to an institution. Incontinence is socially disruptive and may have adverse effects on daily activities and personal relationships.

There are three main types of urinary incontinence. In stress incontinence a small squirt of urine escapes when pressure is involuntarily applied to the bladder during coughing, sneezing, laughing, weight-bearing or strenuous activity. It especially affects women who have had babies and whose urethral sphincters – the muscle rings that close off the urine outlet tube – have been stretched. It is also commonly caused by the weakening of the pelvic floor muscles in pregnancy and childbirth, urinary tract infections, bladder stones or by a downward displacement of the womb.

If the desire to urinate is resisted too long, the pressure in the bladder rises to a point at which involuntary and uncontrollable contraction occurs so that it empties completely – so-called urge incontinence. In some cases urge incontinence occurs at any time and during any activity, even at rest. It may even be triggered by a sudden change of position. Much of this problem is caused by the inability to get to a toilet in time and a great deal more could be done to make reasonable toilet facilities more readily available and accessible to older people. This may improve as the proportion of elderly people in the population rises.

In irritable bladder, for various reasons the bladder muscle contracts intermittently, pushing out a little urine into the beginning of the urethra. As soon as this happens, the pressure of urine at this point in the urethra causes an intense desire to relax the sphincter and pass urine.

Any form of incontinence calls for medical attention. If it is caused by bladder infection, this can be treated. Examination of a sample of urine is necessary and often reveals the cause. Ultrasound scanning or X-rays using a dye that is rapidly excreted and shows up on the plate (intravenous urography) detects obstructions, stones and structural abnormalities. The muscle and nerve function of the bladder can be tested by measuring the internal bladder pressure. Sometimes it is necessary to examine the inside of the bladder directly by passing a narrow viewing tube (a cystoscope) along the urethra. This may reveal stones, polyps or tumours. All these can be treated.

Weak pelvic muscles can be strengthened by pelvic floor exercises, which can help to restore sphincter function. Occasionally, surgical tightening of the muscles may be needed. In extreme cases, an artificial sphincter that can be controlled from the outside can be implanted around the urethra. Rarely, the solution may be to bypass the bladder altogether. In men, prostate gland enlargement (see pp. 37–40) is responsible for a high proportion of cases of incontinence. These cases are best treated by surgery.

Urge incontinence can often be treated with drugs in the anticholinergic groups. These include propantheline (Pro-Banthine), oxybutynin (Cystrin) and imipramine (Tofranil), all of which can be taken by mouth three or four times a day. In addition, smooth muscle relaxants such as flavoxate (Urispas), taken by mouth three or four times a day may help some affected people. The calcium channel blocker drug nifedipine (Adalat), also taken by mouth, has been found helpful in some cases. These drugs must be taken only under proper medical supervision and only on a doctor's prescription.

There are some special objections to anticholinergic drugs. Propantheline, for instance, should not be given to people with dementia. Imipramine and nifedipine may cause severe dizziness on standing up due to a drop in blood pressure. In addition, anticholinergic drugs may work too well and cause retention of urine and overflow incontinence.

While treatment and cure are obviously best, many affected women prefer to use an alarm clock to get them up at night to empty the bladder. In extreme cases in which specific treatment is inappropriate or undesired, special incontinence clothing or urine collecting devices can be used. The convenient, plastic male urinal bottle can be adapted for women by a simple, shaped collecting part that is pushed into the neck. These devices can be discreetly used on long car journeys. Self-catheterization, to keep the bladder empty by draining it through a tube, is used successfully by some people, with a surprisingly low incidence of infection. In irritable bladder, drugs are sometimes used to relax the bladder muscle.

Faecal incontinence

Apart from when associated with dementia (see chapter 4) faecal incontinence is relatively uncommon and, with the exception of faecal impaction, the condition is nearly always due to disease. Repeated occurrence calls for medical investigation. The causes of faecal incontinence in elderly people include:

◆ injudicious use of purgatives
◆ faecal impaction
◆ prolapse of the rectum
◆ cancer of the colon or rectum
◆ diverticulitis (inflammation of the diverticula – sacs or pouches of tissue protruding through the lining of an organ – of the intestine)
◆ colitis (inflammation of the colon)
◆ diarrhoea from various causes.

The incontinence may be associated with loss of local sensation or with loss of the ability to close the external sphincter voluntarily. In dementia, actual neurological damage may disrupt the mechanism that controls the normal tendency for the colon to contract after a meal.

Faecal impaction is one of the commonest causes of soiling among elderly people. This is a form of overflow incontinence, and the end result of prolonged constipation. Persistent constipation leads to faecal drying and hardening and progressive packing of the rectum. Eventually the rectum gets too tight and is emptied involuntarily. Such constipation does not call for purgatives but for investigation of the cause. This may be inadequate roughage in the diet from lack of fibre, physical inactivity, or piles, fissures or other painful rectal conditions. If these are put right the problem will be solved.

Parkinson's disease

Often called paralysis agitans, this disease usually starts between the ages of 40 and 70, and progresses steadily over the years, eventually often causing severe physical disability. It is more common in men than women. Its features include:

◆ an involuntary tremor of the hands at rest, with finger movements resembling 'pill-rolling'
◆ rigidity of the muscles
◆ slowness of body movements
◆ a mask-like face
◆ quiet, monotonous voice
◆ slow speech
◆ minute handwriting
◆ forward inclination of the body on standing
◆ great difficulty in starting to walk
◆ short, tottering steps
◆ the appearance of falling forward.

In most cases the intellect remains unaffected but some sufferers develop mild dementia. Depression is often a feature of the condition.

Parkinsonism affects about one person in 1000 of the general population but one in 100 of those over 60. It is due to changes in the connections between the areas of the brain called the substantia nigra and the corpus striatum, resulting in loss of pigment and of dopamine-producing cells. (Dopamine modifies the nerve pathways that control muscle contraction.) It may be caused by:

◆ certain drugs used in psychiatric treatment
◆ (possibly) by arterial disease affecting the brain
◆ poisoning with carbon monoxide, carbon disulphide, manganese or other substances
◆ (very rarely) brain tumours
◆ repeated head injuries

◆ boxing injury to the brain (the 'punch-drunk' syndrome)
◆ inflammation of the brain (encephalitis).

In most cases, the cause of Parkinson's disease is unknown.

The condition is treated by dopamine replacement. The drug levodopa has been proven to produce striking improvement in two-thirds of affected people. Other drugs, which stimulate dopamine receptors in the brain, can be used. Experimental treatment with transplantation of a sample of the patient's own adrenal tissue or implantation of fetal cells to try to restart dopamine production in the substantia nigra, have been tried but the results are uncertain. Mexican workers claimed remarkable improvement, but their reports have been criticized.

Shingles

This painful and sometimes seriously debilitating disease is an increasing problem in older people. Most sufferers are over 50 and the frequency rises with age. Half of those who reach 85 will have had at least one attack, and an attack does not necessarily confer permanent immunity. Every year about 200,000 people in Britain suffer from shingles, and about half of them have severe and persistent pain.

Shingles is not an infection; it is caused by the same virus that causes chickenpox (the varicella zoster virus). The virus is acquired, as a general rule, during childhood when it causes an attack of chickenpox – usually a mild and transient illness, which may even go unnoticed. In the course of the attack of chickenpox, varicella zoster virus is believed to enter the sensory nerve endings in the skin and travel up the nerves to the collections of nerve bodies (the ganglia) near the spinal cord. The virus has been isolated from these ganglia at post-mortem examinations of patients who died while suffering from shingles. Many years after the attack of chickenpox, the viruses may become reactivated and produce an acute inflammation in the ganglion. This is the cause of the pain experienced in the area supplied by the nerve, prior to the onset of the rash. Reactivation occurs because of a drop in the efficiency of the immune system which had been keeping the virus in check.

Replication of the viruses now produces a large number of new individuals and these travel down the nerve to the skin where further reproduction occurs and the characteristic rash, from cell damage, appears.

The first indication of shingles is usually a tingling sensation in the area which will become affected, followed by (often severe) pain in the same area. The area involved is the skin distribution of one or more sensory nerve roots supplying a strip of the skin of the chest or abdominal wall on one side, or on the face, above the eyebrow, also on one side. There is often fever and sickness and on the fourth or fifth day after the onset, the skin becomes red, and typical crops of small blisters appear in the area affected.

These are initially full of clear fluid, which is teeming with herpes viruses, but about three days after they appear, they turn yellowish and within a few days flatten, dry out and crust over. In the following two weeks or so, the crusts gradually dry up and drop off, leaving small, pitted scars. Occasionally, the rash is more widespread and the blisters may join up to form large confluent areas of damaged skin. In these cases healing may take many weeks and residual scarring may be severe. Shingles of the face, which occurs in 10 to 15 per cent of cases, is especially distressing, for the eyes may be involved and the vision affected, sometimes permanently.

The complications of shingles include rash infection by secondary organisms, causing deep tissue damage and scarring; skin contractures around the chest and eyes; local loss of skin pigment, leaving white areas; occasional damage to the middle and inner ears, with deafness and vertigo; the Ramsay–Hunt syndrome, in which there are:

- ear problems and paralysis of the facial nerve (Bell's palsy) on the same side
- ulceration and permanent scarring of the cornea
- loss of sensation in the cornea
- inflammation of the iris

Persistent pain in the site of the rash, which is known as post-herpetic pain, is the real reason why shingles is so important. As a rule, the pain and discomfort of shingles settles in two or three weeks from the onset. But in a proportion of cases this is not so and the pain continues for months, sometimes even years. This affects about 30 per cent of shingles patients over the age of 40, and the older the person and more severe the pre-rash pain, the more likely this is to happen. Persistent pain of this kind can have a devastating effect on the lives of sufferers. Many are old and frail and ill-equipped to tolerate the resulting debility and the deeply depressing effects of unremitting pain.

Shingles cannot be avoided, but an important treatment has made it possible to minimize its effects. This is the anti-herpes drug acyclovir (Zovirax), which should be given in large doses as soon as the diagnosis becomes clear. The earlier the drug is given, the more effective it is.

Thyroid underactivity

The thyroid gland in the neck produces a speed-up hormone called thyroxine that acts on almost all the cells of the body, stimulating them into activity. Too much and your body operates too quickly; not enough and you have a condition known as myxoedema, used to describe the general effects of severe underactivity of the gland.

Myxoedema occurs in women five times as often as in men. The effects are devastating but come on gradually and may not be recognized until a late stage. The signs of myxoedema are:

◆ dry and scaly, cold, thickened and coarse skin
◆ scanty, coarse and brittle hair
◆ gradual weight gain
◆ intolerance to cold conditions
◆ hoarseness of the voice
◆ thinned or even partly absent eyebrows
◆ thickened and mauve-coloured lips
◆ bad breath.

The affected person may be deeply depressed but does not complain. He or she may show signs of lethargy, fatigue and a slowing of body and mind, and may suffer constipation, muscle aches, deafness, anaemia, angina pectoris, heart failure and even coma and death. Short of the latter, all these effects can be reversed by the administration of thyroxine. The victim begins to feel better within two or three weeks and then makes a rapid recovery. Restoration of normal skin and hair may, however, take as long as six months.

It is important to bear the possibility of thyroid underactivity in mind, so that it is not overlooked as an explanation for general slowing of body and mental functions.

If surgery becomes necessary

Having to face a surgical operation is daunting. If you are scheduled for surgery, no matter how courageous you may be, you would be less than human if you were not feeling anxious, perhaps even fearful. Perhaps you are wondering whether your operation is really necessary, although your surgeon should have taken time to discuss it with you and to explain why you need surgery and what is to be done. He or she has a legal obligation to ensure that you do understand. Your consent must be informed. So if you are in any doubt, ask. Don't sign the consent form until you really know what is involved.

It is possible that you may have misunderstood something the surgeon has said to you and it is just possible that the proposed operation is not as essential as you think. More probably, your operation may be more critical to your health than you realize. You are entitled to know the facts, and it is perfectly proper for you to approach your surgeon, either directly or by letter, to find out all you want to know. It is always better to know the facts so that you can clearly understand what you are facing. The truth may be unpleasant, but it is something most people can face up to and cope with. For many, ignorant fear proves much worse.

When you go into hospital for your operation, you will be asked a lot of questions, many of which you may already have answered. Be patient: the more that is known about you the better. You will be asked about such things as:

- your general fitness
- any tendency to breathlessness
- palpitations
- ankle swelling
- persistent cough
- eating habits
- bowel action
- urinary difficulty or incontinence
- getting up at night to go to the toilet
- sleeping problems
- allergies
- smoking and drinking habits
- overseas travel
- any medication you may be taking
- whether you are diabetic.

These questions and the examination that follows are designed to make your operation safer by bringing to light, and dealing with, any matters that could cause complications.

You will be disturbed at regular intervals to have your temperature, pulse rate and blood pressure checked and recorded. It is customary to do certain routine tests on all patients, whatever the reason for their admission. You are likely to have some blood taken for tests of your haemoglobin levels, and red and white blood cell counts. You are also likely to be asked to give a specimen of urine for routine urinalysis.

Don't be surprised if you are given a very complete examination. A doctor may:

◆ re-check your pulse and blood pressure
◆ check the colour of your skin for jaundice
◆ look at the insides of your lower eyelids for anaemia
◆ look in your mouth and check the state of your teeth and tongue
◆ feel for lymph nodes in your neck, armpits, groin and elsewhere
◆ examine your chest, tapping it to check for normal resonance and listening to your heart and breath sounds with a stethoscope
◆ test your tendon jerk reflexes.

The examination may then focus on the particular problem for which the operation is to be done. This may involve careful feeling and possibly manipulation. If you have an abdominal complaint the doctor will carefully feel for tenderness or masses. A rectal or vaginal examination may be an essential part of the check. For these latter, the doctor wears disposable plastic gloves and uses a gel lubricant; both procedures are painless and there is no need for embarrassment. The doctor has done this so often that all he or she is interested in is what can be found out from the examination.

After checking the notes and confirming the type and site of the operation to be done, the doctor may mark your skin with a felt pen, making an arrow or other mark to ensure that the right operation is done in the right place. It may be necessary for a nurse to shave your skin at and around the site of the operation. This is done less often than formerly, but long skin hair can be a nuisance to the operator, especially when stitching up an incision, and many surgeons prefer the area to be shaved.

You will be visited by your anaesthetist who will want to be satisfied that you are fit to have the anaesthetic and that you have medication to help you to sleep the night before the operation. He or she will also prescribe drugs to ensure that you return from theatre feeling as little pain as possible and that the recovery period causes you the minimum of discomfort.

chapter three

Taking Care of Yourself

F orget the old superstition that a loss of mental and physical ability is an inevitable feature of old age. If this does happen, the chances are that you have some unsuspected medical problem. So any suggestion of loss of capacity is an indication for a visit to your doctor. When you go, be wary of comments like 'Well, of course, we must expect this kind of thing at our age, mustn't we?' The answer to that is a categorical 'No.'

Remember that many diseases are commoner in old age – diseases that can seriously prejudice the quality of life. They include atherosclerosis, cancer, diabetes, malnutrition (especially vitamin deficiency), underaction of the thyroid gland, osteoarthritis, osteoporosis, pernicious anaemia, cataract, shingles and depression. The most important of these are dealt with in Chapter 2. More than one of these disorders may be present at the same time. Some of them are obvious, but others remain concealed unless looked for and as a result many elderly people do not receive the standard of medical care they need.

There are several reasons why persistent (chronic) ill health in elderly people tends to be concealed. Many old people expect to be frail or unwell and feel that they should not complain. Many are remarkably stoical. Older people often have a lowered sensitivity to pain or even a lowered level of general awareness. Most are anxious not to be a burden to others. Sometimes failure to complain is due to genuine mental impairment, but an appearance of unconcern may be the result of physical disorder and lack of stimulation. Sensory deprivation is especially important. Many old people, who could be restored to self-sufficiency by a cataract operation or the provision of a hearing aid, remain lethargic and indifferent and require constant attention.

It is important that the elderly have full and regular medical attention. Millions of old people suffer unnecessary invalidism, distress and disability because of remediable conditions. Gradually developing anaemia, bedsores and malnutrition may go long unnoticed and conditions such as dehydration and hypothermia may affect those in all social circumstances. Given reasonable standards of medical and nursing care, these and other conditions need never occur. Make it your business to ensure that these things do not happen to you.

Self-neglect is common in older people, especially in those living alone, and its consequences may be serious. This is occasionally the result of unsuspected dementia, but in many cases it is due to no more than mild confusion, forgetfulness, mild depression and increasing physical difficulty resulting from organic disease. Those in greatest need of help include people recently discharged from hospital, those handicapped by poor vision and deafness, recently bereaved people and those who are lonely. Such people should never be left solitary for long periods. If you are in this kind of situation, do everything you can to maintain contact with others.

Check your home environment carefully. Adequate heating and good lighting make for comfort and safety and encourage reading, sewing and other activities. Accidental injury from falls is a common danger to the elderly (see pp. 95–7) and for this and other obvious reasons, if you live alone you should ensure that you are provided with an effective alarm system so that you can summon help reliably and quickly.

Voluntary agencies and public health authorities do much to help, and you should make full use of available facilities. The Home Help service can provide more than merely domestic assistance. Home helps keep a watchful eye on their elderly charges, noting signs of difficulty and calling in professional assistance when necessary. Volunteers providing meals on wheels can also offer a valuable monitoring service. The concept of sheltered housing, in which older people enjoy the benefits of custom-designed accommodation while remaining under unobtrusive surveillance, has much to commend it. It is an excellent system that should be more widely adopted.

Adequate social intercourse, mental stimulation and the encouragement of activity are essential. If necessary, you can achieve these by regular attendance at day health-care centres, at which various facilities such as bathing, chiropody and launderette are provided; at workshops for the elderly; clubs for older people; and, if arranged by your GP, even day hospitals. The latter are valuable institutions, offering full medical investigation and assessment, rehabilitative treatment and the means of health maintenance on a daily attendance basis. Your relatives will be encouraged to participate in any discussion of future management at home and to learn how you can achieve maximum activity and independence.

A major cause of distress to some older people is the feeling that they no longer matter to others, that their dependence is irksome and their presence a nuisance. This particular aspect of the ageist stereotype is readily fostered by the apparent neglect or unconcern of younger relatives. Their refusal to let older people participate usefully in the home is wounding and damaging, both physically and mentally. They should be encouraging elderly relatives to be active, not passive and unwanted. Older people with grandchildren are well aware of how therapeutic their close association with children can be, especially when, as is usually the case, their grandchildren love and value them. Ideally, older people should be able to take it for granted that they are expected to take a share in child care.

Living alone

Many people live alone by choice but many more by necessity. Often in older people the solitary state is the result of bereavement. You may have heard stories about death rates being higher among bereaved people than others of the same age. But the statistics do not necessarily indicate that it is the death of the partner that causes the higher risk. Researchers amalgamated all the cases of death following bereavement and found that the death rate was higher than in people who had not been bereaved. But couples share the same, possibly unfavourable, environment, or tend to have the same unhealthy habits, or even suffer the same diseases, so the reduced life expectancy of the survivor need have nothing to do with being bereaved.

The figures show that men often do badly, especially in the first six months, and that the mortality in that group is higher than in a comparable married group of the same age. In this case, there are several possible explanations. Many men have been accustomed to being looked after by their partners and some simply don't know how to look after themselves. In addition, it is clear that women often do keep men's bad habits in check and that widowers tend to 'go to the dogs'. Many widowers fail to feed themselves properly and smoke and drink far more than is good for them. Cirrhosis of the liver and lung cancer are common causes of death in such men.

At least one study of over 500 bereaved people showed that, for women, bereavement seemed actually to be protective. There was no significant increase in the chance of dying during the first six months and the life expectancy appeared to be slightly increased at about two years after the death of the husband. Other studies, and they are in the majority, show that the risks for widows are slightly greater at about two years, but that this increased risk soon passes off.

Suggestions that people left solitary by bereavement are seriously at risk of an early death can be dismissed. Nevertheless it is important to take an interest in the special health factors affecting bereaved people.

Stress

Stress, of course, is not confined to those who live alone. But many of its worst effects are experienced by those who do live alone, when adequate social stimulation may be lacking.

Much of what is written about stress is simplified and exaggerated. The fact is that stress is an essential and normal part of life and we all experience it, to some degree, all the time. The list of stress-producing events is endless and includes such things as:

◆ worrying
◆ suffering embarrassment
◆ having new experiences
◆ mastering a difficult task
◆ watching horror films
◆ having a sense of social inferiority
◆ taking exercise
◆ suffering infection
◆ suffering pain
◆ fright
◆ cold
◆ shock.

To cope with these demands, our bodies respond, to an appropriate degree, by the production of a number of hormones. The most important of these are cortisol and adrenaline. Most people are well aware of the effects of adrenaline – anxiety, 'butterflies' in the upper abdomen, fast pulse, rapid breathing, sweating palms and so on.

Cortisol, like adrenaline, is produced by a pair of small glands sitting on top of the kidneys, known as the adrenals. Nowadays, physiologists define stress as any event which causes an increased output of cortisol. Cortisol, also known as hydrocortisone, is a natural steroid ('sterol-like'), essential for health and normal living – without it we would die. The substance was synthesized in 1950 and became available to doctors for use as a valuable and often life-saving drug. One of its actions in the body is to remove protein from the muscles and to stimulate its conversion into the fuel, glucose, which is essential for coping with the stress. This action is the reason why children exposed to severe stress, or children given steroids, may fail to grow properly. Another action of cortisol is to tighten up arteries so as to prevent a dangerous fall in blood pressure.

When cortisone is given in very high dosage it has a powerful effect in reducing inflammation; this is medically valuable in allergy, arthritis and other diseases. But inflammation has to do with the body's resistance to infection and that is closely connected with the immune system. Cortisol, in large amounts, prevents vessels from widening so that they are no longer able to bring the full complement of essential blood to a part of the body in need; it reduces the ease with which important scavenging white cells (phagocytes) can get to an area where they can combat infecting organisms; it interferes with the action of lymphocytes ('B' cells and 'T' cells) so that antibody production is reduced and lymphocyte control of virus infection, and even of cancer, may be prejudiced.

Large doses may also accelerate the development of high blood pressure, precipitate diabetes, promote stomach ulcers and, most seriously of all, may hasten the development of atherosclerosis (see pp. 17–25).

Note that these effects result from the relatively enormous doses which doctors have been able to give since cortisol was synthesized and even more powerful steroids developed. We simply do not know for certain whether persistent 'natural' rises in cortisol can have the same catalogue of ill effects. The probability is that, to an extent that varies from person to person they do. We know that different people produce different levels of cortisol for apparently the same stress, and that these differences tie in with characteristic personality types. We also know that people with 'stressful' personalities do have a greater tendency to develop those diseases which excess cortisol can lead to.

But data on these matters is statistical and can be misleading. There seems to be little doubt that prolonged high levels of stress are undesirable, but it is also clear that there are plenty of people who thrive on them. Ageing is often a time of loss – loss of friends, partners, status, sometimes affluence – and the degree of stress depends on how badly you take the loss or how important it is to you. If you have reason to suppose that you are having high and continuing stress from this, or other causes, you should certainly watch out for and report the earliest signs of illness.

Effective relaxation can lower stress of all kinds. The inter-relationship of the mind and the body is so close that everything that affects one, affects the other. An unhappy state of mind produces tension and other bodily reactions which are damaging. But it is also true that if you can somehow succeed in releasing these tensions, you may be able to induce a measure of serenity of mind. This can be difficult, and stress-induced tension usually requires training for its release. Try on your own, by all means. If you live in a town, you will almost certainly find that evening classes in relaxation – or in yoga or meditation, which many people have found to help in relieving stress – are available, for example. But if you find you need more help, ask to see a physiotherapist or occupational therapist.

Pets

If you live alone, consider the advantages of keeping a pet. Dogs and cats provide company, comfort, sometimes protection, and may have a major role in promoting social intercourse. Dog owners who take regular walks tend to meet others engaged in the same activity or working in their gardens. You cannot pass the same person repeatedly without forming some kind of a link – however tenuous. A nod leads to a chat and then to a discovery of common interests.

Pets provide a sense of being needed and a source of living touch. Affectionate cats who sleep on laps promote a sense of peace and well-being, lower stress levels (it's difficult to stroke a cat when you are tense) and fulfil, to some extent, the basic biological need for regular contact with some other living thing. Some owners believe that they have a high level of communication with animals, to whom they attribute many human character-istics. The obvious display of emotional reaction by many dogs and the ease with which animals can be conditioned to react predictably to various stimuli, foster this conviction. That this is partly an illusion in no way diminishes its value to the lonely and friendless.

But there is a cost to everything, and you must remember that pets can tie you down and limit your travel possibilities. Remember also that some have short lives and that, if you become too devoted, you may have to go through another loss.

The dangers of living alone

Most doctors, especially those working in hospital accident and emergency departments, are familiar with the special risks run by people who live alone and who have no regular visitors. Such people are often helpless and in a poor state; some are even found dead on the floor of their homes. People who are so debilitated that they cannot look after themselves are liable to all sorts of risks and misfortunes such as chest, skin and urinary infections, pressure ulcers (bedsores), body cooling (hypothermia), fluid deficiency (dehydration), fractures and immobilization from falls, and so on.

Remember that, however healthy you feel, you can always have an accident. Every year, one quarter of all people over 70 have at least one fall (see pp. 95–7). In half of these cases the person who falls is unable to get up without help. Dying alone and without human contact is not the way you should go, but it often happens. People living alone are at least as liable as others of the same age to suffer strokes, heart attacks, diabetic or hypoglycaemic coma, debilitating weakness that precludes survival action, or accidental drug overdose from medication.

These dangers are not confined to poor people: many of the people who die alone at home or who are brought into hospital in a precarious state are by no means impoverished. Many are living in expensive houses in well-to-do neighbourhoods. Having a healthy bank balance is of no value if you are unable to spend your money in ways to help yourself to a safer and happier lifestyle.

In spite of all that modern medicine can do, the consequences of falling alone remain serious. About half of the people brought into hospital for this reason require intensive care and only about one-third can eventually return to their own homes. Ten per cent die in hospital and the rest have to be transferred to nursing homes or other forms of residential care.

What can you do to avoid this problem? Firstly, acknowledge the risk. If you are independent and determined not to rely on others for help, that is your right. It may be that after social neglect by your relatives you feel that you don't want to make any demands on them. But you must still be clear in your mind that if you become ill or disabled, you will be in real trouble if you can't communicate with anyone.

Relying on others is not a denial of your independence. You need a plan to secure your own safety. Ideally, such a plan might work to the mutual advantage of yourself and someone else. Try to set up an arrangement with an elderly neighbour for a mutual visit or phone call. This way you will not be beholden to anyone and will be doing someone else a good turn. Failing such a solution, see if you can arrange for a weekly visit by a nurse. You may have to pay for this but it will be money well spent.

Personal alarm systems can be useful, but there are snags. Batteries may become exhausted and the device must be constantly accessible. They are sometimes subject to repeated false alarms so that they may, in the end, be ignored. You may resent the need to carry such an alarm at all times and the attendant implication that you may not be able to look after yourself. If you use an alarm system, make sure that anyone within the audible vicinity is aware of its significance. And, of course, never abuse the system by using it for trivial purposes.

Consider sheltered accommodation. There may be a lot of money locked up in a house that is really far too big for you. You could have a comfortable income with no risk if some of that equity were released. But be sure to take professional financial advice before making any major decisions of this kind. Your bank can be relied on to help with this.

Sheltered housing units may be provided by local authorities or by a housing authority or private speculator. They can be bought or rented, and usually consist of small bungalows or flats grouped together in clusters of up to about 40. In some, you are on your own and treated as entirely independent individuals. Others provide some communal facilities with living-in overseeing wardens, alarm systems and arrangements for regular daily checks. These facilities may provide central cooking with meals-on-wheels, help with the domestic work, laundry facilities, window-cleaning, gardening and extensive home care. Although wardens always pay a daily visit, it is not their responsibility to provide personal assistance, but they will contact a relative or GP, or call an ambulance if any real problems arise.

The rest of what follows in this chapter is applicable whether you live alone or not, but you should be aware that some of these problems are more acute in those who do live on their own.

Nutrition

Most younger people eat too much and, in general, this tendency is reduced with age. But if your intake is normally small and, for whatever reason, you become depressed, the further reduction in food intake could be dangerous. If you don't eat, your body still needs fuel to keep going. First, it uses up all the fat stored under your skin and elsewhere, converting it into glucose which the body burns for energy. When the fat is all consumed – and this will not take very long if you are naturally slim – your muscles are called on to supply the vital fuel and these soon waste away. This is serious as it leads to weakness and disability and you will find it difficult to put the bulk back into the wasted muscles. Persistent loss of appetite is especially dangerous in those people whose muscles may already be weakened and wasted by disuse.

Some older people take so little interest in food that, although they do eat, they subsist on a fixed and insufficiently varied diet, perhaps just buns and tea for example. This kind of a diet provides calories but is so short of vitamins that sooner or later you will begin to suffer from vitamin deficiency diseases. It is hard to believe that elderly people living in our affluent society can suffer from scurvy – the vitamin C deficiency disease which used to affect sailors on long sea voyages whose diet consisted only of sea biscuits and salted pork – but this is so. Bleeding from the gums, massive bruising, severe arthritis from bleeding into the joints and other unpleasant effects can occur after about three months on a restricted diet.

It is easy to get enough vitamins and any diet, however meagre, which contains a little fruit and fresh vegetables, some milk, fish and cheese, and an occasional chicken leg or some minced beef, will give you all you need.

(What is said here about vitamins refers to an adequate dietary intake to avoid deficiency diseases; the use of vitamins in larger doses as antioxidants is a different matter, dealt with fully in chapter 6.)

Exercise

The body is amazingly responsive, even in old age, and given time will adapt to perform much of what you ask it to do. This was demonstrated by a trial carried out on over 100 people in their 70s and 80s in California. These people were started on gentle exercising, well within their capacity – walking, jogging, swimming, stretching and yoga. Many could hardly walk when they started but, with careful progression of the exertion, excellent results in terms of improved physical ability were obtained. Many men were able, within six months, to jog for 2 km (1 mile) without stopping. Their lung air capacity increased by about 20 per cent and the amount breathed in, in a given time, rose by as much as 35 per cent.

This important study brought out the fact that you are never too old to enjoy an improvement in physical capacity. But the adaptability of the body works in the opposite direction also. Too much rest is dangerous. Enforced bed rest, as a result of illness, leads to loss of power which may take much longer to recover from than the length of the period spent in bed. For this reason, most doctors minimize bed rest, and get patients moving as soon as possible (see chapter 2).

Aim to take a reasonably long walk at least three times a week. The more often, the better; the longer the better; the brisker the better. If you can walk up a hill and down the other side, do so rather than going round on the flat. Regular physical exercise is as good for the mind as it is for the body. It relieves depression, induces a sense of optimism, encourages constructive thought and prompts the imagination. Wordsworth used to walk for hours composing poetry in his mind, then go home and write it all down.

The benefits of exercise

Exercise brings with it many benefits. Among them are improved muscle strength and flexibility, both of which will help to keep you mobile for longer. This can mean anything from reaching behind to do up a dress zipper to stretching to get something down from a high shelf (or bending easily to pick something from a low one). Exercise can counter or postpone some of the worst effects of osteoporosis. A greater range of mobility will improve your posture – which will help alleviate such common problems as back ache – and your coordination. It will also encourage the production of endorphins, sometimes called 'the happy hormones', thereby reducing depression. And, going to bed pleasantly tired physically helps promote good sleep. Exercise burns calories and increases the metabolism, making such conditions as constipation less likely.

But perhaps the major reason for exercising is that it improves the fitness of your cardiovascular system, causing your heart and lungs to work more effectively. As you exercise your muscles demand more oxygen to work, so your heart beats faster to pump the blood – which contains oxygen – to those muscles that need it. This not only has an effect on your heart, but also on your lungs, breathing and circulatory systems. In time, as long as you sustain exercise, your body starts to take oxygen from the blood more effectively, so that your heart beats more strongly, and more slowly. In effect, it has to do less to achieve what you are asking of it. An improved circulation means you will suffer less from such common problems as cold fingers and toes, or swollen ankles.

What to choose

Walking is one of the easiest ways to start exercising because, apart from comfortable shoes and a waterproof jacket, you need no special equipment and no outside help. Gentle jogging, once you have built a reasonable level of fitness through walking, is a good next stage. Many people find it helps to have a partner to walk or jog with; others find that they enjoy the solitude as an opportunity to organize their thoughts, perhaps work through a problem that has been bothering them.

One of the most common misconceptions about leisure centres and gyms is that they are for the young and fit. And it is true that most of the people who use the weights rooms, for example, and pack them in the early evening fit this bill. But centre managers realize that for most of the working day Monday to Friday they would be largely empty if they catered only for this age group. Among the facilities for the older age group (either through specific classes or set times of the day) you may find at your local leisure centre are:

◆ swimming
◆ aquarobics (aerobics in water so that most of your weight is supported in the water, reducing the risk of damage)
◆ low-impact aerobics.

Some leisure centres also offer yoga and dance classes (ballroom, line, and so on). If you extend your search a little farther afield you may find facilities for senior players at a local golf range, ski slope, tennis club or bowling green. See also pp. 174–5.

If you don't have a good motive to walk, provide yourself with one – get a dog, for instance (see p. 88).

Principles of exercising for older people

- Don't rush into strenuous exercise without medical advice.
- Remember the benefits – see p. 91 – and use these facts as motivation to continue.
- Build up your exercise capacity gradually.
- Make walking a central exercise activity to start with but do not neglect loosening-up and stretching exercises.
- Try to increase the range of movements of all joints, but be careful to avoid damage to ligaments by forcing this.
- Ensure that your footwear is suitable.
- Have a good stretch before starting any exercise.
- Stop at once if exercise causes pain – especially if you suffer from any form of arthritis.
- Aim, if possible, at a steady increase in your tolerance to exercise.

Smoking and drinking

The first priority in the life of any person who smokes should be to stop. Everyone knows that smoking damages health, but less well known is that it is one of the chief risk factors for sudden death from a heart attack and is regularly a cause of angina pectoris, coronary thrombosis, severe disablement from disease of the arteries supplying blood to the legs and from what is called chronic obstructive airway disease.

How to quit

For many people the best way to stop smoking is simply to stop, now. Throw away any cigarettes you have in the house, resolve not to buy any more and determine to say no if anyone offers you one. You are stronger than your need for tobacco.

If you have tried that in the past and failed, try again. If you still can't do it, cut down drastically now with a view to quitting completely in the next month. Find something else to do with your hands, such as knitting, starting a large complicated jigsaw puzzle, digging the garden or making bread.

Most people who really want to stop smoking do so in one of these ways. But if neither works for you, you could also consider

- nicotine patches (available from a chemist)
- nicotine gum (also available from a chemist)
- stop-smoking classes (good if you need the support of others, particularly if you live alone)
- acupuncture
- hypnosis

Smoking is one of the major risk factors for atherosclerosis (see pp. 17–25). The direct effect on the lungs – apart from the cancer risk – is to encourage chronic bronchitis and emphysema and progressively to reduce the efficiency of the respiratory system. Respiratory cripples suffer from constant exhausting, laboured breathing (even at rest in bed), blue lips and heaving shoulders fighting to get enough air. Their only prospect is progressive deterioration.

Alcohol is easily abused, especially by solitary people. Many people living alone fall quickly into habits of over-indulgence, perhaps feeling justified by their depression and insomnia. The risks are addiction, liver damage, pancreatitis and eventually brain damage. Women are especially susceptible.

Danger signs of alcohol abuse

◆ Thinking a lot about alcohol
◆ Forming regular patterns of taking more than one drink
◆ Drinking early in the day, or regularly at lunchtime
◆ Alcohol beginning to interfere with normal activities
◆ Progressive need for larger quantities to satisfy you
◆ Feeling bad every morning.

Don't worry about regular moderate drinking. A daily habit doesn't mean that you are in danger. There is a lot of evidence that it may even be good for you. Just watch the quantities. Estimate your intake in units. A unit is a glass of wine, a measure of spirits or half a pint of beer. A man who exceeds three units (and a woman two) a day, every day, is at risk of injury. This is not to suggest that a maximum of this number of units a day is necessarily a safe level of drinking – susceptibility to alcohol damage varies considerably from person to person – but you would be unlucky if it did harm you.

Cirrhosis of the liver

This is a dangerous and insidious disease in which functioning liver tissue is progressively replaced by scar (fibrous) tissue that can perform none of the vital processes of the liver. The trouble with cirrhosis is that it never gives any warning of its presence until a critically late stage. The chief cause, and the one which makes it a major menace, is long-term alcohol abuse. In this respect, as in others, women are far more sensitive to the adverse effects of excess alcohol than men. In middle-aged people, it is the third cause of death after heart disease and cancer.

The effects of cold

Even in the most severe winters, the numbers of cases of hypothermia in Britain is small. In only about 25 cases a year is hypothermia given on death certificates as the underlying cause of death. But the effects of cold on older people are much more widespread and serious than this figure suggests. We now know that cold is a major contributing factor in heart and lung disease in old people and in causing their death from these conditions.

Every year, there is an immediate rise in the death rate among old people when mean temperatures drop below freezing, and this rise continues for over a month after the extreme cold has passed. About 40,000 more people die each average winter, in England and Wales, than during a comparable period in summer, and the majority of these are elderly.

Body heat production is less efficient in old people, many of whom use up body fuel at a slower than normal rate. Even more important, shivering may be less effective in producing heat, because of diminished muscle bulk. Shivering is the most important way of raising a falling body temperature. Heat is normally lost from the body by a widening of the blood vessels of the skin and conserved by a narrowing of them, so that less blood flows through the skin. Because of age-related changes in the walls of these blood vessels, elderly people's skin vessels are often unable to constrict, and so older people may be denied this method of conserving heat. The control of heat regulation in the brain can also be less efficient in the elderly. These factors lead to an increase in the thickness of the blood and a rise in blood pressure. Low temperatures also reduce the ability of the linings of the bronchial tubes to resist infection and can induce asthma. The net effect is a substantial increase in the death rate from serious heart and lung disorders.

In cold weather, take special care to keep warm, both by effective domestic heating and by insulating your body so as to minimize heat loss. Multiple layers of garments are more effective than heavy material. Don't forget that you can lose considerable heat – up to 25 per cent – from the top of your head. There is much to be said for wearing woolly hats, indoors, in winter time.

Falls

There are several reasons why falls are common in older people. These include:

- defective (often unsuspected) vision
- unsteadiness
- slower reflexes

- ◆ vertigo
- ◆ stiffness
- ◆ muscle weakness.

In addition, falls are usually far more serious in elderly people than in the young. Osteoporosis makes older people, especially women, particularly susceptible to fractures, even from minor stumbles, and the resulting immobilization and decline in the level of activity can have grave effects. Chest and urinary infections commonly supervene and these may tip the balance against survival. Delicate skin can tear and bruise easily and stretched or torn muscles are slow to heal. Long periods of pain, discomfort and disability may follow an apparently trivial fall. And even after physical recovery from a fall, there is often considerable disability from the fear of another fall.

Because of these risks, you should make every effort to avoid hazards in your environment. Watch out for, and avoid, loose mats on polished floors, damaged floor coverings, carelessly disposed electric cables, loose stair carpets and stair rods, poorly lit stairs or corridors and icy paths. Highly polished floors may massage your pride in the standards of your housekeeping, but the risks really don't justify them.

If you live alone you are especially at risk, and some form of alarm system which will enable you to summon help, even if immobilized, is essential. Don't take chances.

Walking aids

Walking sticks can be helpful if you have a one-sided weakness or a painful knee or hip joint on one side. The correct length is that which allows you to stand upright with the tip of the stick on the ground and your arm bent a little at the elbow. Walking sticks can be used in two ways. Usually the stick is held on the strong side, so that it is forward when the foot on the weak side is also forward. But if one leg is particularly weak, it is sometimes better to hold the stick close to the leg on that side so that it acts as a kind of splint. People suffering from instability may benefit from a walking stick with a broader base consisting of three or four small feet.

If you have a greater tendency to fall, you may find the light alloy frame 'walker' (Zimmer frame) a useful aid to mobility. Your progress must necessarily be slow and tedious, but a walker often allows people with severe weakness or disability to get around and perhaps gain strength for greater mobility.

The older design of armpit crutch, which could injure the nerves under the head of the upper arm bone, has been replaced by light forearm-support or elbow crutches. These offer good mobility and can be used in several ways. For the most disabled, 'four point' walking is used in which only one foot or one crutch tip is moved forward at a time. In 'three point' walking, both crutches are moved forward together then, while the weight is supported, one foot is moved and then the other. For the more agile, the crutches can be used to support the whole weight of the body while both legs are swung forward together. You may need a bit of courage at first, but you will soon get the hang of it and feel safe. The only thing to avoid is leaning backward. On stairs, it is usually best to discard one crutch and use the handrail on that side. It is convenient, therefore, to have three crutches so that one can always be left at the top or bottom of the stairs.

Pressure sores (skin ulcers)

Older people who are too debilitated to move much and who spend a great deal of time lying in bed or confined to a chair are liable to suffer sustained compression of the skin in the areas taking the weight of the body. This leads to local loss of blood supply, loss of feeling and, eventually, local tissue death with breakdown of the skin (ulceration). Pressure ulcers, usually known as bed-sores, are especially likely to affect the buttocks, heels, elbows and the back of the head. They are particularly common in people who have suffered loss of skin sensation from neurological damage as a result of a stroke or a disease of the nervous system. The skin can remain healthy and intact only if it has a constant supply of blood, bringing oxygen, sugars and other essential nutrients. Local pressure squashes the small skin blood vessels, and the supply is cut off.

Bedsores, technically known as decubitus ulcers, may be large and the ulceration may progress to complete local loss of skin with exposure of the underlying tendons or bone. They are common in poorly nursed unconscious patients or in those suffering from extreme weakness or paralysis. Diabetics, and those with compromised blood supply to the limbs from arterial disease, such as atherosclerosis, are especially liable and require special attention.

Bedsores can be avoided by regular changes of position. But for many debilitated people the only real solution is skilled nursing by a qualified person who can detect and deal with early signs of trouble. All kinds of ingenious beds which, by sequential air inflation of bed segments, or movement of fluid, constantly alter the sites taking the body weight have been devised. If you can afford it, one of these beds can greatly help to reduce the risk of pressure sores, but they do not eliminate the need for regular passive body movement and skilled nursing care. The nurse will inspect your skin daily and ensure that it is kept clean, dry and in good condition.

Residential care

Many older people dread the prospect of having to resort to residential care. It is worth pointing out that residential homes and nursing homes are not the same thing. Residential homes are places in which a person can live under a closer degree of care than is provided by sheltered housing. People in residential homes have bed and board, communal recreation facilities and, as necessary, help with eating, toilet, washing and dressing. Many such homes are provided by the local authority, others are run for profit by private organizations. Naturally, the quality of life of the residents depends almost entirely on the motivation and goodwill of the managers and staff. Such homes must be registered with the local authority and are inspected at least twice a year. Remember that the tales of atrocities that appear occasionally in the papers do so because they are rare. Most of the residents of such places are contented and able to live satisfying lives.

Nursing homes, most privately run, provide full-time nursing care by properly qualified and often highly experienced nurses. They are appropriate for people who, by reason of ill health, disability or senile deterioration, require long-term professional care. Nurse–patient ratios (two full-time nurses for every three occupied beds) are stipulated by law. These homes, too, must be registered with the local authority and are also inspected at least twice a year.

Before considering a move to a residential institution, decide whether it is near enough to be accessible for visits by your friends and relatives. Are there local amenities – post office, library, shops, church and so on – within easy reach or are there arrangements for residents to get to them? Take plenty of time to inspect the premises and meet the people so that you can be assured of certain important factors. First and foremost, assess the current residents and staff. Are these the kind of people with whom you could comfortably live? The residents are unlikely to put on a performance for you, but the staff might. They will, of course, be anxious to persuade you to stay, so make due allowance for this. You should expect courtesy, a measure of respect and friendliness but not undue familiarity, and certainly not a patronizing attitude on a brief acquaintance. Carers who patronize their charges do not respect them.

Make a list beforehand of your minimum requirements and check whether these are really available.

◆ Would you have immediate access to a telephone?
◆ Are there any restrictions on the use of the phone?
◆ Is there strict regimentation on times of getting up, mealtimes, bedtimes, and so on?

- Confirm whether you would have a bedroom of your own or would be expected to share or even to sleep in a small dormitory.
- Would you have your own toilet and washing facilities?
- What arrangements are there for the storage and protection of personal belongings?
- How much personal material will you be allowed to bring to the home?
- Is TV communal, so that you are restricted in the choice of programmes, or would you have your own TV set?
- How many books are you allowed to have?

These are all important questions that could have a major effect on the quality of your future life and you are entitled to enquire into them in detail. Don't be either embarrassed or intimidated.

The question of finance must inevitably brook large in your considerations. It will also be of some interest to your children. Whether you select a private home or one run by the local authority, you are still liable to have to meet all or part of the cost. Currently, people with capital or savings of over £16,000 are required to pay the full cost. This may apply even if your capital is tied up in property and you may be required to sell it. If your holdings are less than £16,000, the deficit will be paid by the council. If they are less than £3,000, the whole of the fee will be paid by the local authority.

Prescription drugs and old age

Because older people often suffer from more than one disorder at a time, there is a tendency for doctors to prescribe many drugs. Although more than four separate remedies should be exceptional, there are plenty of people taking as many as ten. Sometimes these interfere with one another. This is called drug interaction and it may cause the effects of the drugs to be more severe than they should be (see below). The normal side-effects of some drugs may become more severe with age. Some researchers have suggested that as many as 10 per cent of admissions of elderly people to hospital are related to the effects of prescription drugs, whether from inappropriate prescribing or other causes.

If you are taking several different drugs, you are entitled to try to make sure that you are not being harmed. It is a good idea to write down the name of everything you are taking and how many per day. If possible, put down what you think the medication is for. Write down, too, any herbal or non-prescription medicine you are taking. Don't miss anything out just because you have been taking it for years. Write down, also, any symptoms or effects you have had since starting any of the medicines. Then take your list to your doctor and ask him or her to check it. You are likely to find that several drugs will be struck off the list.

Ask your doctor whether all these medicines are really necessary, whether any of the symptoms you are having may be caused by them and whether any of the drugs have been prescribed to treat the side-effects of others. This is sometimes unavoidable but is often just the result of hasty medical management. In such cases, you are entitled to expect your doctor to think again.

Most drugs are absorbed at the same rate as in younger people, but the drug levodopa is absorbed much more readily. Other drugs that seem to have a more marked effect than in younger people include:

- the benzodiazepam sleeping pill nitrazepam (Mogadon)
- the beta-blocker propranolol (Inderal)
- the anticoagulant drug warfarin (Marevan)
- the heart drug digoxin (Lanoxin)
- some of the antibiotics such as the penicillins and the aminoglycosides gentamicin (Cidomycin, Genticin) and kanamycin (Kannasyn).

Digoxin and these antibiotics may have a greater effect than expected because they are eliminated from the body more slowly in older people. This may be an advantage in the case of the penicillins but with the aminoglycosides there is a real danger that unexpectedly high levels of the drug in the body may cause permanent damage to the sensitive mechanism in the inner ears and lead to permanent deafness.

Diuretic drugs – drugs that increase the output of urine – such as bend-rofluazide (Aprinox) and hydrochlorothiazide (Hydrosaluric) can cause problems in older people because the average intake of potassium in the diet of older people is often less than the amount lost from the body as a result of the diuretic drug. The resulting potassium deficiency can have serious effects, especially on the heart. It may also cause muscle weakness, loss of appetite and constipation.

Following the doctor's advice

Many of the ill-effects or failures of drug treatment in older people are due to their not complying with their doctors' orders – perhaps failing to take the whole course of antibiotics. You are entitled to ask your doctor to write down his or her instructions, especially if these involve a number of different drugs and different times of taking them.

Over-the-counter drugs can cause problems, especially if used in dosages that exceed the recommendations on the package. Aspirin and indomethacin (Indocid) and other non-steroidal anti-inflammatory drugs (NSAIDs), used to relieve the pain of arthritis, can cause stomach and duodenal irritation that can amount to ulceration. Bleeding into the bowel from such drugs is quite common.

When taking prescription drugs, always be on the lookout for side-effects. Different drugs may cause different side-effects, which may include:

♦ nausea
♦ vomiting
♦ loss of appetite
♦ diarrhoea
♦ constipation
♦ drowsiness
♦ tiredness
♦ a dry mouth
♦ blurring of vision
♦ a rapid heartbeat
♦ difficulty in urinating
♦ impotence.

Some drugs can lower your blood pressure and cause fainting. Drugs that act on the nervous system, such as sedatives, narcotics and tranquillizers, can affect mood, judgement, memory and motivation – usually for the worse. These drugs may even disturb your coordination and affect balance. But remember that vertigo, occurring for no known reason, is quite common in older people so this may not be an effect of any drug.

Drug interactions are the adverse effects that can occur when separate drugs are taken simultaneously, and the drugs act on each other in such a way as to increase the toxicity or reduce the effectiveness of one or both. Drug interactions may be dangerous. The commonest interaction is well known – the additive effect of similar drugs or of drugs having similar actions – and the commonest example is the additive effect of alcohol on any of the sedatives or tranquillizers. This can lead to a dangerous degree of sedation and may, for instance, make driving hazardous. The law does not excuse you simply because it was a drug, rather than drink, that led to the crime.

Sometimes drugs combine to reduce the effect of both. One drug may interfere with the absorption of another. Drugs are commonly bound to, and carried by, proteins in the blood. One drug can sometimes displace another from its bound form, releasing it so that its action is stronger. Much of what happens in cells is controlled by thousands of different chemical activators called enzymes. Drugs can interfere with enzyme action, either enhancing or interfering with it. Drugs are often broken down by enzymes, so that they do not act for so long. Some other drugs, by interfering with the breaking-down enzymes, allow the first drug to act for much longer than normal. Some drugs prevent the action of others by blocking the receptor sites on cell membranes where many drugs act.

Elderly people have far more trouble from prescribed drugs than younger people. Often without knowing it, they suffer adverse effects directly attributable to the medication they are taking. Every time this problem has been investigated, alarming facts have come to light – people being seriously overdosed, people taking drugs which react dangerously with one another, people taking medicines whose actions cancel one another, and so on. Often more than one doctor is involved, so each may be unaware of what the other has been prescribing. It is not unknown for doctors to diagnose senile dementia or Alzheimer's disease when, in fact, the trouble is due to over-treatment with sedatives or other drugs.

Elderly people often feel unhappy about troubling their GPs and prefer to buy additional over-the-counter remedies from a chemist. Some, unwisely, may even take medicines recommended and given to them by their friends from well-stocked bathroom cabinets. Some herbal remedies contain active and potentially harmful ingredients and overuse of these can add to the problem. They may even interact with prescribed medication. The only really safe policy if you are on one or more prescription drugs is to avoid taking any other form of medication.

Caring for elderly people

Although this part of the book is concerned with looking after yourself, it may well be that you also have responsibilities for the care of another person, perhaps older than yourself. It is estimated that there are as many as six million carers in Britain. Surveys also indicate that more than a third of those who have accepted the care of people over 65 are themselves over 70. Most carers are women.

Caring can involve many stresses and sacrifices – of time, money, social freedom, emotion and sometimes limited physical strength. If you are in this situation you probably need all the help and advice you can get. Sometimes the responsibility as a carer comes on gradually as a relative, spouse or partner slowly becomes less capable of self-care. The situation is often much more stressful if this responsibility is suddenly thrust upon you as a result of the sudden illness – a stroke for example – suffered by the other person.

The most difficult problems for carers arise when their charges constantly behave badly – usually from dementia or the effects of stroke – or behave in such a way as to cause loss of sleep. Incontinence, with the attendant repeated necessity to wash clothes or bedding, also often adds greatly to the burden.

Many carers seem to make no attempt to get help, but simply shoulder the whole burden. One survey showed that 45 per cent of carers received no assistance from anyone. About one-third get some help from another relative but only 14 per cent get help from the social services. Carers, by their voluntary efforts, save the government billions of pounds each year but many of them seem unaware that they are entitled to financial help in the form of attendance allowance and invalid care allowance. Often, by accepting these responsibilities, they are denied the possibility of earning income for themselves.

Many carers need information, advice and guidance on lightening their load. In many cases, the person they are looking after needs medical help and this, in itself, can relieve the burden by improving the general condition of the patient and increasing the range of self-care. But a GP has another function – to ensure that the carer is provided with all the help to which he or she is legally entitled. Obtaining the full financial allowances, getting domestic help from the local authority, meals on wheels, domiciliary nursing care and access to the appropriate organizations can all help to improve the quality of life of carers.

In the appendix are useful addresses, such as those of the Carers' National Association, the Alzheimer's Disease Society, Help the Aged and Age Concern. In the section on references and bibliography are suggestions for reading that you may find helpful.

chapter four

The Psychology of Ageing

I
n the absence of diseases that damage the brain, mental processes show
only one confirmed characteristic with increasing age – a degree of
slowing. Expressed in psychological language, from the highly respected
psychiatry textbook *Companion to Psychiatric Studies*, 'The major change with
ageing is the decline in psychomotor speed, while other cognitive functions
show little in the way of consistent change.' The size of the vocabulary remains
constant or increases with age and, apart from the factor of speed, verbal
learning shows little or no decline with age.

These facts tie in with the observation that there is only limited loss of brain
cells at more advanced ages and they are not challenged by other observations
of apparent degenerative changes in a small proportion of the brain cells and a
reduction in their connections. The fact is that the built-in redundancy in brain
nerve tissue is enormous, far greater than the redundancy in other organs. In
this context, the word 'redundancy' means a generous superfluity of cellular
richness, far in excess of what is ever used. It is only in conditions such as
Alzheimer's disease (see pp. 117–21), in which an enormous proportion of the
brain cells is destroyed, that mental functioning is significantly affected by loss
of neuronal tissue.

That declining mental function is an inevitable concomitant of ageing is a
myth.

Ageing and memory

From one point of view, the quality of a human being is a measure of that
person's memory. Certainly there are people with a rich memory who do
nothing with it but, in many contexts, the possession of a large store of
information determines a person's effectiveness and usefulness. Professional,
business, academic and scientific hierarchies are, largely, hierarchies of
memory status. And society in general tends to treat those whose memories
have been destroyed by various forms of dementia as of less significance.

The processes involved in human memory – defined as the ability to store and retrieve information – are highly complex. Nevertheless, a great deal has been discovered in recent years, and the precise nature of human memory is gradually being uncovered. All biological and medical scientists agree that memory is a function of the brain and there are very few scientists who do not believe that memory is actually stored in the brain. The term 'memory' is used both for the actual information store and for its content. Memory, in the sense of a store, however, is not a discrete and recognizable part of the brain in which data is stored, like the hard disk in a computer. There is no single part of the brain that could be damaged by disease or injury, thereby destroying our whole memory store. There is no single part corresponding to the long-term store – no unique part corresponding to the disk drive.

There are, however, certain known parts of the brain that can deprive us of access to the memory store. These parts are concerned with the temporary storage, registration, processing and recall of information that is to be permanently stored. Information enters our bodies by way of our sense organs – eyes, ears, noses, mouths and skin – and is complex. This suggests that there may be many different kinds of memory – visual, auditory, olfactory (smell), gustatory (taste), tactile (touch). Also, the incoming data to be memorized is never presented to us in simple form. Our information input takes many different forms – pictorial, verbal, numeric, and so on – and these complex masses of information are analysed by our sense organs and converted into streams of frequency-modulated nerve impulses.

The brain is able to put these nerve impulse data into their context because it 'knows' where they come from, because of the part of the particular sense organ that is stimulated. The brain 'knows' that it is perceiving blue sky because it 'knows' that blue-sensitive cones on the lower parts of the retinas are the ones sending it messages. Light coming from above hits the lower parts of the retinas. And the brain 'knows' that it is seeing sky because a large amount of other information has already been received that 'tells' it that if we are out of doors and we look up and see something bright and blue, the chances are that we are looking at the sky.

So data always arrives as part of a complex matrix in which it is embedded. The context of the data is likely to form part of the memory; indeed daily experience shows us how important context and associations are for effective memorizing. For example, a single item of information conveyed to us by way of speech will be accompanied by a considerable context of other data – the appearance of the speaker's face, its spacial relationship to other things, the quality of the voice, the indications of emotion, and much other information. There is no reason to believe that all this material is stored in the same place, and good reason to believe that it is distributed to those parts of the brain known to be concerned with the different sensory functions. Visual information, for instance, always goes right to the back of the brain; olfactory information is perceived near the front. All the areas of the brain concerned with the many modalities of sensation have been mapped out.

Short-term memory

The storage capacity of the human brain is immense but there is no way that complex perceptions of this kind could all be stored separately at each moment of perception. If this were happening, the brain would soon be filled up. So some kind of analysis and selection is necessary to determine what should be registered and stored. It seems almost certain that familiar contexts are stored and that only significant changes in them are registered. But this kind of analysis and selection can only be performed if the data are temporarily stored so that they can be operated upon. This implies the existence of short-term stores or 'buffers' that are constantly in use.

In fact, individual experience suggests that there are several short-term buffer stores for different types of memory – speech sounds, non-verbal sounds, touch, vision and so on. There is almost certainly a short-term store that codes for the articulation of a sequence of words that we intend, shortly, to use in spoken conversation – most of us have had the annoying experience of having forgotten what we were about to say. This is probably because delay led to the loss of the content of the short-term store or something else overwrote it. Again, we obviously have a short-term memory for small items of new data that need only be remembered for a short time. This buffer has to be constantly refreshed. Most of us can look up and remember a new telephone number if we repeat it internally until we dial it. But if someone speaks to us or we think of something else, the number is lost as new incoming data displace the current contents of the buffer.

There is also a strict limit to the actual length of any item of new data if it is to be held in this short-term buffer. Most of us can readily hold a seven- or eight-digit number, but not a 12-digit number. The human buffer can be emptied by a blow or an electric shock to the head. All these facts suggest that short-term memory operates via some kind of dynamic neuronal circuit, possibly of circulating nerve impulses.

Understanding these normal features of memory may help to eradicate some of the anxiety older people have when they find they have forgotten something and attribute this to imminent dementia.

The importance of mnemonics

Each of us carries in the brain an almost immeasurable quantity of data, recorded via short-term memory and preserved, often for a lifetime, in permanent storage. This mass of data is highly organized in terms of meaning and association and the better it is organized the more accessible it is to us. The efficiency of retrieval depends on clues, mnemonics (anything designed to aid the memory) and, in particular, cues, all of which seem capable of addressing the appropriate part of the memory store. If you were asked to recite the beginning of Hamlet's celebrated soliloquy you might be stuck. But if you were asked for the three words that follow the cue: 'To be or . . .' the chances are that you would come up with the continuation: '. . . not to be'.

The difficulty most older people have in remembering names is a case in point. If we are presented with the name of a person we know well, there is an instant flood of data about that person. But the linking associations obviously do not work nearly so well in the opposite direction. We can rehearse in our minds numerous details about a person but still fail to come up with the name. This may be because the memory system does not operate by applying labels. Or it may be that a name is, neurologically, a less efficient way of identifying something or somebody than the mass of sensory data the brain 'prefers' to deal with.

Efficient and reliable registration for long-term storage demands good organization and strong association. Scholarly people with a profound grasp of their subject assimilate new information on their speciality with the greatest of ease, so long as it can be related to existing stored data. Entirely new matter, unrelated to any previous experience, is much more difficult to memorize.

The interface circuits

Clinical studies of people with brain damage have shown us the exact sites in the brain through which sensory data must pass to be stored in the memory. These 'interface circuits', through which long-term memory is recorded and recalled, are contained in two large structures on the inner surfaces of the temporal lobes of each half of the brain – two massive collections of nerve cells known as the amygdala and the hippocampus. Together they are known as the limbic system. The amygdala is connected to all the sensory areas of the cortex by two-way pathways. The hippocampus also has extensive connections. Destruction of these two structures leads to profound loss of memory.

Long-term memory

The actual physical basis of long-term memory continues to elude scientists. Several theories have been put forward. The sheer size of the database in relation to the size of the brain implies that the unit of information – whatever its nature – must be very small. This has led some scientists to suggest a protein molecule as the basis.

There is a good deal of evidence that the sites of memory are the same areas of the brain where the corresponding sensory impressions are processed – the various parts of the outer layer (the cortex). It now seems almost certain that, in memory recall, the amygdala and the hippocampus engage in a kind of feedback dialogue with the appropriate part of the cerebral cortex, playing back the same kind of neurological activity that occurs during sensory experience.

This being so, it seems likely that long-term memory store takes the form of the interconnection of many nerve cells in a particular way. There is evidence that particular connections – activation of the nerve-to-nerve junctions (synapses) – are built up as a result of repeated stimulation of the kind that occurs during sensory experience. The way in which repeated stimulation leads to permanent link-up is also beginning to be understood. The addition of a phosphate group (the process of phosphorylation) to a brain protein, called F1, as a result of the action of an enzyme, protein kinase C, is now known to be capable of causing the necessary changes in the synapses. Unfortunately, protein modified in this way has a limited lifespan, ranging from minutes to weeks. Ingenious suggestions for ways around this difficulty have been proposed by various scientists. These include processes that automatically regenerate protein molecules and a special form of gene expression that gives rise to longlife protein.

Brain damage and memory loss

There are several conditions, such as Alzheimer's disease, the alcohol-induced Korsakov's syndrome and persistent shortage of blood supply to the brain, in which destruction of brain cells is clearly associated with loss of memory. This has led many people, including some doctors, to conclude that the normal forgetfulness of middle and old age (the kind that makes us come out with statements like: 'I saw what's his name yesterday, you know, the one that what's her name married . . .') is simply a minor form of this kind of disorder and is due to loss of brain cells. This idea has been promoted by the introduction of the phrase 'age-associated memory loss'.

Such labels persuade a lot of people that the thing they seem to be referring to actually exists, but they are no substitute for disinterested research to discover the truth. Nor does the fact that some drug manufacturers, mainly in the USA, have put a lot of money into research into 'age-associated memory loss' mean that there is such a thing, rather that they hope there is and that they will be able to find a pill that millions of people will buy to combat it. The American Food and Drug Administration (FDA) has hesitantly admitted that the disease of 'age-associated memory loss' might exist, but its job is simply to protect the public against damage from drugs: it has to look into everything the drug manufacturers produce whether it is for a real condition or not.

The fact is that there is no convincing evidence for the supposition that there is any such thing as 'age-associated memory loss'. There are certainly age-associated brain diseases that cause memory loss, but that is quite a different matter. The distinguished biochemist, Professor Steven Rose, who has held numerous prestigious appointments in brain science and written extensively on the subject of brain function and memory, acknowledges that mental processing slows with age but insists that there are no grounds for the belief that normal ageing brings memory loss.

The efficiency of brain functioning is due to the richness of the connections between individual brain cells. As we learn and store away information, the number of connections between our brain cells increases. The number of brain cells is at a maximum at around the time of birth. Thereafter we lose cells at a rate of approximately a million a day; that is 40 billion cells in a long lifetime, a negligible proportion out of many thousands of billions.

What is much more important is that the space in our brains that is left by this daily loss of cells is made up by a corresponding increase, as we experience and learn, in the number of dendritic and synaptic connections between brain cells. Dendrites are the tiny branches that bud out from brain cells to connect with others, and synapses are the chemical links between the ends of nerve cell fibres (axons) and other cells. There may be as many as 1000 dendrites to a single brain cell, and it is the complexity of these connections that makes our brains such wonderful and hard-to-understand entities.

Age and mental disorder

This section is mainly concerned with the most distressing features of age-related mental disorder – dementia and Alzheimer's disease. But first we must deal with defence mechanisms – which are so common as to be considered almost normal – and some other psychological disorders as they affect older people: neurotic disorders, depression, delusions and delirium.

Defence mechanisms

These are important patterns of behaviour by which the mind copes with the anxiety caused by conflict between spontaneous desires and socially approved behaviour and beliefs. They are largely unconscious and relieve us of the need to contemplate our own inadequacies and faults. They vary from person to person but some of them are present in all of us. In any particular person, the defence mechanisms tend to become a fixed feature of the personality. They include:

◆ exclusion from consciousness of threatening desires and feelings (repression)

◆ refusal to recognise the existence of emotionally threatening external factors (denial)
◆ explaining away of unacceptable personal actions as being logically justified or the result of external circumstances (rationalization)
◆ making exceptional efforts to achieve success in an area of real or imagined inferiority (compensation)
◆ transfer of one's unacceptable qualities and desires to others (projection)
◆ exaggeration of tendencies and impulses which oppose those perceived within oneself (reaction)
◆ transfer, to a second person, of unacceptable feelings about a first (displacement).

Defence mechanisms in other people often seem illogical and annoying, but it is important to remember and recognize their importance to the individual. If you bear this in mind when you are relating to other people and remember that much interpersonal strife arises from unwise attempts to point out and demolish each other's defence mechanisms, you may be regarded as a more tolerant person. Try also to analyse, if you can, your own defence mechanisms.

Respect for other's defence mechanisms is particularly important in cases in which they are employed as a major expression of neurotic disorder.

Neurotic disorders

A neurotic disorder is any persisting mental disorder which causes distress to the person concerned, which is recognized by the sufferer as being abnormal, but in which contact with reality is retained. People who have been neurotic all their lives often achieve some kind of accommodation with the disorder by the time they reach old age, but they do not cease to be neurotic and they do not cease to suffer from this disabling complaint. Older people who show what seem to be neurotic traits for the first time are not neurotic, but are most likely to be suffering from depression (see below).

There is no obvious cause of a neurotic disorder and the behaviour of the sufferer does not grossly violate social norms. Earlier classifications included anxiety neurosis, phobic neurosis, obsessive-compulsive neurosis, hysteria, depressive neurosis, narcissistic neurosis, depersonalization and others, but clinical experience showed these ideas to be much too clearcut and that it was often impossible to apply these labels accurately. Because of this, the tendency today is to recognize that most neurotic people suffer from anxiety which is either experienced directly or expressed through various defence mechanisms, and appears as one or more of a variety of symptoms, such as a phobia, an obsession, a compulsion or as sexual dysfunction.

The current classification of mental disorders does not include an overall class of neuroses. These conditions are probably best regarded as being the result of early conditioning or programming inappropriate to the generally accepted patterns of society.

For younger people, the most effective treatment currently seems to be some form of behaviour therapy. Bearing in mind that neurosis can be considered as a personal response, or even adaptation, to social and other difficulties, many older people with a neurotic problem would probably prefer to continue to live with it rather than to be forced by therapy to adopt a new and probably painful way of life. With increasing age, however, psychological mechanisms for coping with stress – such as hope and expectations for the future – may become less effective. This may lead to a considerable increase in anxiety among neurotic people and medical help may be badly needed.

Depression
Depression is a mood of sustained sadness or unhappiness with marked loss of motivation. Since, for most people, one of the primary objectives in life is the pursuit of happiness, depression of any degree is a serious matter. Severe depression, since it often drives people to suicide, may be the most serious calamity of all. Depression in older people is essentially the same, in its effects, as in younger people.

Of course, we all feel a bit down from time to time when things are going wrong, but it is important to make a clear distinction between this kind of normal reactive unhappiness and genuine depressive illness, or clinical depression. Clinical depression involves a degree of hopeless despondency, dejection, fear and irritability out of all proportion to any external cause. Often there is no apparent external cause, so this kind of trouble is sometimes called endogenous depression – that is, depression that comes from 'inside'. Features of clinical depression are a general slowing down of body and mind, slowness of speech, poor concentration, confusion, self-reproach, self-accusation and loss of self-esteem. There may be restlessness and agitation. Insomnia, with early morning waking, is common. Sexual interest may be lost and there is always the risk of suicide.

It is quite common in older people for depression to be confused with dementia. Depression causes the same kind of slowness of mind and a reduced performance in tests designed to check mental function. This is a serious error. In such a case, a correct diagnosis and proper treatment can restore an apparently demented person to bright, lively normality. Depression also causes loss of appetite and (often) a hypochondriacal preoccupation with minor symptoms. This can lead to confusion with organic illness. At the same time, however, serious illness can often cause depression, and this aspect of the problem may require treatment.

Depression is especially common in older people, women more than men, and the highest incidence of first attacks occurs between 55 and 65 in men and between 50 and 60 in women. It is usually triggered by a distressing major life event, such as a bereavement, retirement or loss of status. Post-menopausal depression is a reason for the higher incidence in women overall. This is often attributed to the loss of oestrogen hormone but there is no positive proof of this.

The causes of depression remain speculative and many theories have been proposed. Cognitive psychologists regard depression as being the result of a negative view of oneself as being unwanted, unloved, undesirable and worthless. The depressed person, they believe, views the world as a hostile place in which failure and punishment are to be expected and suffering and deprivation inevitable and probably deserved. The increased prevalence in women indicates that they are particularly vulnerable. In some, this may be due partly to a feeling that their physical attraction and energy are declining. It is often said that some women's awareness, after the menopause, that they can no longer bear children adds to their sense of uselessness. Perhaps the recent demonstrations that this is not actually true may help to remove this illogical cause.

Men are, of course, often just as preoccupied as women with their sexual attractiveness, but the knowledge that, in theory at least, most of them are still capable of reproduction to an advanced age, may help to limit this cause of depression.

Recognizing depression

The recognition of medically abnormal (pathological) depression is very important so that urgent treatment can be given. This is one reason why older people living alone should not be left unvisited for long periods. Even a regular telephone call is better than nothing. It is not too difficult to assess, in the course of a chat over the phone, whether the spirits are normally high. Partners are, of course, far better placed to observe signs of depression in each other.

Since depression can, in most cases, now be relieved no time should be lost in getting or seeking help. Many depressives who could have been restored to a normal emotional and social life have committed suicide. Effective anti-depressant drugs, the tetracyclic and tricyclic anti-depressants, the monoamine oxidase inhibitors and serotonin re-uptake inhibitors, such as Prozac, are available. These drugs work, yet many depressed old people are denied their benefit. Note particularly that most anti-depressant drugs do not show their effect until about two weeks after starting the treatment. This is important and the person taking the drug should always be repeatedly and positively told that they take time to act. In very severe depression, electro-convulsive therapy (ECT), done under a brief general anaesthetic, can produce remarkable results. Great age is no bar to this treatment, but it is restricted to the worst cases.

Delusions

These are fixed beliefs, which cannot be shaken by argument or demonstration, however reasonable, in something that is manifestly absurd or untrue. It is not always easy to distinguish delusions from strongly held opinions that are generally rejected by society, especially if these are shared by a group. But most delusions are so intrinsically improbable or so obviously based on defective reasoning as to indicate serious mental disturbance.

There are various types of psychotic delusion, the commonest of which are delusions of persecution, also known as paranoid delusions. Others include:

◆ delusions of grandeur
◆ hypochondriacal delusions
◆ delusions of abnormality of body shape
◆ delusions of unreality or depersonalization
◆ delusions of being influenced by others or by malignant forces
◆ self-deprecatory delusions of unworthiness.

This last class is commonest in severe depression.

Delusions sometimes serve useful purposes by providing an acceptable explanation for what would otherwise be too unpleasant to be borne. They often have an inherent logic which, given the defective premises on which they are based, cannot be faulted. Paranoid disorders occur in dementia, in which they follow no particular pattern and tend to change rapidly, and in depressive disorders, in which they are usually persistent and relevant to the condition. In paranoid delusions, the conviction of persecution might, for instance, be deemed by the sufferer to be justified because of some delusory earlier guilty conduct. The principal paranoid disorder of old age is, however, known as late paraphrenia and corresponds to the paranoid schizophrenia of younger people.

Paraphrenia is about seven times as common in women as in men and there is often a family history of schizophrenia. It tends to affect people who have had great difficulty in forming good relationships and who, as a result are often solitary and socially isolated. Most affected people have never married. A surprising number of them have been severely deaf for a long time – a misfortune that, in itself, can cause social isolation.

The usual pattern in paraphrenia is a delusory conviction by the affected person that other people are talking about him or her, spreading malicious rumours, or even plotting against him or her. The victim of the disorder may complain of having actually heard such talk. Paraphrenia responds well to drug treatment in the sense that drugs may remove all overt indications of any disorder. But the delusions may still be preserved and often re-emerge if the medication is stopped.

Delirium

This is an important form of mental disorder in older people, especially in relation to other illness. Delirium is a short-term disturbance of the mind with a fluctuating course resulting from organic disorder of brain function. It features:

◆ confusion of thought
◆ disorientation
◆ restlessness
◆ trembling
◆ fearfulness and often fantasies
◆ unwarranted convictions (delusions)
◆ disorders of sensation (hallucinations).

Sometimes there is maniacal excitement. Disorganized thinking causes rambling, incoherent or irrelevant speech. The affected person is unable to sustain attention and is easily distracted. Sometimes, he or she may simply go on repeating the same words or actions, over and over again.

Delirium may be caused by high fever, head injury, drug intoxication, drug overdose and drug withdrawal. The commonest form of this is probably delirium tremens, due to alcohol withdrawal after a long period of over-indulgence, but delirium may be induced by cocaine (especially 'crack'), marijuana, and other abused substances. Delirium may be the presenting indication of pneumonia or a heart attack.

Delirium in the elderly is remarkably common in hospital. In one study it was found that 35 per cent of patients over 65 were either delirious on admission to hospital or developed delirium during their stay. Delirium developing in the course of a physical illness is a bad sign, associated with roughly a doubling of the mortality. Those who recover from the delirium, however, and many do, have a good outlook. In such cases, delirium is not an indication of future dementia.

Dementia

Dementia is a syndrome of failing memory and progressive loss of intellectual power due to continuing degenerative disease of the brain. This brain damage may occur in several different ways. About half of all cases diagnosed as dementia are due to the brain shrinkage (atrophy) of Alzheimer's disease (see opposite), but the next most common cause – about 10 per cent – is progressive destruction of brain tissue by blood supply deprivation. Other causes, such as alcoholic damage from long-term over-indulgence, brain tumours, 'water on the brain' (hydrocephalus), long-term drug intoxication and Huntington's chorea do not concern us here. Most of the remainder are either of unknown origin or are caused by one of a variety of other diseases such as:

◆ liver failure
◆ pernicious anaemia
◆ syphilis
◆ thyroid disease
◆ multiple sclerosis
◆ Creutzfeldt–Jakob disease
◆ epilepsy
◆ Parkinson's disease.

The early signs of dementia are subtle and are likely to be noticed only by close relatives or friends. There may be a loss of interest in work or hobbies, an increase in forgetfulness and easy distractibility. Reasonable discussion of problems becomes impossible. Later it is found that only the simplest of instructions can be followed correctly, orientation in familiar areas becomes defective and the affected person may get lost near home. Judgement is impaired. The main defect is in memory and in the use of language. Nuances of meaning are lost, vocabulary becomes simplified and limited and conversation becomes repetitive and garrulous, full of clichés and stereotyped phrases.

Sudden anger or inappropriate tearfulness is common at this stage and the mood tends toward depression and bad temper. The emotions are abnormally changeable (labile) with quick swings from laughter to weeping. Standards of personal care and hygiene decline. There is indifference to social convention and to the opinions of others. Physical deterioration is a constant feature and there is almost always eventual loss of appetite, emaciation and high susceptibility to infection.

In the end, the demented person stays in bed, inaccessible to stimuli, incontinent but indifferent to discomfort or pain, mute and mindless. People in this condition are totally unaware of their vegetable state and often succumb to infection, usually pneumonia. To strive officiously to keep them alive, by intensive antibiotic treatment, is not part of a doctor's duty.

Alzheimer's disease

The possibility of acquiring this disorder is a central concern to many people as they get older. About one in five of all people over the age of 80 develops dementia (see above) and 50–70 per cent of these cases are due to Alzheimer's. But there is hope on the horizon and, for many, knowledge of the condition, in spite of its unpleasant features, is more reassuring than ignorance.

In 1907, the German neuropathologist Alois Alzheimer (1864–1915) reported the changes in the brain of a 51-year-old woman who had died after five years of progressively worsening dementia. These findings have since been confirmed and extended and we now know that the disease causes the brain substance to be severely shrunken from massive loss of nerve cells. The convolutions of the brain are narrowed and the grooves between them widened. The spaces within the brain (ventricles) are symmetrically enlarged. Microscopic examination of the nerve cells shows that they have lost many of their interconnections and that they contain tangled loops and coils of fibre-like material, and numerous tiny plaques of a material called beta-amyloid protein, never found in normal brains. Most researchers now believe that an abnormal beta-amyloid protein, resulting from a gene mutation is the principal cause of the disorder. Changes of this degree are inevitably fatal and Alzheimer's disease almost always results in death, 5 to 15 years after onset. It is by far the commonest cause of loss of the higher brain functions. Alzheimer's disease is not confined to elderly people and has been described in people as young as 30. There is a definite hereditary form, but this accounts for only 5 to 10 per cent of all cases.

The disease starts with gradual, almost imperceptible, loss of brain function, usually first noticed as loss of memory, and progresses to ever more profound loss of intellectual function with disorientation and confusion and eventual grave disablement. The features vary from case to case, but three broad stages can be recognized. First, there is mere forgetfulness that can be compensated for by keeping memo pads and lists. The loss of memory, however, often causes anxiety. Secondly, there is a gradual increase in the severity of the memory loss, particularly for recent events. The recollection of events in early life may be good and reminiscence will be free. Sometimes this stage includes an element of confusion and even invention (confabulation) to fill the gaps. At the same time there is progressive loss of awareness of current time or place (disorientation), with uncertainty even in familiar areas and inability to give the date or even the year. Concentration declines with inability to find the right word (dysphasia). These difficulties cause alarm and frustration, and sudden and unpredictable mood changes. Microscopic changes, said to be specific to Alzheimer's disease, occur in the hair. These include twisting, changes in the cuticle, local swellings and areas of loss of pigment. These findings are unnecessary for the diagnosis which, by this stage, is becoming obvious.

In the final stage there is severe disorientation and confusion. There may be perception of non-existent sights, sounds and smells (hallucinations) and false ideas of persecution (paranoid delusions). These are usually worst at night. It is now that people with Alzheimer's become especially hard to live with. They become demanding, suspicious, sometimes violent. They disregard personal hygiene. Incontinence of urine and faeces is common. In the end, the burden on relatives becomes too heavy, and institutional care becomes necessary. Once the affected person is bedridden, complications such as deep vein thrombosis, bedsores, urinary and chest infections, rapidly supervene and death from pneumonia is common.

Theories concerning Alzheimer's

One of the most widely held theoretical ideas about Alzheimer's disease is that people have only a certain limited amount of brain power, known as cognitive reserve, and that brain damage related to ageing uses up this power. Those who develop dementia early may have less cognitive reserve than people who get it later or never. This theory has gained some support from a series of remarkable observations made by researcher Susan J. Kemper at the University of Kansas.

Her work concerns a group of 700 retired nuns of the teaching order of the School Sisters of Notre Dame, all of whom wrote short essays about themselves when they were novices, usually around the age of 20. Kemper studied these essays and discovered that all of those whose essays were written in a simple, short-sentence style with no subsidiary clauses died showing signs of Alzheimer's disease. By contrast, none of the sisters whose early essays were written in a more elaborate style with longer sentences and with subordinate clauses showed any signs of the disease.

This was too improbable to treat as mere coincidence. Kemper concluded that the nuns who wrote in very short sentences had an inherent deficiency in the short-term memory necessary to work out more elaborate sentences. In other words, they may have had a small amount of cognitive reserve that got used up when they were older.

Other research indicates that there are a number of ways in which a predisposition to Alzheimer's disease can be detected. There are familial patterns of the disease; PET scan studies (positron emission topography, which produces a three-dimension image of the metabolic and chemical activity of tissues) of the brains of people known to be positive for the gene for Alzheimer's have shown that differences in the metabolic functions of the brain can be detected in people in their 50s, long before any sign of memory loss appears.

What is the cause?

The cause of Alzheimer's disease is still unknown, but a great deal is now known about what happens to the brain in the condition that has a bearing on the cause. We also know quite a lot about the genetics of the disease. Alzheimer's is a feature of Down's syndrome and there is a family history of Down's syndrome in 15 per cent of those with Alzheimer's disease. Recent research has concentrated on the isolation of the gene for a normal substance called amyloid precursor protein (APP) found throughout the body, including the brain cells.

In people with Alzheimer's disease and in older people with Down's syndrome, an abnormal substance called beta-amyloid protein is released from APP. The gene for APP is on the same chromosome (chromosome 21) of which an extra copy is present in every body cell of people with Down's syndrome, and the high incidence of Alzheimer's in people with Down's syndrome is attributed to this extra gene for APP, probably in a mutated form. The region of the chromosome containing the gene for the amyloid precursor protein has been established. A number of cases of Alzheimer's disease have been positively linked to mutations of the gene for APP. The current view is that the plaques start as amyloid precursor protein and that this passes through a fibrillary stage before forming the plaques of beta-amyloid. It seems clear that the brain cells that contain the characteristic fibrillary tangles and plaques – the hallmarks of Alzheimer's disease – are those that die off.

The hereditary familial forms of Alzheimer's disease start around 50 years of age and progress very rapidly. No one has been able to show any pathological or clinical difference between common Alzheimer's disease and familial Alzheimer's disease. Some evidence has recently appeared as to the cause of late onset Alzheimer's disease. In 1991 it was found that there was a genetic linkage to chromosome 19 in familial groups of people with Alzheimer's disease starting after the age of 60. This linkage relates to a variant (e4) of a gene for a protein known as apolipoprotein E. This variant of the gene is present twice as often in people with Alzheimer's as in people without. Of those who do not have this gene only 2.9 per cent have Alzheimer's disease; of those with the gene on only one of the chromosome 19 pair, 7.6 per cent have Alzheimer's; and of those with the gene on both chromosomes, 21.4 per cent have the disease. The scientists concerned in this study claim that about a quarter of all cases of early Alzheimer's disease can be attributed to this gene.

It is now clear, however, that the apolipoprotein E variant gene is not the cause of Alzheimer's disease. Its presence is neither necessary nor sufficient to cause the disease. It appears to act as a modifier that lowers the age at which the common form of age-related Alzheimer's disease starts. Its presence is associated with a greater number of senile plaques and it seems probable that it can affect the rate at which beta-amyloid protein is produced from APP. Even so, a person can have both pairs of mutated genes and reach old age without any sign of Alzheimer's. The real culprit is almost certainly beta-amyloid protein. In October 1995, at a conference sponsored by the American National Institute on Ageing, the Alzheimer's Association and other interested bodies, it was decided that DNA checking for the apolipoprotein E variant gene was not recommended as a test for Alzheimer's and that it should not be used as a screening test for the disease. To do so would be to cause often unjustified anxiety in many people.

A third gene mutation related to Alzheimer's disease has been detected on chromosome 14. This gene, situated on the long arm of the chromosome is now held to be responsible for about three-quarters of cases of early-onset (age 32 to 52) familial Alzheimer's disease of dominant inheritance. In 1995 this gene was cloned and various mutations identified. With this discovery most of the genetic basis of the disease appears to have been established.

Research reported in *Nature* in March 1996 into beta-amyloid protein has shown that one of its effects – possibly its major effect – is to damage the lining of small blood vessels. It does this by producing free radicals which are a principal cause of cell damage in disease. Free radical effects can be countered by antioxidants. The research has shown that beta-amyloid damage is effectively controlled by a natural body antioxidant called superoxide dismutase. This could, of course, possibly lead to a preventive treatment for Alzheimer's disease.

Other interesting implications follow from all this research. The genetic advances make it likely that we will soon be able to detect those at risk from Alzheimer's disease, even before they are born. This, of course, would raise major ethical issues. But if the structure of the various genes, and the way they modify the synthesis of beta-amyloid protein, can be established, it may be possible to do something positive, by way of gene therapy, to prevent or treat the disorder.

Another possible means of prevention was reported at a meeting of the American Academy of Neurology in April 1996. Research done as part of the Baltimore Longitudinal Study on Ageing showed that people who took regular doses of non-steroidal anti-inflammatory drugs such as ibuprofen, naprosyn or indomethacin were half as likely to develop Alzheimer's disease as those who did not take the drugs. No positive explanation for this finding has been put forward but it seems likely that it is related to some response of the immune system, perhaps to the action of beta-amyloid protein. There are, of course, serious drawbacks to the use of these drugs over a period of years, especially the production of stomach and duodenal ulcers, and this is not currently being recommended. The importance of the finding is that it opens yet another window of understanding into the nature of Alzheimer's disease.

It is extremely important not to assume that every person who seems demented or seriously forgetful has Alzheimer's disease. Forgetfulness, especially for names, is a characteristic of a heavily stocked elderly mind. In addition, at least 10 per cent of people with dementia-like symptoms have a treatable disease such as thyroid underactivity (myxoedema), simple depression (pseudode-mentia), a brain tumour or a blood clot pressing on the brain (subdural haematoma) following sometimes apparently minor injury. Full investigation is necessary to ensure such treatable disorders are identified. Pseudodementia, unlike Alzheimer's disease, commonly starts suddenly and the change of mental state is immediately obvious. Antidepressant drugs can often cure such cases.

At present, there is no definitive treatment for established Alzheimer's disease and, of course, once the brain cells have been destroyed, there is no chance of recovery. But much can be done with mood-controlling drugs (tranquillizers) and other forms of medication, to reduce behaviour problems and ensure sound sleep. The burden on the family can be relieved by the use of day-care centres. The final move to hospital or nursing home should not be delayed once the sufferer's awareness of his or her surroundings has gone. It is often difficult for relatives to realize the extent of the loss of functioning brain substance and, in consequence, of mind, but it is important that they should do so, so that they can understand how little the profoundly demented person actually suffers.

chapter five

Sexuality and Ageing

S exuality is such a deep-rooted element in human biology that it affects all our relationships, intimate or otherwise. In close human associations, satisfactory mutual sexual expression leads to confidence, happiness and contentment. 'Sexual expression' does not simply mean physical sexual intercourse, but includes all the effects of the partners' awareness of the physical, mental and emotional differences between them. The sexual act itself is, or should be, an 'expression' or demonstration of the feelings of love, appreciation, gratitude and solidarity experienced by partners. In younger people, the purely erotic and sensory element may assume an overwhelming importance, but in a mature relationship sex can, perhaps more easily, be directed outward so that the concern is more with the partner. The resulting warmth and closeness may be one of the most important sources of contentment, and its absence a cause of distress. Sexuality can also be used destructively, sometimes as a means of gaining power over the partner, and negative sexual relationships of this sort can damage the quality of life.

We live in a society in which a powerful emphasis is placed on sex and there is often an unthinking equation of sex with youth and vigour and a widespread assumption that elderly people are 'past' sexual activity. But sexuality is so fundamental to human nature that it is not going to go away. Sexual interest is as perennial as life itself. Older people, for reasons of discretion, dignity, patience and an awareness of their declining attractiveness, tacitly conform to the stereotype and seldom if ever protest their rights. In this way, the myth of elderly sexlessness is perpetuated.

To some extent, this idea of sexlessness in older people has been promoted by misguided moralism. Earlier writers on morality and religion have hailed old age, approvingly, as the time when the individual is freed from the sinful lusts of the body. A 'purification' occurs, they imply, that is complete to the extent that sexuality is extinguished. This philosophy is deeply embedded in our culture and affects us all.

But sex is not sinful and the elderly are not sexless. Many older people are more aware of their sexuality than they were when younger. There may, perhaps, be less emphasis on the erotic elements and on physical beauty, with more concern for character and achievement. But the preoccupation, nevertheless, is with another person and the emotions involved may be every bit as strong as those felt by younger people. The capacity to experience, and perhaps inspire, sexual desire or love may sometimes decline with age but it often survives undiminished throughout life. There are numerous instances of well-known men and women who have retained a high level of sexual vigour – of body as well as of mind – until an advanced age.

The father of the Duc de Richelieu married for the third time when he was 70. This great libertine was still leading a life of sexual debauchery when his distinguished son was in his 60s. At 78 the old man, in spite of having a wife and a mistress, was also having affairs with actresses from the Comédie Française. He liked to spend his evenings with prostitutes and sometimes brought them home. At 84 he married yet again and his wife was soon pregnant. But he was not satisfied with one woman and continued his patterns of sexual promiscuity right up to the time of his death at 92.

The French writer and statesman François Chateaubriand (1768–1848) left a manuscript entitled *Amour et vieillesse – chants de tristesse*, a harrowing account of what it is like to be an old man who still feels the power of the pangs of sexual love. Chateaubriand was so upset by the signs of ageing that he saw in his mirror that he refused to sit for his portrait. At the age of 61 he reacted rather badly to the sexual advances of a young woman. 'I'll be horrified,' he said, 'if you tell me you love me like a father; and if you love me as a lover, I will not believe you.' The novelist Honoré de Balzac (1799–1850) has also, in his collection of novels entitled *La Comédie humaine*, often illustrated this sometimes painful situation.

Sexuality in women persists at least as strongly as in men, perhaps more so. Surveys have shown that, although older women may be less active sexually, there is no reason to suppose that they are less inclined for sex. Many older women are seriously frustrated by the lack of opportunity for sexual activity and tormented by desire, for which the only relief is masturbation. It is common for elderly women who are widowed to find, quite soon after the death of the husband, that they desire desperately the sexual attentions of a man. Some have confessed that they have gone out to look for a man, to give themselves to the first man who offers. Many long to marry again. Many women can tolerate the ageing of their bodies if they believe they are desired and are found attractive. But the first indication of lack of interest by men, on account of age, may make them aware of the full impact of bodily deterioration.

The belief that there is an exact correspondence between general physical decline and decline in sexual interest is mistaken. There is certainly a general decline in the frequency of sexual intercourse, but this is as much because of loss of opportunity as because of lack of inclination.

Sex and the menopause

The belief that the menopause signals the end of a woman's sexual life is the commonest myth of all. In fact, the relief from the risk of pregnancy, and the increase in privacy following the departure of children as they grow up commonly leads to a new and more satisfying phase of a woman's sex life. The only likely problem is vaginal dryness, which is usually remedied by HRT, and can be alleviated – for those women who choose not to have HRT – by an oestrogen vaginal cream or even a lubricant, such as K-Y jelly.

Loss of sexual capacity with age

For most men, sexual capacity – the ability to achieve an adequate erection and to perform sexually – declines with age. In the case of women, there may also be reasons, related to oestrogen deficiency (see Chapter 2), for diminished sexual capacity. But sexual performance is not the same as sexuality and, in any case, these difficulties can be overcome, especially for women. Older men do not reach orgasm so easily as young men, and it is important to dismiss the notion that sex is incomplete or unsatisfactory without an orgasm. This is often merely a matter of pride, related to the significance of retained fertility. If the woman experiences orgasm, but the man has not, this may often be a happy point at which to stop. It is deeply satisfying to most men to induce an orgasm in their partner.

Sexuality directed to a single individual over a period of time should be manifested not simply in the desire for erotic gratification, but also in other important elements such as love, friendship, protectiveness and so on, built up over an extended period of attachment. Male sexuality, however, commonly leads to sexual interest in more than one person within a short period and the result is trouble. Male promiscuity brings unhappiness, often severe, and not only to its female victim.

Women are sometimes less troubled in this way than men because female sexuality usually has a wider base and, in general, is concerned more with love than with eroticism. Women's sexual interest is thus less likely to be promiscuous.

Sexuality and ill health

Advanced age can bring with it sexual problems relating to ill health. Sexual feelings do not disappear simply because a person may have become disabled. The need for sexual expression may even be greater after such a disaster. The aspirations, feelings and desires may be very strongly experienced whatever the possibility of physical expression, and to ignore or be unaware of this may harm a relationship. On the other hand, because it is the state of mind that matters, a reduction in the ability to express sexual feeling physically may be less important than might be imagined.

In 1974 the British Association to Aid the Sexual and Personal Relationships of the Disabled (SPOD) carried out an intensive study of the sexual problems of disabled people. This was the largest research project of its kind ever carried out and the results were as significant as they were sad. Over half of the disabled interviewed had severe sexual problems, damaging to their happiness. And the more severe the disability, the worse the difficulties experienced in obtaining sexual satisfaction. Many of these problems arose from destructive mental and emotional attitudes toward sex and the disabled. And many of the people interviewed were badly in need of advice, help and encouragement.

As in all human endeavour, state of mind and quality of motivation decree the outcome. Enlightenment, determination and courage are needed. There must be open and realistic attitudes to sex, and the conviction that, even with disability, a full and gratifying expression of love through sex is possible.

Sex and physical problems

There are several reasons why normal sexual expression may be affected by serious illness. A heart attack or stroke, for example, is an alarming and distressing experience which tends to turn people inward, away from others. It can also induce severe anxiety about the possibility of a more serious recurrence. (Conversely, some people find their libido heightened, as if sex is an affirmation that they are still alive.) Some surgical procedures attack the heart of our sexuality. A mastectomy, for example, may make a woman feel less than whole, which may have serious consequences on her perception of herself as a sexual being, and on her notion of herself as sexually attractive. Loss of a limb in either sex may have similar consequences. These reactions commonly involve a reduction in sexual energy. But there are many other conditions which may make men and women sufficiently depressed as to be reluctant to have sex.

In a long-term relationship of mutual trust, reassurance may be all that is needed to re-establish sexual relations after a medical or surgical problem, once the recovery time recommended by your doctor has passed. Be guided by how you feel: if a scar after surgery is still tender to the touch, ask your doctor about painkillers, avoid the area in your lovemaking, or – if you can't – wait a little longer.

If the healthy partner can make the sufferer feel important, accepted and desired, all may be well. Some couples, however, find that they drift apart sexually after a physical problem. If this happens to you and you can't resolve the problem by talking it through with your partner, ask your GP to refer you for specialist help if necessary. Don't accept that your sex life is at an end, whatever your age, unless you want it to be.

There is a widespread belief that sexual intercourse is actually dangerous to a patient who has had a heart attack or stroke. In fact, the risk is very small and certainly does not justify abstinence if sexual feelings are strong. There have been a few cases, in men, in which a heart attack or a stroke have occurred during intercourse and people to whom this has happened may be reluctant to take the risk again. The danger is mainly from the sharp rise in blood pressure during the male orgasm, but the same kind of pressure rise can result from a wide variety of causes, many of them unavoidable. Any strong emotion or sudden physical strain may raise the blood pressure and, since heart attacks and strokes do not recur every time this happens, it follows that the danger is not very great. But it is sensible to try to take sex calmly. Men, especially, should avoid over-energetic sexual activity.

Stroke
During stroke, damage may be done to those parts of the brain concerned with sexual responses, but it is important not to make assumptions about this, as there are many other causes of loss of libido, some of which are remediable. Stroke can lead to loss of sensation on one side of the body and it can also interfere with normal sexual sensation so that some of the physical satisfaction of sex is lost. It is important for the healthy partner to be aware that skin caressing, on the side on which feeling is absent, may be emotionally damaging. (But talk about this: a partner who watches your loving caresses may be aroused by them, even if he or she cannot feel them, another instance of the power of the mind in sexuality.) Actual paralysis need not be a barrier to satisfactory sexual expression, particularly if the partner is well-motivated, loving and imaginative.

Stroke sometimes causes such a profound change in personality that a partner may feel that he or she is living with a different person – often, although not always, a less pleasant one. This can certainly cause difficulties. It is not uncommon for the personality change to involve a much greater interest in sexual expression than before. This is sometimes directed away from home and serious interpersonal problems, calling for great strength of character and tolerance, may arise. Medical advice is warranted in such cases.

The effects of stroke may make the patient less attractive than before. And, in cases where physical dependence is great, the need for the partner to provide constant bodily attendance may have a negative effect on interest in sex. Much depends on the extent to which the patient retains the love, respect and affection of the partner and this, of course, depends on the degree of mental change. It is difficult to live indefinitely on memories of past attitudes and it may often be true that the stroke victim has become, in more ways than one, 'a different person'.

Colostomy

In a colostomy part of the large intestine is passed through an opening in the abdominal wall to allow faeces to bypass the rectum and be discharged into a bag attached to the stomach. The bag is changed after a bowel movement. It takes a few weeks to get over the operation, after which the person affected can hope to resume his or her normal life.

Physically the bag may have little impact on sex, as long as positions for lovemaking are chosen with care. Mentally, however, you may be unwilling to let a partner see the bag, and worry about him or her feeling it and what effect it may have. It helps to avoid eating or drinking for an hour or so before sex and to change the bag before sex.

Arthritis

Something of an umbrella term, arthritis is inflammation of the joints. It can vary in severity from a mild ache and stiffness in one joint, to severe pain in several, and may eventually lead to deformity of the joints.

Mild arthritis usually causes no problems sexually. But if you are in severe pain, you may not want to contemplate lovemaking. Many arthritis sufferers find the pain more acute at certain times of the day than others, so you could try to time sex for your least painful hours. Also, time medication so that you are in least pain when you want to have sex. If your joints are becoming deformed, support yourself with pillows or cushions for maximum comfort.

Mastectomy

The removal of part or all of a breast can affect a woman's sexuality in many ways, often depending on how much tissue has been removed. It is not simply that the breasts are erogenous zones, but also that they are so intrinsically linked with fertility and this perception exists even after the fertile years have passed.

Reconstructive surgery may be offered which can help to foster a feeling of 'wholeness' again. Reassurance from a partner is important. Discover new areas where sensation is strong together. Some women find it helps to establish relations with the scar covered, perhaps by a new nightdress, until they feel confident of their sexuality again; for others this simply postpones acceptance of a truth that must be faced. Talk to your partner and to your GP if you need more help.

Heart problems

Apart from the fear that strenuous lovemaking may provoke a recurrence of the problem (which is highly unlikely if your doctor has given you the all-clear to resume sexual relations), heart problems may make you feel too tired for sex, or you may still suffer pains in the chest. Medication to relieve any pain should help; and try to choose the time of day when you feel least tired to make love.

This is another instance when the healthy partner should take the initiative and adopt positions that minimize any strain on the sick partner.

Sexual potency after illness

Fear of losing sexual pleasure is natural and justified, but it is a mistake for a man, for example, to equate sexual potency with masculinity and status as a male. Men may become impotent after a stroke or a heart attack, but loss of potency can result from so many causes, both psychological and organic, that it is very difficult, even after full medical investigation, to be sure of the cause. As a general rule, if after a stroke control over the functions of the bladder and bowel are retained, the organic sexual function should be unimpaired. Erection and ejaculation can operate satisfactorily even if the lower part of the spinal cord is completely disconnected from the brain by an injury such as a fractured spine.

However, organic factors other than the effects of the stroke may be operating. For instance, if there is high blood pressure which needs to be treated, the drugs used may cause some loss of potency. Some of the new, more selective, drugs used for high blood pressure are much less liable to have this effect. Other drugs which may cause impotence are alcohol, barbiturates, sedatives such as Valium, drugs used in the treatment of cancer and Parkinsonism, Cimetidine (Tagamet) for peptic ulcer, Lithium and various other drugs used for depression and other mental disorders. Diabetes is a fairly common cause of male impotence, as a result of diabetic nerve damage.

Studies have shown that at least a quarter of all men of 70 or over have experienced a substantial loss of coital ability, even in the absence of any organic disorder. This usually means that they cannot obtain or sustain a full erection, and this problem may call for more direct and positive genital stimulation than was necessary before. But it is unwise to jump to conclusions, since many such men have been shown to be capable of a full erection during sleep.

The principal cause of impotence following serious illness, however, is the psychological effect of the catastrophe on the victim. In most cases, the remedy is, literally, in the hands of the partner. The loving embrace, the caress, sexually stimulating touching and holding – all potent symbols of caring and need – are the best treatments for psychological impotence. Anxiety must be dispelled, relaxation and freedom of touch encouraged, humour promoted and patience enjoined. Failure must never be made a cause of overt distress.

The most powerfully erotic sexual stimulus is the sexual excitement of a partner. Unless you have been so severely disabled as to be motionless, remember that your own contribution is essential. The variety of sexual positions available may be limited, so your partner may find it necessary to become dominant, both in a physical sense and also by taking the initiative in lovemaking. This can also add variety and interest. Prudery about discussing and changing methods and positions can deny couples much-needed satisfaction and comfort. There is no reason, except for shyness or inhibition, why anyone should not have access to a great range of information on the subject of sex. Hundreds of books are available and no one need be bashful about purchasing such helpful aids.

Loving touch
The whole area of the skin is potentially sexually sensitive and whether or not it becomes so depends largely on the sensitivity and enlightenment of the partners. Those who hasten to immediate genital contact, or engage in sex fully clothed, are not only omitting an essential stage in the process of arousal but are also denying themselves a great deal of pleasure. Imaginative and patient touching, holding, stroking and caressing can form the basis of greatly heightened sensuality. Experiment, open-mindedness and a willingness to make clear responses, are necessary. No part of the body should be considered taboo and often tactile stimulation of the most unexpected areas may give intense pleasure. Interestingly, those areas most likely to be avoided by the prudish, may be the most productive of pleasure and a sense of intimacy. Unequivocal attention to parts of the body secretly thought to be uninteresting or unattractive to the other, may be good for the ego and, in turn, for the attitude toward the partner.

Many disabled men who have suffered reduced libido require stimulation to be applied with both sensitivity and continuity. It may be difficult for the man to convey this to his partner, for any attempt on his part to guide her may have a negative effect. Discussion is essential. Skin stimulation, when effective, produces at least some degree of erection and this must be cherished and promoted by a progress to direct, tactile stimulation of the penis. All too often, a promising erection may be lost. Often it will be necessary for the woman to sustain the penile stimulation right up to the point of penetration and, even then, any fumbling or delay may result in its loss. The method of penile stimulation must also be skilful and acceptable to the man. There is no substitute for frank discussion and demonstration.

Inadequate erection is common, but this need not prevent rewarding sex. The strongest stimulus to erection is the feeling of penetration. One way or another this should be achieved. Vaginal lubrication is important and is in itself strongly stimulating to the man. If nature needs some help, try K-Y gel available from pharmacists. Sexual positioning is dealt with comprehensively in books, CD-ROMs and video tapes, but imagination is cheaper. The principles are that nothing is unnatural except that which causes pain or distress and that variety is the spice of loving. Within the limits imposed by any existing disability, the greater the variety the better.

Oral sex

If full genital sex is not an option for whatever reason, oral sex can be a good substitute as long as there is a level of trust between you. Oral sex takes away any pressure to 'perform', so answers any reluctance against strenuous love-making after a health problem.

Performed on a woman, oral sex offers good lubrication, if that is a problem; and it often results in orgasm, which may not be true of other forms of lovemaking, especially after a health problem. Giving oral sex to a man may stimulate an erection more easily than manual touch alone and may make it easier to sustain an erection once achieved.

Masturbation

Sexual pleasure that is shared is one of life's greatest joys, but that does not mean that sexual pleasure alone – through masturbation – is wrong, nor does it mean that mutual masturbation has no place in a physical partnership.

Masturbation is an important means of achieving sexual satisfaction for those who are incapable of full intercourse. Skilfully performed by a partner, it can be an eloquent expression of love and regard. If mutual masturbation has not been a part of your relationship up to now, discussion and an open mind may be all that are needed for it to become one.

If you are alone and sexually frustrated, acknowledge that masturbation is an acceptable means of achieving sexual satisfaction. Never feel guilty about masturbation.

chapter six

Free Radicals, Antioxidants and Ageing

Thousands of medical and scientific papers have been published on free radicals and antioxidants in recent years, and there are even medical journals devoted exclusively to them.

Free radicals can do you a lot of harm. If your body fails to combat them effectively, they will kill you. We now know that most of the major diseases that kill people prematurely or ruin the quality of their lives, do their damage by means of free radicals. This applies particularly to some diseases that characteristically affect older people.

Free radicals are constantly attacking body proteins, carbohydrates, fats and DNA, causing potentially serious damage if unchecked. Every cell in your body suffers an estimated 10,000 free radical hits each day. Needless to say, the body strikes back, as we shall see. There is no way you can avoid free radicals, but there is a lot you can do to cut down the numbers produced in your body and to ensure that the maximum number of those that are produced are neutralized.

What are free radicals?

Medical interest in free radicals is very recent, but chemists have known about them for over 50 years. They are involved in many important chemical reactions, such as the deterioration of stored foodstuffs, the formation of plastics (polymers) and the perishing of rubber. Some free radicals are among the smallest things that exist. One of them consists of a single atom, others of two atoms linked together; some are larger. Those that we are mainly interested in each consist of two atoms. But these are not ordinary atoms. Ordinary atoms have two electrons in their outer electron shell and are quite stable. Free radicals are different in that they have only one electron in the outer shell: it is this difference that makes them dangerous to our bodies.

Water consists of hydrogen and oxygen atoms linked together and it has long been known that these atoms can be separated. But about 50 years ago it was discovered that under certain circumstances the water molecule can split in a previously unknown manner. If water is exposed to radiation such as X-rays or gamma rays, the bonds between the oxygen and the hydrogen atoms can briefly split, leaving one electron on a hydrogen atom and one on an oxygen thereby creating two radicals, both electrically neutral but both having only one spare electron. Thus, momentarily, we have two atoms each with only one electron in an outer orbital.

These radicals are known respectively as the hydrogen radical and the hydroxyl radical, and both are highly active, due to this unpaired electron. A group with an unpaired electron is highly unstable, desperate either to pick up another electron from somewhere, or to give up its solitary electron. The hydroxyl radical is the most reactive free radical known to chemistry and will attack almost every molecule in the body in its need to achieve stability.

A free radical, therefore, is any atom or group of atoms that can exist independently, however briefly, and that contains at least one unpaired electron. Not all free radicals are small, like the hydrogen or hydroxyl radicals but, from the medical point of view we are interested mainly in two free radicals – the hydroxyl radical (– OH) and the superoxide radical, which consists of two linked oxygen atoms (O_2) with a single, unpaired electron.

Free radical chain reactions

These oxygen free radicals, each with its single electron, can attack and damage almost every molecule in the body. They are so active that, after they are formed, only a small fraction of a second elapses before they join on to something. Whether they hand over their unpaired electron or capture an electron from some other molecule to make up the pair, the radicals become stable but the attacked molecule is itself converted into a radical. This starts a chain reaction that can zip destructively through a tissue.

The hydroxyl free radical does not under normal circumstances occur in living systems because of the strength of the bonds holding the water molecules together. But if anyone is exposed to radiation, these bonds can be broken by the radiation so that hydroxyl radicals result. This is the basis of the damage that occurs in people with radiation sickness. If hydroxyl radicals attack DNA, chain reactions run along the DNA molecule causing damage to, and mutations in, the genetic material or even breakage of the DNA strands. The body does its best to repair this damage by the natural processes of DNA replication, but imperfect repair leaves altered DNA and can give rise to cancer. When strong X-rays and gamma rays are deliberately used to kill cancers they do so primarily by producing large numbers of hydroxyl free radicals.

Radiation is not the only way free radicals are produced, nor are free radicals only produced from water. Radiation is the only common way that hydroxyl free radicals are formed in the body from water. But there are other ways in which hydroxyl radicals can be formed and there are several other kinds of free radicals, especially the superoxide radical, that can be produced in other ways.

Oxygen free radicals in the body

Free radicals can originate in body cells in various ways. External radiation – including ultraviolet light, X-rays and gamma rays from radioactive material – is a potent source. Such radiation acts by breaking linkages between atoms, leaving the radicals with their unpaired electrons to wreak their damage. Free radicals occur in the course of various disease processes. In a heart attack, for instance, when the supply of oxygen and glucose to the heart muscle is cut off, the real damage to the muscle is caused by the vast numbers of free radicals that are produced.

Chemical poisoning of many kinds promotes free radicals, as does excessive oxygen intake from inhaling pure oxygen. The body's need to break down a wide range of drugs to safer substances (detoxication) also involves free radical production. The toxicity of many chemicals and drugs is actually due either to their conversion to free radicals or to their effect in forming free radicals. Free radicals are also produced by:

- metals
- cigarette smoke
- car exhausts
- heat
- lack of oxygen.

Inflammation – one of the commonest kinds of bodily disorder – is associated with free radical production, but the free radicals are probably the cause of the inflammation rather than the effect. However, the body actually uses free radicals to kill bacteria within the scavenging cells of the immune system and when excessive numbers of these are present in an inflamed area the free radical load almost certainly adds to the tissue damage, making everything worse.

Free radicals also arise in the course of normal internal cellular function, or metabolism. The joining of chains of amino acids (polymerization) to form proteins, or the polymerization of glucose molecules into the polysaccharide glycogen, for instance, involve free radical action. In most cases the process is automatically controlled and the number of free radicals does not become dangerously high. Our bodies have become accustomed to coping with free radicals and evolved various schemes for doing so. In the course of metabolism important and potentially dangerous free radicals such as superoxide and hydroxyl radicals are produced.

Magical enzymes

The breakthrough that caused medical scientists to begin to look seriously at free radicals was the discovery that the body actually produces large quantities of an enzyme whose only function is to break down the dangerous superoxide free radical. This enzyme is called superoxide dismutase, or SOD. This and two other enzymes break down dangerous superoxide free radicals into harmless substances. These enzymes are made in our cells under the instructions of a length of genetic code in DNA. Every cell in our bodies contains the instructions for making these (and thousands of other) enzymes. Unless free radicals are important, why would evolution go to such lengths to protect us against them?

Free radicals and your arteries

The very common condition atherosclerosis is the major disease of the arteries. (There are others but all are comparatively rare.) Atherosclerosis is featured in Chapter 2, but it is so important that fuller details are included here.

Arteries carry blood; blood carries oxygen and vital nutrients. If these supplies are cut off, the various organs to which the blood is carried by the arteries die. If the blood supply is seriously restricted they will suffer disorder or malfunction. Atherosclerosis causes narrowing or blockage of the affected arteries. This means that less blood gets through to the organ or part. If the organ is the heart and the narrowing is excessive, the result is a heart attack, possibly death; if it is the brain, the result is a stroke; if it is a leg, the result is gangrene.

Atherosclerosis can affect almost any arteries and kills more people than any other single disease or cause. It also has a devastating effect on the quality of life of millions. Although we have known for years that there is a relationship between diet and atherosclerosis, it is only recently that it has become apparent that the actual damage to the artery that leads to the dangerous narrowing, is caused by free radicals.

Atherosclerosis is a disease of arteries only; it does not affect veins. Arteries are the tough, elastic, thick-walled tubes that carry blood, under fairly high pressure, from the heart to the various parts of the body. This blood is fresh from the lungs where it has picked up a good supply of oxygen and it also carries the body fuel glucose from the liver and the intestines. Both oxygen and glucose are essential for life and health. The brain and the heart are especially sensitive to lack of oxygen and glucose. If the supply of these vital substances is cut off for more than a few minutes death, or severe brain or heart damage, is inevitable. After the oxygen and glucose have been supplied to the tissues, the blood returns to the heart through the low-pressure, thin-walled veins to complete the circulation.

The earliest signs of atherosclerosis – fatty streaks in the linings of the arteries – are present in almost all Western children. The plaques that characterize the fully established disease are white or yellowish-white raised areas on the inner surface of the arteries, varying in size from about 3 mm (⅛ in) across to 15 mm (½ in) across. In severe cases the plaques are so numerous that they run together to form large masses.

Plaques comprise an outer zone of mixed fibrous tissue, phagocyte cells and abnormal numbers of muscle cells with a core consisting of a disorganized mass of cell debris and fatty tissue, mainly cholesterol. Around the edges of the plaques are many tiny abnormal blood vessels that have budded out from the wall of the artery. Cholesterol is not the only culprit; the atherosclerotic plaques are certainly bulging with cholesterol, but there is more to them than that.

How atherosclerosis harms

The arteries most commonly and severely affected by atherosclerosis are the main arterial trunk of the body – the aorta – and its immediate branches. In particular, atherosclerosis affects the coronary arteries – the two branches of the aorta that supply the heart muscle itself with blood; the branches that run down to supply the legs; the carotid branches that run up the neck to supply the brain, and their branches that form a network under the brain. Although the branches to the kidneys and intestines are usually spared, it is common for the openings in the aorta for these branches to be severely narrowed by athero-sclerosis.

Arteries are not usually closed off completely by plaques. What happens is that the surface of plaques becomes rough and is sometimes broken down (ulcerated). This allows the blood to come into contact with the underlying tissue. Blood is designed to clot whenever it comes in contact with body tissue other than blood vessel linings. So clotting on top of atheromatous plaques is common. This is called thrombosis and such a clot can readily close off the artery altogether. Coronary artery thrombosis is the principal cause of heart attacks; cerebral artery thrombosis causes strokes. If small brain arteries are so damaged and weakened by atherosclerosis that they burst, the resulting bleeding around or into the brain is called cerebral haemorrhage and the effects are devastating.

Apart from the risk to the brain, heart and other organs, damage to the aorta itself commonly leads to weakening of the wall and the pressure of the blood in this vessel is so high that the result is often a ballooning out of the aorta – a condition known as aneurysm. An aortic aneurysm is highly dangerous.

Severe atherosclerosis is a condition to be avoided at all costs. Any knowledge about the ways in which it comes about is valuable, and any measures that could retard its progress would be priceless. That knowledge now exists and there is good reason to believe that we do have ways of limiting the worsening of the condition. There is far more to it than simply cutting down your intake of cholesterol. Cholesterol is an essential body ingredient. Every cell contains cholesterol, and each day a large amount of cholesterol comes down your bile duct from your liver, where it is synthesized, and is reabsorbed into your blood. Certainly, a reduced intake of saturated fats will help, but there is always plenty of cholesterol in your body to be laid down in the atherosclerotic plaques, if the process that leads to this dangerous deposition is operating. We are now beginning to understand this process and we know that free radicals are involved.

How free radicals cause atherosclerosis

Cholesterol and other fatty materials (lipids) are transported around in the bloodstream in the form of tiny fatty bodies known as lipoproteins. These are of two main kinds, low-density lipoproteins (LDLs) and high-density lipoproteins (HDLs). The density comes from the proportion of protein present. HDLs have a lot of protein and a little cholesterol; LDLs have a lot of cholesterol and a little protein. LDLs carry cholesterol and other fats from the liver to the tissues – including the arteries – and HDLs carry cholesterol and fats from the tissues to the liver. Low-density lipoproteins are the ones to worry about; high-density lipoproteins are, on the whole, to be approved of.

Scientists have known for several years that if you eat a lot of saturated, mainly animal and dairy, fats – stable fats with no double bonds between the carbon atoms, that are solid at room temperature – you will have lots of LDLs (the cholesterol carriers) in your blood. If you eat only polyunsaturated, mainly vegetable, fats – with many double bonds, that are usually liquid at room temperature – you will have fewer LDLs in your blood. What has not been known is how the cholesterol from the LDLs gets into the atheromatous plaques.

How cholesterol gets into the arteries

Lipoproteins are not, by themselves, much good at penetrating intact tissue. They work by being taken to the site where their materials are required by blood vessels so tiny that they are able to get into direct contact with their target cells. Recent research indicates that LDLs that have been attacked by free radicals and oxidized are so active that they can fight their way through the inner lining layers of the walls of large arteries so that they are able to deposit their loads under the surface layer. Some scientists have also proposed that free radicals also act in other ways: by injuring lining cells and smooth muscle cells in the vessel wall; by preventing scavenging cells (phagocytes) from doing their job; and by promoting the formation of the large phagocyte foam cells in which the cholesterol accumulates in the plaques. Significantly, research has shown that in rabbits with very high blood cholesterol levels, those given the antioxidant probucol – a drug related to butylated hydroxytoluene (BHT, see p. 144) – develop fewer atherosclerotic plaques than those not given the drug. Probucol has also been used in humans.

Current views on the production of atherosclerotic plaques are that LDLs do not, unless oxidized, help to form the plaques. Dr Hermann Esterbauer, of the University of Graz, Austria, a foremost researcher in the field of free radical damage to arteries, speaking at a conference at the New York Academy of Sciences on the health implications of vitamin E, stated that there was strong evidence that free radical oxidation of LDLs was the essential fact and that unless LDLs were oxidized they were not capable of forming plaques. Delegates at the conference were told that the natural antioxidants in the LDLs were depleted by the free radicals to the point where they could no longer prevent damaging chain reactions caused by free radicals.

Vitamin E

At the same conference, Dr K. Fred Gey of Hoffmann-La Roche, Basel, and a Professor at the Institute of Biochemistry and Molecular Biology, University of Berne, reported the results of an interesting survey, co-sponsored by the World Health Organization, into the reasons for the striking differences in the mortality in different countries from heart disease caused by atherosclerosis of the coronary arteries. The study involved 11,000 men aged 40–59 from 12 countries. In some countries the death rates from heart disease were much higher than in others: men living in Scotland and Finland, for instance, were four times more likely to die from heart disease than men living in Italy or Switzerland. Dr Gey suggested that the explanation for this remarkable difference might have been found.

In the course of the survey, the levels of antioxidants (vitamins E and A) in the blood of the subjects were monitored over a four-month period. In those with low levels of these vitamins the death rates were higher than in those with higher levels. This was not a marginal difference. Studies of previous risk factors, such as smoking, high blood pressure and high blood cholesterol, could predict an increased risk of heart disease with an accuracy of only 50 per cent. When the blood levels of these vitamins were also taken into account, the accuracy of prediction rose to 94 per cent. In this context, the fact – reported in the *Scottish Medical Journal* in 1989 – that middle-aged Scottish men eat very little fruit or green vegetables (major sources of vitamins C, A and E) is important.

The most impressive evidence to date in favour of vitamin E, however, was reported in two papers in the *New England Journal of Medicine* in May 1993 by Dr M.R. Stampfer and others at Harvard Medical School. The first of these concerned vitamin E consumption and the risk of coronary artery disease in women. This trial involved 87,245 female nurses aged 34 to 59 in none of whom heart disease or cancer had been diagnosed at the beginning of the trial in 1980. The vitamin intakes of all these women were known. The greatest variation in vitamin consumption was due to the fact that a proportion of these women were taking supplementary vitamin E. During an eight-year follow-up, 552 cases of coronary disease were diagnosed among these women with 115 deaths from coronary thrombosis, and 437 women had non-fatal heart attacks. When those with the lowest vitamin E intake were compared with those with the highest intake, the latter were found to have only 0.66 per cent of the risk of heart attack. Women who took supplementary vitamin E for two years or more had an even greater reduction in risk, to 0.59. Taking vitamin E for short periods did not produce any apparent benefit in reducing the risk. So long-term supplements of vitamin E can, apparently, reduce the risk of heart attack to almost half.

The second paper was concerned with the effects of vitamin E intake on 39,910 male health professionals – doctors, dentists, vets, pharmacists and opticians. This study began in 1986 and lasted for four years. All were believed to be free of heart disease or related conditions such as high blood cholesterol and diabetes at the beginning of the trial. Again, the intake of vitamins was known. There were 667 cases of coronary disease reported during the trial. In the men taking more than 60 mg of vitamin E daily the risk of heart attack was reduced to 0.64 as compared with those taking less than 7.5 mg per day. Those who took supplements of 100 mg or more a day had a relative risk of 0.63 as compared with those who did not take any vitamin E supplements. This trial showed that the association between differences in dietary intake of vitamin E and heart risk was weak; it was only in those men taking the larger doses possible from supplementary vitamin E that there was a substantial reduction in risk.

Neither of these trials proved positively that it was the vitamin E that was reducing the risk. Critics have suggested that people who take vitamin E supplements are, by their nature, more health conscious and may be leading healthier lives. This point was not lost on the authors of the trials, and they adjusted the figures to take into account the effects of such things as exercise, calorie intake, dietary fibre, obesity, smoking, alcohol intake, high blood pressure and routine aspirin-taking. When all these factors were considered, there was still a strong protective effect against heart attacks from vitamin E intake.

Atherosclerosis and mental functioning

The effect of a reduced blood supply to the brain was discussed in chapter 4. There is increasing evidence of the links between general intellectual functioning in elderly people and atherosclerosis of the arteries supplying the brain. Several studies have also shown that there is an association between poor mental functioning, known generally as cognitive performance, and mortality. Some of these studies have also revealed an interesting factor.

A paper in the *British Medical Journal* in March 1996 by Catharine R. Gale and others working at the Medical Research Council Environmental Epidemiology Unit at Southampton University, relates how 1,775 people over 65 were studied as to their total nutritional intake, height, weight, blood pressure, smoking history and drug treatments. They were also subjected to a careful test of their cognitive performance. In this test, a result of 10 was normal, 8–9 indicated slight cognitive impairment, and 7 or less indicated severe cognitive impairment. These people were then followed up for 20 years, during which time 842 of them died. Mortality was significantly higher in those with a diagnosis of atherosclerosis, and those with a cognitive score of 7 or less were more than twice as likely to have died as those with a score of 10.

What was particularly interesting, however, was that the only factor linked with the risk of dying was found to be the intake of vitamin C – a powerful antioxidant vitamin. People with a low intake of vitamin C were more likely to have died; those with high intake were less likely. Apart from vitamin C, there was no independent association between the risk of dying and any other factor assessed, including such factors as blood pressure, blood cholesterol levels, obesity, cancer or social class.

Antioxidant vitamins

All the research results add up to two overwhelming conclusions. Firstly, atherosclerosis is the prime enemy and anything we can do to reduce its likelihood or severity is vital. And secondly, an adequate intake of the antioxidant vitamins C and E are essential if we want to minimize the risk of severe atherosclerosis. These papers are only representative of the enormous numbers of research reports now published that suggest that these antioxidant vitamins have a major part to play in reducing the dangers of atherosclerosis.

The major causes of death in this study were coronary heart disease, stroke, cancer and respiratory diseases. Cognitive function was strongly associated with risk of death from stroke caused by atherosclerosis but was not associated with risk of death from the other causes. The authors of this paper had already demonstrated, in previous research, that low intake of the antioxidant vitamin C was a strong predictor of subsequent death from stroke. They went on to say 'This finding, together with the known link between atherosclerosis and cognitive impairment, suggests that subclinical deficiency of vitamin C may be a determinant rather than a consequence of impaired cognitive function in elderly people.'

Free radicals and ageing

In general terms, the free radical theory of ageing proposes that free radicals are more readily and plentifully formed in older people. We know that free radicals can damage any tissue in the body. The outer membranes of cells, which contain fatty material such as cholesterol, are especially susceptible to damage by fat peroxidation caused by free radicals. Such increased free radical production and damage might result from the cumulative effect of environ-mental influences, or from a reduction in the availability of the natural body antioxidants, or an age-related diminution in their activity.

We have seen how atherosclerosis has widespread and serious damaging effects. This disease obviously contributes importantly to the bodily changes characteristic of ageing. The close link between free radical oxidation of low density lipoproteins and the development of atherosclerosis has also been outlined.

The third link between free radicals and ageing is their undoubted effect on DNA. Not all DNA occurs in chromosomes. All cells contain thousands of tiny energy-producing bodies known as mitochondria and these, too, contain DNA. Mitochondrial DNA is found in the non-nuclear part of the cell and so is derived from the egg, not the sperm. It is thus inherited only from the mother. Mitochondrial DNA is now known to be especially vulnerable to free radical damage, possibly because it is so concerned with oxidative chemical reactions. Any unrepaired free radical damage to this DNA would have a serious effect on the continued functioning of the cell. Scientists have estimated that oxygen free radicals are responsible for about 10,000 DNA base changes (mutations) every day. The great majority of these are automatically repaired, but even the most efficient repair mechanism is unlikely to pick up and correct every mutation.

Another clue to the relationship between free radicals and ageing was proposed in a paper by Dr Earl R. Stadtman, Chief of the Laboratory of Biochemistry at the National Heart, Lung and Blood Institute of the National Institutes of Health, Bethesda, Maryland and published in *Science* in August 1992. This was concerned with explaining how free radicals are involved in the ageing process by their action in oxidizing and damaging enzymes necessary for the continuation of healthy body function. The author points out that enzymes damaged by free radical attack are marked for degradation by other protein-splitting enzymes (proteases) and are normally broken down by them. But since the enzymes that do the breaking down are themselves damaged by free radicals, the result is an age-related increasing pool of damaged protein within cells. This has been shown in animal brain cells to be a feature of ageing; the accumulation of oxidized protein within these cells seriously compromises cell function. These studies showed that pre-treatment with antioxidants can partially prevent the accumulation of oxidized protein within cells so that the damaging effects on cell function do not occur. This research, carried out on gerbils, is described on p. 151.

Dr Stadtman confirmed the general opinion that free radicals are responsible for much damage to cell membranes and DNA, and described in detail the way proteins – the essential building materials of the body – are attacked by hydroxyl radicals, produced by radiation and ozone, and by hydroxyl and other radicals produced in the body. The evidence he quotes suggests that anything up to 50 per cent of the cellular protein in old people might be present in the damaged oxidized form. He ends his paper with the statement: '. . . there is reason for hope that a pharmacological intervention may be found to ameliorate age-related disorders.'

Antioxidants

Free radicals act by oxidation. Oxidation is a kind of burning that is always damaging to whatever is oxidized. Often it is very useful, but in other cases, as when free radicals bring about cell damage in disease processes, we want to try to do something to stop it. This is where antioxidants come in. An antioxidant is any substance that retards or prevents deterioration, damage or destruction by oxidation. In a medical context, antioxidants are comparatively new; but in other branches of science they have been around for a long time.

Chemists have known for years that free radical oxidation action can be controlled or even prevented by a range of antioxidant substances. It is, for instance, vital that lubricating oils should remain stable and liquid and should not dry up like paints. For this reason, such oils usually have small quantities of antioxidants, such as phenol or amine derivatives, added to them. Although plastics are often formed by free radical action, they can also be broken down by the same process. So they, too, require protection by antioxidants like phenols or naphtols. Low-density polythene is also often protected by carbon black to absorb ultraviolet light which causes free radical production.

Food in storage deteriorates by oxidation. When, for instance, fat goes rancid it does so by a free radical oxidation reaction. Since oxidized fats taste and smell horrible, chemists have been actively looking for antioxidants to prevent this for some time. To date, the most popular antioxidant food additives have been BHA (butylated hydroxyanisole), BHT (butylated hydroxytoluene), propyl gallate and tocopherol (vitamin E). These antioxidants act by donating hydrogen atoms to the hydroxyl radical so that water is formed. The equation is simple: $H + OH = H_2O$. In other words, two dangerously active radicals combine to form a harmless molecule, water.

The irradiation of food – which is an excellent way of killing bacteria that can cause spoilage and may be dangerous – can, in itself, cause free radical production that can lead to unacceptable chemical changes in the food. So it may sometimes be necessary to counteract the undesirable effects of food irradiation by using antioxidants.

Natural body antioxidants

The body has its own antioxidants for damage limitation, one of the most effective of which is tocopherol (vitamin E). This vitamin dissolves in fat; this is especially important because much the most significant free radical damage in the body is damage to the membranes of cells and to low-density lipoproteins and these are made of fat molecules. Vitamin C is also a powerful antioxidant, but is soluble in water, not in fat. This means that it gets distributed to all parts of the body. The two vitamins are both highly efficient at mopping up free radicals, and sometimes even cooperate in so doing.

Other natural body antioxidants include compounds such as cysteine, glutathione and D-penicillamine, and blood constituents such as the iron-containing molecule transferrin and the protein ceruloplasmin. These act either by preventing free radicals from being produced or by mopping them up. The body also contains a number of important antioxidant enzymes, especially superoxide dismutase (see p. 136 above).

Vitamins

The greatest popular interest, however, is currently focused on vitamins. Most medical textbooks still discuss vitamins as being necessary in small quantities for the maintenance of health. This is appropriate for the large B group of vitamins (B1, B2, B6 and B12, niacin, pantothenic acid, folic acid and lipoic acid) and for vitamins D and K. If these vitamins are not available in small quantities, various deficiency diseases occur. Vitamin C deficiency causes scurvy, a bleeding disorder; vitamin A deficiency causes serious eye and other problems; vitamin D deficiency causes bone softening, rickets (in children) or osteomalacia (in adults); and so on.

Because many vitamins act in association with enzymes and only tiny quantities are required, convention has it that taking more than the small daily requirement – which is nearly always present in a reasonably balanced diet – is a waste of money. In addition, there have been regular, and well-justified, medical warnings about the dangers of vitamin overdosage, specifically of vitamins A and D. Excessive intake of these vitamins can certainly cause trouble. Too much vitamin D causes calcium to be deposited in the kidneys, arteries and other tissues, which can lead to all sorts of problems, including kidney failure. The dangers of overdosage of vitamins E and A are described below.

In the literature on free radicals most of the emphasis has been on vitamins E and C, and it is worth looking more closely at these substances.

Vitamin E (tocopherol)

Tocopherol first came to notice in 1922 when it was found that female rats required an unknown substance in their diets to sustain normal pregnancies. Without it, they could ovulate and conceive satisfactorily, but within about 10 days the fetus invariably died and was absorbed. Male rats deficient in this substance were also found to have abnormalities in their testes. For these reasons, vitamin E enjoyed a brief reputation as the 'antisterility vitamin' and was recommended as a treatment for infertility, although there was no reason to suppose that the people concerned were deficient in the vitamin. It has also been used to try to treat various menstrual disorders, inflammation of the vagina and menopausal symptoms, but there is no reason to suppose that it is specifically useful in these conditions.

Vitamin E was chemically isolated in 1936 from wheatgerm oil. It was found to be any one of a range of eight complicated but similar molecules known as tocopherols. It is almost insoluble in water but dissolves in oils, fats, alcohol, acetone, ether and other fat solvents. Unlike vitamin C, it is stable to heat and unaffected by acids at temperatures up to 100°C (212°F). If exposed to atmospheric oxygen it is slowly oxidized. This occurs more rapidly in the presence of iron or silver salts. It gradually darkens on exposure to light. Among the richest natural sources are seed germ oils, alfalfa and lettuce. It is widely distributed in plant materials. The international unit is equal to 1 mg of alpha-tocopherol acetate. For practical purposes of dosage, 1 international unit is equivalent to 1 mg of vitamin E.

All the tocopherols are antioxidants and this appears to be the basis for all the biological effects of the vitamin. It is now becoming increasingly clear that vitamin E is involved in many body processes and that it operates as a natural antioxidant, helping to protect important cell structures, especially the cell membranes, from the damaging effects of free radicals. It has been found, for instance, that the vitamin can protect against the effects of overdosage of vitamin A. In animals, vitamin E supplements can protect them against the effects of various drugs, chemicals and metals that can promote free radical formation. In carrying out its function as an antioxidant in the body, vitamin E is itself converted to a radical. It is, however, soon regenerated to the active vitamin by a biochemical process that probably involves both vitamin C and glutathione.

Deficiency of vitamin E is rare because it occurs widely in food, especially in vegetable oils, but when it does occur the effects can be devastating. The need for vitamin E increases if the diet is high in polyunsaturated fats. Deficiency sometimes occurs in premature babies, especially if malnourished, and in people with disorders that interfere with fat absorption. People who are severely deficient in vitamin E for these reasons may suffer, to varying degrees, degenerative changes in the brain and nervous system, impairment of vision, double vision, walking disturbances, anaemia, an increased rate of destruction of red blood cells, fluid retention (oedema) and skin disorders. Some reports have shown that large doses of vitamin E can prevent the progression of the neurological abnormalities or even lead to improvement.

Human vitamin E deficiency occurs only after many months on a severely deficient diet. A daily intake of 10 to 30 mg of the vitamin is said to be sufficient to keep the blood levels within normal limits and this is always provided by a normal diet. Diets that contain other antioxidants decrease the requirement. Breast milk contains plenty to meet a baby's needs.

Dangers of overdosage

Vitamin E is generally regarded as fairly innocuous and few if any warnings are given on the dangers of overdosage. For adults, this is probably reasonable, but there are undoubtedly limits to the amounts that can be safely taken. Since free radical oxidant action is a necessary part of the body's functioning, it is reasonable to suppose that undue interference with it, by excessive dosage of an antioxidant like vitamin E, is likely to be harmful. To do so may be, for instance, to increase the risk of infection. There is no substance of major medical benefit that does not also carry the risk of undesirable side-effects.

Like many other substances, vitamin E is necessary for life and health. But, like many other substances, the amount in the body must for safety be kept within fairly strict limits. The phagocytes that kill and scavenge bacteria and general body debris use free radicals to break up these unwanted materials. Cases have been reported in which overdosage of vitamin E in premature babies has led to the development of a serious intestinal infection. This is probably the result of interference with the action of their phagocytes.

Vitamin C

Vitamin C, or ascorbic acid, is a simpler compound than vitamin E and is water soluble. It was the first vitamin to be discovered, and the disease caused by its deficiency – scurvy – has been known for centuries. The vitamin was isolated in 1928 and chemically identified in 1932. It is readily destroyed by exposure to air and by cooking, especially in the presence of copper and alkalis.

The body's main structural material is collagen, a strong insoluble protein. This forms the main basis of the bones and of most other tissues. Vitamin C is necessary for the proper synthesis of collagen, and deficiency leads to the failure of wounds to heal, weakness of small blood vessels with bleeding from the gums and into the joints and skin, anaemia and looseness of the teeth. Scurvy still occurs in people who live on a restricted diet and the first symptoms appear three or four months after the last intake of the vitamin. In babies and small children scurvy also causes bleeding under the bone membranes, causing very tender swellings so that infants resent being touched.

To prevent scurvy, humans need amounts of the vitamin varying from about 60 mg a day to as much as 250 mg a day. Blood levels are reduced by smoking and by the contraceptive pill. People need more while suffering from infectious diseases, injuries, burns, rheumatic disorders and after surgical operations. A normal, well-balanced diet usually supplies enough vitamin C to prevent scurvy. The vitamin is plentiful in fruit juices, green peppers, cabbages, green vegetables, potatoes, citrus fruits, tomatoes and strawberries. Orange and lemon juices contain about 0.5 mg in each cc (ml). When large doses are taken, there is a correspondingly large loss of the vitamin in the urine.

Vitamin C is a powerful antioxidant and is commonly used for this reason to preserve the natural flavour and colour of processed fruit, vegetables and dairy products.

Vitamin C in medicine

No one disputes that vitamin C is of great value in the treatment of scurvy. As soon as the vitamin is given in adequate dosage, improvement occurs and, within a few weeks, all the symptoms and signs have gone. The real dispute has been whether the vitamin has any value in people who are not suffering from scurvy. Until recently, the orthodox medical view has been that the vitamin does no good to such people. In spite of this view, however, there have been over the years repeated enthusiasms for trials of the vitamin in all sorts of conditions. Even before the current interest in free radicals and in the use of antioxidants, vitamin C had many supporters. One reason for the medical scepticism is clear; most of the trials of vitamin C in the management of conditions like the common cold failed because the doses given were little more than the minimum daily requirement to prevent scurvy. It is becoming clear that, used as an antioxidant, much larger doses than the minimum daily requirement are needed.

A safe dosage

The late Linus Pauling in his *Vitamin C and the Common Cold* made an interesting point while considering vitamin C in an evolutionary context. Assuming that early peoples must have eaten whatever they could get their hands on, he decided to work out how much vitamin C they would have taken in if, as must often have happened, the total daily calorie requirement (about 2,500 calories) was met from a single foodstuff. The results were surprising. If they had eaten enough peas and beans to get 2,500 calories, they would have taken in 1,000 mg of vitamin C. Vegetables with a low vitamin C content would have provided 1,200 mg; vegetables and fruits with an intermediate content would have provided 3,400 mg; foods rich in vitamin C like cabbage, cauliflower, chives and mustard greens would have provided 6,000 mg per day; and foods with a very high vitamin C content like blackcurrants, kale, parsley, peppers and broccoli would have provided no less than 12,000 mg (12 grams) per day.

Since humans evolved in an environment providing quantities of vitamin C of this order, Pauling inferred that the ideal daily intake for most adults should be somewhere in the range of 2,300 to 9,000 mg. The very large vitamin C intake throughout a large part of the evolutionary period implied that big doses of this vitamin should be regarded as 'natural'.

Pauling was awarded the Nobel Prize for chemistry and is regarded by many as the greatest chemist of the 20th century. His book *The Nature of the Chemical Bond* revolutionized chemical thought.

Possible dangers

Vitamin C has an excellent safety record and has been taken in 1,000 mg plus doses by millions of people with no apparent disadvantage. To balance this is a handful of reports on the ill effects of very large doses thought to be due to the vitamin. One of these concerned a man who was given a course of vitamin C in a dosage of 40,000 mg (40 g), by intravenous injection, three times a week, plus 20,000 to 40,000 mg every day by mouth. This huge dosage was continued for a month with no obvious change in his condition. The intravenous dose was then doubled to 80,000 mg. The next day he became breathless and feverish and his urine turned black, indicating that many red blood cells had broken down, releasing haemoglobin which was passing out in the urine.

Investigation showed that this man had sickle cell trait and exceptionally fragile red blood cells. Many drugs in common use can cause the red cells to break down in this condition. The patient was given lots of fluid to drink so as to flush through his kidneys, and on the third day the urine was clear. He made a complete recovery from the red blood cell breakdown. There is every reason to suppose that, had his red cells been normal, he would have suffered no ill effects from the enormous quantities of vitamin C he was taking. Dosages of this order are exceptional and there are very few active drugs that can, with perfect safety, be taken in quantities of 20 or 30 times the customary dosage. The report does, however, indicate that there are some people who ought to be particularly cautious about taking any drug, even one as apparently safe as vitamin C.

Beta-carotene
Popular books and articles, as well as advertising literature on antioxidants, imply that vitamin A is in the same class as vitamins C and E as an antioxidant. This is not so. Part of the reason for this view was the coincidence that the three vitamins formed the word 'ACE'. As a result numerous references and book titles have given the misleading impression that these three vitamins are equally important as antioxidants.

The plant pigment beta-carotene is also known as provitamin A because it is converted into vitamin A (retinol and other forms) in the liver. It is found in whole milk, butter, cheese, egg yolk, liver, yellow and green vegetables and fish, especially fish liver. The same foods also contain a number of different carotene-like substances (carotenoids) that cannot be converted to vitamin A and so are wasted. Retinol and its related substances have many important functions in the body. They are necessary for the growth and health of the surface and lining tissues and the bones; for the health of the immune system and for protection against cancer; for normal vision and for the health of the corneas; for protection against various skin diseases; and for protection of the skin against sunlight radiation and ageing changes. People deficient in retinoids suffer night blindness and dryness of the eyes (xerophthalmia). Babies may suffer devastating melting of the corneas of the eyes with permanent blindness. Severe deficiency is a common cause of death in small children after severe damage has been sustained by most systems of the body.

A normal, well-balanced diet provides enough retinol to prevent any such effects. If taken as a dietary supplement, 1 mg per day is equivalent to the recommended daily allowance and this dose is probably double the amount needed to prevent deficiency.

Dangers of overdosage
Unlike vitamins C and E, vitamin A cannot safely be taken in large doses. Very large doses of vitamin A cause chronic poisoning with skin dryness, itching and peeling; drowsiness, irritability and an irresistible desire to sleep; headache; loss of appetite; enlargement of the liver and spleen; and painful and tender swellings over the bones. The vitamin accumulates in the body and the effects take weeks to wear off. Inuits and their husky dogs never eat polar bear liver

(which contains huge quantities of vitamin A) because they know of these effects: 1 g of polar bear liver contains up to 12 mg of retinol, 12 times the minimum daily requirement. Vitamin A is also dangerous to the fetus if taken by the mother in doses of 7 to 12 mg a day during the first three months of pregnancy, and can cause congenital abnormalities.

There is another good reason why vitamin A should not be considered as a routine antioxidant. The results of the trials of this antioxidant are much less convincing than those of vitamins C and E. Some major trials of carotenoids have been stopped prematurely because the results in people taking them seemed to be worse than in those who were not. The *Lancet* for 27 January 1996 contained a report that a major American trial of beta-carotene plus vitamin A against lung cancer in a high-risk population of smokers and asbestos workers had been stopped 21 months early because of 'increased morbidity and mortality in the supplemented group'. Another trial in Finnish smokers had also shown increased lung cancer and mortality with beta-carotene supplements. Two other important trials in low-risk groups were also stopped because they had shown no effect on disease or death rates.

These trials had shown what was already known from previous research that people with higher blood levels of beta-carotene were less likely to get cancer or suffer from heart disease than people with low levels. In addition, they showed that the people with the highest blood levels of beta-carotene did not have higher rates of lung cancer, heart attacks or death. It appears that it is only in the high-risk groups – essentially the cigarette smokers and those exposed to asbestos – that vitamin A supplementation is dangerous.

The research workers conducting these trials are puzzled by these results and are currently trying to produce possible explanations. While they do, it might be best to get enough vitamin A but not too much, in other words, to chop the A out of ACE.

Flavonoid antioxidants

Flavonoids are natural antioxidants of a chemical class known as polyphenols. They are found in fruits, vegetables such as onions, tea and red wine. Numerous research projects have been carried out in recent years to determine whether they are medically valuable. This research has shown that flavonoids reduce the tendency for blood to clot in the blood vessels. This effect, alone, can be valuable since it is the clotting of blood on top of atherosclerotic plaques that causes occlusion of arteries. But it has been shown that flavonoids interfere with the oxidation of low-density lipoproteins, the cholesterol carriers that are implicated in the formation of atherosclerosis.

A research project, reported in the *Lancet* in October 1993, by M. G. L. Hertog and others working at the National Institute of Public Health in Bilthoven,

Netherlands, describes a study of the flavonoid intake of 805 men aged 65–84 in 1985. The researchers measured the flavonoid content of 28 vegetables, 12 fruits and 9 beverages and were thus able to get an accurate figure for the flavonoid intake of the men. In each case, a full medical history was recorded, blood samples were taken, cholesterol levels checked, blood pressure measured, height and weight recorded, and smoking history determined.

The men were then followed up for five years. During that time 43 died from coronary thrombosis. The flavonoid intake – mainly from tea, onions and apples – was found to be inversely related to the incidence of heart attacks. Those with a high intake were less likely to have attacks; those with a low intake were more likely. Perhaps there is some truth in the old adage 'an apple a day keeps the doctor away'.

A similar trial, reported in the *British Medical Journal* in February 1996 involving 5,133 Finnish men and women from 30 communities in different parts of Finland over 26 years, showed substantially the same results. Low flavonoid intake was associated with a significantly higher risk of heart attacks from coronary artery disease. Again, apples and onions were the main source of flavonoids.

A number of research papers have suggested that the high flavonoid content of red wine may account for what has been called the 'French paradox' – the remarkable fact that in spite of a high intake of saturated fats and other 'unhealthy' dairy products, the French as a nation enjoy a strikingly lower incidence of coronary heart disease than, for instance, the British.

The role of safe antioxidants

There is a positive and important link between diet and longevity. In many animal species, lifespan can be increased up to 50 per cent by suitable modification of the diet. Whether this enhancement is due to a reduction in free radical action so that bodily antioxidants can more readily cope, remains to be seen. There is evidence that rats on low-calorie diets suffer less free radical damage to their body proteins than those on unrestricted diets. This may be because they have larger quantities of the important enzymes that protect against free radicals. Antioxidants are unlikely to be the whole story, for rats living longer on restricted diets are known to have more of certain genes in their liver tissue.

There is, however, some more direct evidence of increased free radical action with age. Scientists at the University of Kentucky have been studying the performance of gerbils in running mazes. Old gerbils, on average, make twice as many mistakes as young gerbils. But if old gerbils are given the free radical-trapping antioxidant butyl-alpha-phenylnitrone (PBN) for two weeks, their performance improves so as to be as good as that of young gerbils. When the PBN was stopped, they went back to making as many mistakes as before.

Proteins that have been damaged by free radical oxidation can be detected by highly sensitive tests for traces of amino acids (carbonyl groups) that are released in the course of the damage. Post-mortem examinations on human brains have shown more of these groups in old people than in those of young people. The probability is that antioxidants can make up for progressive, age-related deficiencies of the natural antioxidants that mop up free radicals in younger people.

The researcher Thomas Johnson of the University of Colorado has been able to breed a strain of roundworm with a lifespan more than twice that of others of the same species. The remarkable thing about these long-living worms is that they have significantly higher levels of the enzymes superoxide dismutase and catalase than others. These enzymes are natural antioxidants and are exactly the same as those that protect humans against free radicals.

As long ago as 1956, the research scientist D. Harmon, writing in the *Journal of Gerontology*, suggested that free radicals are probably involved in the ageing process. Since then the free radical theory of ageing has become widely accepted. Gerontologists now generally believe that free radical damage to tissues is a central factor in the development of most age-related diseases – atherosclerosis, arthritis, loss of muscle and heart efficiency, cataract, lung disorders, skin deterioration and, probably, cancer.

Free radicals and your heart

In 1991 the British magazine *The Lancet* carried a report produced by the heart research unit in the Department of Cardiology and Medicine of the University of Edinburgh. The report, by Dr R. A. Riemersma and colleagues, described a research study into whether there was any connection between the levels of certain vitamins in the body and the risk of angina pectoris. The vitamins concerned were vitamins C, E and A and the substance beta-carotene that is converted by the liver into vitamin A. There was more to the trial than immediately meets the eye.

About angina

Angina pectoris is not a disease but a symptom. It is the often agonizing tight gripping, constricting pain 'like a steel band around the chest' felt by the sufferer after a certain, often predictable, amount of exertion. Angina usually comes on after walking for a particular distance, comes on more quickly on a cold day or when walking against the wind, and especially when walking uphill. It may be brought on by anxiety or emotion. Sometimes the pain passes down the arms, especially the left arm; sometimes it radiates through to the back or up into the neck.

Angina is caused by asking the heart to work harder than it comfortably can with the limited oxygen and glucose supply it has available. This supply is limited because the arteries that carry the blood to the heart muscle – the coronary arteries – have been narrowed by atherosclerosis. Atherosclerosis is the disease; angina is the symptom. In the case of most affected people – usually men – the heart can beat satisfactorily when the person is at rest. But during exertion, the heart has to work harder to pump additional blood to the muscles and there comes a point at which the narrowed coronary arteries cannot supply the necessary increase in blood flow. When this happens, the heart complains. Waste materials accumulate around the heart muscle cells and stimulate pain in the nerve endings. Many people with angina go on like this for years, but in some the condition gradually worsens until it may occur even at rest. In others the angina becomes more rapidly unstable and there is a serious risk that a coronary artery, or a large branch of one, may become completely blocked, causing coronary thrombosis, or a heart attack.

Angina and vitamins

Dr Riemersma's paper was interesting for several reasons. First, there is an obvious relationship between angina pectoris and the risk of heart disease; both are caused by atherosclerosis. Second, the vitamins it studied are antioxidants that attack free radicals. Perhaps most interestingly of all, the study implied a presumption that there might well be a connection between free radicals and heart disease. The results of the study confirmed this presumption. No connection was found between vitamin A levels and angina. The results for vitamin C were confused by the fact that vitamin C levels are lower in smokers than in non-smokers; and since smoking is an established risk factor for heart disease this could not be attributed to low levels of the vitamin. But so far as vitamin E was concerned, there was no doubt about the result. Even after taking into account smoking, blood pressure, obesity and blood cholesterol levels, the facts were clear. Men with low blood levels of vitamin E were significantly more likely to have angina than men with higher levels.

The authors of the paper concluded that '. . . some populations with a high incidence of coronary heart disease should supplement their eating habits with more cereals, vitamin-E-rich oils, vegetables, and fruit.' The paper brought out other interesting points. Low-density lipoproteins (LDLs) altered by oxidation by free radicals are believed to be the main factors in the development of the plaques that narrow arteries in atherosclerosis. The authors of this paper drew attention to American research that showed that when vitamin E is added to cells grown in culture in the laboratory, it blocks the oxidation changes in LDLs. They also point out that the protective polyunsaturated fats are vulnerable to attack by free radicals, which can start a chain reaction causing them, in turn, to become free radicals. This chain reaction can be prevented by vitamin E.

This is but one of many hundreds of professional articles dealing with free radicals and heart disease that have been published in recent years; almost all support the view that free radicals have a significant part to play in causing heart disease.

Free radicals and heart attacks

A heart attack is different from angina. It is the consequence of an actual blockage of a coronary artery or one of its branches. In some cases the heart attack is caused by a temporary spasm of a coronary artery so that it almost closes off for a time. The effects are the same. Heart attacks are not related to exertion, like angina, but come on at any time. The pain is similar in nature but often more severe and it does not pass off on resting, but goes on and on. There may also be a sense of impending death, often justified.

When a part of the heart muscle is completely deprived of its blood supply it becomes swollen and dies. This weakens the heart's action and may sometimes weaken the wall of the heart, but is not necessarily fatal. With luck the dead patch of muscle forms a strong scar and the heart continues to beat satisfactorily, although it is capable of less powerful action than before. Sometimes this process is repeated several times, and with each attack the heart is damaged further. In such cases, heart failure – the inability to keep the blood circulating adequately – is likely to occur.

Modern research suggests that the most important effect of free radicals occurs, not at the time of the blockage, but when the damaged tissue, especially that around the dead zone, is trying to recover by widening nearby blood vessels. This response is called reperfusion and it is during this period that more oxygen becomes available and the maximum danger from free radicals occurs. This fact was illustrated in a paper published in *The Lancet* in April 1993. Free radical research has now progressed to the stage at which evidence of the presence of free radicals can actually be obtained by analysing a small sample of the blood emerging in a vein from the area concerned. Such blood is examined by electron paramagnetic resonance spectroscopy. Samples have to be stored at very low temperatures in liquid nitrogen until they can be examined.

The paper describes the case of a 61-year-old man who was treated in hospital two and a half hours after having a heart attack. A kind of X-ray called angiography showed that one of his coronary arteries was blocked. A fine tube (catheter) with a small balloon at one end was passed into the affected artery, pushed along to the obstruction, and the balloon inflated. The artery was successfully opened up. So far, the matter was routine. (The procedure of coronary artery balloon angioplasty is routine.) What was different about this case was that, before passing the balloon catheter, a second narrow-bore tube had been passed into the patient's heart so that the tip lay near the opening of the vein – the coronary sinus – that returns the coronary artery blood to the circulation. This allowed samples of the blood passing through the affected area to be taken throughout the procedure. These were immediately frozen to await spectroscopy.

An hour later, the coronary artery closed again and the procedure had to be repeated. Again, samples of blood emerging from the affected area were obtained and processed. This time, the artery remained open long-term and all was well. When the blood samples were studied it was found that, in both episodes, each time the artery was opened up a flood of free radicals poured out of the area.

This was an important confirmation of the widely held view that a great deal of the damage that occurs in the course of a heart attack is caused by free radicals that are released during the recovery phase, whether from the body's natural recovery response by opening up nearby blood vessels, or due to medical intervention. The experts currently believe that it is the increased availability of oxygen, at this point, that initiates the production of free radicals.

Later free radical damage

As soon as heart muscle is damaged by loss of its blood supply, millions of phagocytes move into the area to start cleaning it up so that healing and scar formation can proceed. What was not known until recently, is that this so-called leucocyte infiltration, is also associated with a burst of free radical production. Phagocytes actually use free radicals in their cleaning-up operations. The monitoring of free radicals in this study was continued and between 9 and 24 hours, there was a rise in the output of free radicals that went even higher than when the coronary artery was opened up on the first and second occasion. Such free radical production is probably necessary, but there is a real possibility that it is also responsible for further damage to the heart. Phagocyte free radical over-production has been investigated in several other diseases.

Practical implications

Scientific medicine looks for explanations of disease processes before attempting to find cures. 'Try-it-and-see' methods are all very well and adopted if the evidence for their efficacy is strong enough. But until there is a demonstrable explanation of how they work, there is always a lingering doubt, and this doubt is sometimes later found to have been justified. Now that so much is known about the role of free radicals in the production of disease damage, the stage is set for attempts at intervention to try to minimize this damage. Such intervention must obviously take the form of an attack on the free radicals, either by the use of various antioxidants or by other means.

Medical interest in this possibility is now intense and many trials are being conducted. From the earliest stage, everything possible should be done to prevent narrowing and obstruction of the coronary arteries. Since free radicals play an important role in causing the arterial disease that brings about this narrowing, there is one obvious line of approach.

The whole picture

It would be totally wrong to deflect attention from the importance of the already established risk factors – smoking, obesity, high blood pressure, lack of exercise and a diet high in saturated fats. Free radicals are not the whole story and anyone who thinks that a regular daily dose of vitamins E and C confers a licence to continue the life of an over-eating, overweight, cigarette-smoking couch potato would be foolish.

Free radicals and cancer

Since cancer is such an important cause of death and morbidity in elderly people it is important to consider the relationship of free radicals and antioxidants to this group of diseases. The significance of free radicals in relation to cancer is much less clear than in the case of arterial and heart disease, and no real breakthrough has yet been achieved. Free radical and antioxidant studies are by no means in the forefront of cancer research, at least at the moment, and we still don't know whether they will ever be. Nevertheless, apart from the huge amount of general cancer research in progress a great deal of research specifically into the question of free radicals and cancer is under way. At least 28 human trials, sponsored by the American National Cancer Institute, are in progress to discover the role of dietary factors, including vitamin E, in the development of cancer. In Britain, too, much research is in progress. The Imperial Cancer Research Fund, the Medical Research Council, the Dunn Nutrition Unit and the Department of Community Medicine at Cambridge University, among many other authorities are engaged in long-term studies, involving thousands of subjects, into the effects of dietary elements on the incidence of cancer. Monitoring includes the subjects' intake of vitamin C, E, A and beta-carotene. Similar projects are also under way in France, Germany, Spain, Italy, Denmark, Sweden, the Netherlands and Greece.

Free radical activity markers

Hundreds of thousands of samples of blood and urine are being taken and analysed and, although it is impracticable on such a scale to detect the free radicals themselves, these samples will among other things be examined for signs of free radical action. This is done by looking for markers of high levels of oxidation. These markers include the substances malonaldehyde, fat dienes (hydrocarbons with two double carbon-to-carbon bonds in the molecule), damaged protein thiols (sulphur-containing organic compounds), and the blood proteins such as albumin that take up free radicals. The greater the free radical activity, the higher the levels of these substances in the blood sample.

Another way of assessing free radical action, of special significance in the cancer context, is the degree of free radical damage to DNA. This, too, is being monitored by careful examination of the DNA in white blood cells in the samples. We know that free radicals can promote damaging chain reactions in DNA and that DNA damage can cause cancer. Examination of the DNA in white cells can show indications of severance of the double helix, appearing as regions in which there has been random rejoining. In smokers, DNA damage can be detected in cells from the lining of the air tubes, where lung cancer starts. These cells are constantly being coughed up and can be examined for the number of fragments of DNA lying free in them – an index of the amount of DNA damage by free radicals.

Preliminary findings

Reports to date suggest that vitamins C and E do offer protection against certain cancers, such as those of the lungs, gullet, stomach and large intestine. In particular, vitamin C is believed by some experts to be the body's major protective element against stomach cancer. This, is true, is especially important because stomach cancer is one of the most dangerous and least easily detected kinds, and is often fatally advanced before it is diagnosed.

We are still a long way from fully understanding the role of free radicals in the development of cancer. We do not even know whether their contribution is major or minor. There are, however, some very suggestive points in the story and since many cancers are so devastating and antioxidants – vitamins C and E – so safe, it is perhaps not surprising that many of the researchers engaged in this work take regular daily doses of these vitamins.

Free radicals and your eyes

As the medical literature on free radicals and antioxidants grows, an increasing number of body systems and medical conditions are shown to be affected by them. Although so far the visual system has received comparatively little attention, interest is growing and it seems probable that before long free radical damage will be implicated in many eye disorders. Cataract is a major eye disorder affecting millions of older people.

Cataract is due to a denaturing of the protein fibres in the internal lenses of the eyes. It is becoming increasingly obvious that oxidation of the lens protein is an important factor. The fine protein fibres of which the internal lenses are made are transparent. The transparency of the lens as a whole depends on the uniformity of diameter of these fibres and the evenness and parallelity with which they are laid down in the lens. When protein is damaged, this uniformity of structure is lost, and the fibres, instead of transmitting light evenly, cause it to be irregularly refracted and even reflected. The result is severely defective vision.

The view that age-related cataract may be due to free radical damage is indirect but strong and based largely on the differences between the levels of antioxidants in the bodies of people with cataract compared with those in comparable people with clear lenses. These trials have been reported in various medical and scientific journals such as the *British Medical Journal*, the *Archives of Ophthalmology, Annals of the New York Academy of Science*, and the *American Journal of Clinical Nutrition*.

One of the most impressive studies was carried out in the Department of Biomedical Sciences, University of Tampere, Finland, and published in the *British Medical Journal* in December 1992. In this project 47 people with cataract and a carefully selected comparable group of 94 people with clear lenses were compared. The normal 'controls' were selected to be as similar as possible to those with cataracts in terms of age, sex, occupation, smoking history, blood cholesterol levels, body weight, blood pressure and the presence or absence of diabetes. All had blood samples taken that were analysed for levels of vitamin E and beta-carotene.

The results showed that there was a significant relationship between the levels of vitamin E and beta-carotene and the likelihood of having cataract. Low blood levels of these antioxidant vitamins were found in the cataract group; higher levels in the clear lens controls. People low in both vitamins were two and a half times as likely to have cataracts as those with higher levels. The authors of the study concluded: 'Low serum concentrations of the antioxidant vitamins alpha-tocopherol (vitamin E) and beta-carotene are risk factors for end stage senile cataract. Controlled trials of the role of antioxidant vitamins in cataract prevention are therefore warranted.'

Another study carried out in Canada and reported at an International Conference, involved 175 cataract patients and the same number of people with clear lenses. Again, this study showed a meaningful difference in the intake of vitamins E and C in the two groups. Those who had taken extra C and E vitamins for five years or more were significantly more numerous in the clear lens group than in the cataract group. The epidemiologist Professor James Robertson, head of the project, said: 'Supplementary vitamins C and E are associated with a significant reduction in risk of cataracts.'

Free radicals and ultraviolet light

Many scientists now suspect that at least one source of cataract-producing free radicals is ultraviolet light, present in large quantity in sunlight. Some have even suggested that this is the reason why cataracts occur much earlier in countries such as India than in more temperate areas. It is already well established that ultraviolet radiation produces free radicals in tissue. Ultraviolet light is the cause of sunburning and of the age-related damage to skin found in people with a history of long exposure to sunlight. These are free radical effects. It is also the cause of much external eye irritation and of the condition of pterygium in which a fold of the membrane covering the white of the eye (the conjunctiva) moves across over the cornea. Since surface eye tissues are transparent, they are very susceptible to ultraviolet light and it seems almost certain that these changes are induced by free radicals.

Because the internal lens of the eye is protected by the cornea and by a layer of water behind the cornea, both of which partially absorb ultraviolet light, ophthalmologists have been less ready to accept that ultraviolet light is an important cause of cataract. In recent years, however, this view has gained increasing support. The idea that free radicals are involved is supported by research conducted at the University of Maryland by Professor of Biochemistry Shambu Varma. Isolated lenses exposed to strong light stresses became cloudy, but this could be prevented if the solution in which the lenses were placed contained antioxidants. Professor Varma also recommended that people should take supplementary vitamins C and E, at least from around the age of 40, to protect the lenses against later cataract formation. The evidence for the protective value of vitamin C and E against cataract is persuasive.

Skin ageing and free radicals

Doctors have known for years that sunlight damages the skin. A direct comparison of the skins of white people living cloistered lives with those of people who spend their days in the open, especially in tropical and subtropical areas, shows that, while the former remain smooth and elastic, the latter become wrinkled, discoloured and lax. Many sun-loving people of European or American origin who lived for years in hot areas suffer devastating skin damage, with drooping, sagging folds, extensive wrinkling, and a much higher than average incidence of the three most common skin cancers (see chapter 2).

This damage is caused by radiation – specifically ultraviolet radiation from the sun. The most obvious effect of this radiation is on the elastic collagen protein of the skin which becomes reduced in quantity and altered in quality. Loss of support to the small blood vessels leads to their expansion and prominence, as 'broken veins' (telangiectasis). Skin specialists, recognizing that these changes are the result of light damage over long periods, call them photo-ageing.

Tretinoin and ageing skin

The new knowledge concerns the way in which ultraviolet radiation causes the damage. In 1986 a paper appeared in the *Journal of the American Academy of Dermatology* entitled 'Topical tretinoin for photo-aged skin'. This paper recounted how the ratio of sun-damaged to normal skin collagen could be markedly reduced by treatment with tretinoin (all-trans-retinoic acid, the active form of vitamin A in all the tissues of the body except the retina; it is a powerful antioxidant). This was followed by similar papers in other journals including one in the *Journal of the American Medical Association* entitled 'At last, a medical treatment for skin ageing'. Some trials involved large numbers of patients treated with tretinoin over a period of several months. (Taking tretinoin is not the same as taking vitamin A.)

We now know that the ultraviolet light causes production of free radicals and that it is these that do the damage. By the time this became clear, dermatologists already knew that they could partially reverse the effects of solar radiation on the skin by using tretinoin. In a typical trial of this treatment, one side of the face of volunteers was treated with 0.05 per cent tretinoin cream once a day and the other side treated with the cream base without the tretinoin. At the end of 12 weeks skin thickness, measured by ultrasound and other methods, had increased by 10 per cent.

Other trials of longer periods of treatment showed improvement in skin thickness, in the roughness of the skin and in fine wrinkling but did nothing to help sagging, age freckles (lentigines) or broken veins. The thickening of the outer skin, or epidermis, was in many cases remarkable, and could be as great as two and three-quarter times. Almost all the people in the trial suffered some degree of minor inflammation with itching and a feeling of tightness, but this side effect settled on stopping the cream applications for a day or two and the treatment could then be safely resumed. These trials make it clear that people whose skin has already been severely damaged by the sun are likely to derive much less benefit from tretinoin treatment than people who have had less exposure to solar radiation. Tretinoin, under the trade name of Accutane, is also widely used in the treatment of the adolescent skin disease acne, in which it is highly effective. It was introduced in 1982 and has been used by over a million people.

Risks from tretinoin

The manufacturers repeatedly warned that this drug was capable of producing birth defects or even the death of the fetus, and stated that it should not be taken by women during pregnancy. Even so, a number of cases of congenital malformation were reported in fetuses born to women using the drug. There was no positive way of knowing whether these were due to the tretinoin. Congenital malformations and spontaneous abortions also occur in women who were not taking or using tretinoin. Reports in the popular press of very large numbers of cases of malformations were almost certainly exaggerated. A study reported in the *Lancet* in May 1993 showed that the number of major fetal abnormalities occurring in the case of pregnant women using tretinoin preparations on the skin was the same as the number in the case of women not using the drug.

Malignant melanoma

In the last 40 years or so there has been a dramatic increase in the number of cases of the skin tumour malignant melanoma. There is now some evidence that antioxidant treatment with tretinoin can reduce this risk. Trials have suggested that the drug can normalize the early changes in the pigment cells (the melanocytes) that can progress to melanoma. They also suggest that tretinoin can retard the growth of melanomas and reduce their tendency to spread. This research is still in an early stage.

Prevention is better than cure. Sunbathing is a bad habit; if you must indulge, protect your skin with an effective sunscreen preparation.

Free radicals and stroke

Stroke is the devastating consequence of a loss of the blood supply to a part of the brain. Threatened strokes are called transient ischaemic attacks (TIAs). These are mini-strokes lasting for less than 24 hours and then, apparently, reversing. Any of the manifestations of a full stroke may occur and TIAs are clear indications of risk.

The *Lancet* for 27 June 1992 carried a paper from the Department of Neurology at Brussels University. This described a study of 80 people who were showing definite signs of being at severe risk of developing a stroke. In this study, patients with TIAs lasting for more than three hours were matched against similar people who had never had TIAs, and the outcome assessed after 21 days. Blood levels of vitamin E were assessed but no significant difference was found between those with below or above average concentrations of this vitamin. It was found, however, that people with more than average vitamin A in their blood were significantly more likely to make a complete recovery than those with average amounts or less. The trial indicated that those people whose symptoms and signs persisted for more than 24 hours, and whose blood levels of vitamin A were higher than average, suffered less neurological damage than did those with low blood concentrations of the vitamin.

Destruction of nerve cells in stroke and pre-stroke conditions is known to be partly due to oxidative damage by free radicals. The body does what it can to protect against these free radicals, but its capacity to do so is limited. We know that vitamin E is highly effective as a free radical mop in the presence of high concentrations of oxygen. But stroke and TIAs occur because blood is not getting through to carry oxygen to the nerve cells. This may be why vitamin E seems ineffective in this case. Vitamin A, on the other hand, is a powerful antioxidant in conditions of low oxygen concentrations, and this may account for its apparent value in these cases. It is, of course, possible, that it also has valuable effects other than simply free radical trapping.

It would seem from this study that each antioxidant has its optimum range of action, and that several different antioxidants are needed to ensure comprehensive cover. But taking antioxidant vitamins is not an effective substitute for a healthy lifestyle that minimizes the risk factors for stroke – smoking, overweight, a diet high in saturated fats, low vegetable and fruit intake, and lack of exercise.

Medical interest in free radicals

Reports of free radical research continue to appear with increasing regularity in the medical press. Other conditions in which free radicals have been implicated or suspected of being important include:

◆ pressure sores
◆ red blood cell damage
◆ paraquat poisoning
◆ carbon tetrachloride poisoning
◆ ozone damage
◆ skeletal muscle damage
◆ liver cell damage
◆ spinal cord injury
◆ diabetes
◆ (possibly) cancer caused by electromagnetic fields from power lines.

Free radicals have also been found to be active in alcohol toxicity and in bringing about the destructive action of anti-cancer drugs.

Papers on free radicals have appeared in numerous medical and other journals from all over the world. In addition to those already mentioned, they have appeared in the *British Journal of Hospital Medicine, Annals of the Royal College of Surgeons of England, Journal of the American College of Cardiology, Nature, Journal of Biological Chemistry, Cancer Research, American Journal of Clinical Nutrition, Journal of Pharmacology, Biochemical Medicine, American Journal of Epidemiology, Toxicology and Applied Pharmacology, Annals of Clinical Biochemistry, Acta Physiologica Scandinavica, Gastroenterology, International Journal of Epidemiology, Journal of Inorganic Biochemistry* and the journal devoted exclusively to the subject, *Free Radical Biology and Medicine.*

Many researchers in this field and many doctors who have read the literature take supplements of 1000 mg of vitamin C and 400 mg of vitamin E every day. Such dosages appear to be harmless and there is evidence that they can do a lot of good.

chapter seven

Eugeria: the Art of Ageing Well

Eugeria is derived from the Greek *eus*, meaning good, and *geras* meaning old age. So eugeria simply means ageing well. It implies working for the maximum degree of health – using the word in its widest sense – in the latter part of life. The word is introduced in this book in the hope that it will catch on.

There are several components to the art of ageing well, and some of these – notably the maintenance of good physical health – have already been touched on, in chapter 2, in particular. But fundamental to them all is the state of the mind – attitude, outlook, motivation and, above all, determination to live fully and to resist being caught in the stereotypes of the 'age trap'. Nature helps us here: it is the almost universal experience that, internally, we hardly age at all. The image we carry of ourselves, unthinkingly, is that of the person we were years before. Life may have battered us a bit and we all acknowledge that in some unimportant respects we have deteriorated slightly but, in the essentials, we simply go along with the assumption that we are still young.

Typical of this is the experience of the English dramatist and novelist J. B. Priestley (1894–1984) who, like most highly productive people, had no time for ageing. When he was 79 and had just published his 99th work, someone asked him what it was like to be old. This is what he replied: 'It is as though while walking down Shaftesbury Avenue as a fairly young man, I was suddenly kidnapped, rushed into a theatre and made to don the gray hair, the wrinkles and the other attributes of age, then wheeled on stage. Behind the appearance of age I am the same person, with the same thoughts, as when I was younger.'

Many teenagers and young adults would be surprised to gain a sudden insight into the mental attitudes of most people of 60 or 70. They would find that these oldies still have youthful aspirations, the same hopes and fears, the same ambitions as half a century ago. To think of much younger people as our contemporaries is right and proper; it is entirely in order to be shocked when a younger person refers to you as as 'that old woman' or 'that old man'.

The ageist stereotype

People who choose, for whatever reason, to behave as they think old people should behave; people who give up trying because they have reached some statutory age such as 65; those who think that it is inappropriate, at such an age, to be looking forward to some new challenge and activity in life – are going against nature, and will suffer for it. It is also unnatural to be gratified when people say. 'Isn't he wonderful?' or 'She really is marvellous!' when what they really mean is, 'Considering he has one foot in the grave, it's rather remarkable that he can still manage to totter to the Post Office for his OAP.'

To combat the stereotype, we must recognize it and know all about it. According to the image, old people are rigid in their attitudes and beliefs and incapable of forming new opinions. They are prejudiced, tied to views formed years ago, and totally preoccupied with their own petty affairs. Everything about them is slow – their movements, thoughts and understanding. They are cantankerous and irritable and yet, because they are feeble, they can do nothing about the causes of their irritability. Many younger people reading this description are likely to agree with it and, up to a point, they have reason to believe it: there are old people like that, plenty of them.

But the important point is that there are also just as many young people like that. Perhaps younger people prefer to think that these are features of old age. There is in many a deep prejudice against the elderly, based on a fear of ageing, and this is reflected in derogatory attitudes toward the old.

Lasting personality traits

Old people do not have a monopoly on rigidity of attitude, prejudice, slowness to change, irritability and incapacity. These are not characteristics of age; they are characteristics of a certain type of personality; such people show these features from early adult life or sometimes even from adolescence. Naturally, they nearly always preserve these characteristics into old age. But when these features are observed in an old person, the fact that they may have been lifelong features is ignored and they are simply attributed to old age.

Old age, of course, commonly involves some degree of slowing down. It also involves the cumulative effect of illness and injury and a natural loss of physical power. But old age also involves wisdom derived from experience, an absence of impulsive and often dangerous behaviour and a degree of caution that has resulted from the knowledge of the ill effects that have, in the past, resulted from incaution.

One important feature of the stereotype is the conviction that after the age of 50 it is all downhill. Some people, of course, are old at 30 but for most the peak is taken to be 50. One of the purposes of this book is to show that this is nonsense. The appendix (see pp. 237–66) contains plenty of examples of the achievements of people of far greater age than this – achievements well beyond the scope of many people in their prime. Eugeric people also look on 50 as an important point, but for quite a different reason: 50 is the age at which a person may be supposed to have reached a reasonable degree of maturity. By that age, the learning process, in the widest sense – the sense of learning about life – has covered the elementary steps. The person concerned may now consider himself or herself fit to start applying this learning to good effect.

Another aspect of the ageing stereotype is that most old people are so incapable of looking after themselves that they have to be locked up in institutions or 'homes'. This, too, is nonsense. At any one time, close to 95 per cent of all people aged 65 or over are living independent lives in the community. Most of these people are, for a variety of reasons, fiercely determined to continue to do so, and it is only physical or mental health that may cause some of them, at some stage, to lose their independence.

Old people are also often looked on as unproductive, costly and a drain on the economy. This may be true of some, and the Welfare State may have something to do with this. But many who have now ceased to be able to earn their own livelihood have, throughout a long working life, paid for their support in old age through large pension payments. Millions more have sought and achieved financial independence in their old age by working hard and by thrift and investment. Today, more than ever, an enormous amount of private money is in the hands of the elderly. By their investments and interest-bearing savings, these people are contributors to rather than takers from the economy. Younger people who choose to express this particular pejorative view of the aged ought to bear these facts in mind and to remember that they too, if they are lucky, will reach old age and may live to smile tolerantly at the injustice of such unthinking criticisms.

Familiarity with the ageist stereotype may help people of all ages to avoid it. But it is most dangerous of all in the elderly because of its damaging effect on their incentives.

Motivation

Motivation – the desire to do things and to arouse and sustain interest or drive – is everything. After the age of 50 there is, in many people, a tendency to lose motivation. It is not the power to act that is weakened but the desire to act. The maintenance of a youthful outlook throughout life is not particularly easy, but it is essential, for another of the stereotypes of ageing – perhaps the most insidious – is that it is normal to lose the characteristics of youthfulness, such things as optimism, curiosity, the determination to learn, kindness, belief in moral values and belief in reason. There are some grounds for the perpetuation of this stereotype. Many people have found optimism misplaced; many are too preoccupied to investigate new fields of knowledge and hence stimulate new curiosities; many have become soured by bitter experience of the conduct of others and have lost their innate tendency to kindness; many, observing the apparent flourishing of the unrighteous, have concluded that ethical conduct doesn't pay; many have just found the whole business of living so difficult and fraught with pain that they have given up trying to reason it out.

This stereotype can lead to a dangerous downward sequence of motivation that starts with 'Why should I keep trying?', then proceeds to 'Why trouble to go out into the world? It's boring', then 'Why bother to leave my room?', then 'Why not just stay in bed?', then 'What's the point of living?' And finally, 'Why not just do away with myself?'

The maintenance of motivation ties in closely with objectives and interests. We must all have objectives if we are to live, and we must be careful to avoid, if possible, factors that undermine or destroy motivation. It is hard to maintain motivation, objectives and interests if we are solitary and we should try to cultivate and nourish relationships. All kinds of relationships are valuable but special, one-to-one relationships – whether of marriage, cohabitation or close friendship – are the most important of all. For most people, only one such full relationship is possible. There are difficulties in achieving high quality in such relationships, but this is well worth striving for. Older people, with the benefit of experience of earlier mistakes, are better placed to succeed here than the young who often form such relationships on the basis of sexual attraction and immature values which are later seen to have little or no relevance to the realities of life. This is how biology ensures the continuation of the species, but it does not necessarily lead to long-term fulfilling relationships.

Promoting good relationships

To promote and sustain mature relationships, objectives should be acknowledged and tacitly approved by partners. Because we are all interested in our own objectives, we speak about them. Each partner should recognize that the objectives of the other are of central importance to him or her and that repeated reference to them is inevitable. This may sometimes be boring if ruling passions are not shared, but failure to acknowledge the other's interests can be damaging both to motivation and to the relationship. Reciprocity is vital. Listening intelligently is important. Statements should not be casually dismissed, however pointless they may at first seem. So far as honesty allows, always look for merit in the other's statements. Never take offence and avoid attributing blame. Censoriousness is a great destroyer of relationships (see below).

Ill health can seriously interfere with our chances of success, because suffering and the inability to live life to the full obviously add to the difficulties. Many sufferers are sustained by admirable courage and patience and partners cannot fail to admire such qualities in each other and to respect determination to make the best of things. Suffering can be ennobling and there are many whose characters have been refined by it; but it is often true that suffering is more damaging than improving to character and, as a result, to the quality of relationships. It may be that we cannot truly understand the pain, distress and shock of the suffering of others unless we, ourselves, have experienced similar trauma. In this sense, suffering can strengthen us as whole individuals.

The ability to relate well to each other also calls for acceptably healthy functioning of the thoughts, emotions and will. There is no real borderline between the normal and the abnormal in any of these three divisions. It is all a matter of degree. We are all, from time to time, seriously mistaken in our thinking, but we do not all believe that the neighbours are plotting against us; we are all a bit low sometimes, but few of us reach suicidal depression; we all occasionally lack energy and drive, but few reach the stage of mute, stuporous withdrawal of all interest characteristic of the catatonic schizophrenic. Some degree of anxiety, the odd phobia, occasional mild depression, a touch of hysteria, a slight feeling of persecution, a few delusions are all features of normal mental life: only when exaggerated are they signs of mental illness.

Achieving good relationships is easier for some people than for others. We start with different degrees of handicap. Some are born with a hereditary disadvantage or suffer early and damaging environmental influences. Since these are outside our control we can, if we wish, blame them for our present difficulties. On the other hand, we can be more positive and determine to make the best of the material we have to work with. In spite of the pervasive effect of these early influences we can, at any age, do a good deal to improve the state of our psycho-social health.

Psychological normality

Mature psychological normality involves most of the components of mental and social health and also points to the direction in which we should be striving. The capacity for, and constant engagement in, clear thinking; a controlled but deep emotional life; and an effective determination to act are the ideal general characteristics of the mature, healthy personality.

Fully mature, psychologically healthy people show, to varying degrees, certain qualities:

- in all ordinary matters, they are self-sufficient and can manage their own affairs effectively
- they are reliable and trustworthy and always strive to meet obligations in full
- they avoid getting into debt
- they have a realistically sceptical attitude to assertions and claims, especially those of advertisers or others who have something to gain from them
- they have a social conscience and are willing to play a part in ventures requiring cooperative activity
- in their work they prefer to make a contribution to society rather than to be concerned solely with their own advantage
- work is important to them and they take satisfaction in it
- they have a reasonably accurate perception of themselves and neither over-estimate nor under-estimate their own abilities
- they accept the world as it is and try to make the best of it
- their personalities contain no obvious contradictions
- they are achievers
- they tend to look outward rather than inward
- they show respect for others and are able to relate easily to them
- they always try to see things from the other person's point of view.

Assuming they are not too inhumanly perfect, they are respected and liked by all to whom they relate. Such paragons are, of course, rare and very few of us score high on all of these characteristics. But many, if not most, of these qualities may with effort be cultivated. It is possible at any age to strive after this kind of maturity. But only those who believe that trying is necessary or is worth the trouble, are likely to make the effort.

Imaginary or feigned illness

Malingering is not a particular feature of old age, but it can be more damaging to the elderly than to younger people, so it is worth looking at. A fair proportion of what is commonly called 'neurotic illness' is consciously calculated to manipulate others and achieve some advantage. Many people with this trait are deeply in need of reassurance and may crave affection, but are incapable of expressing the need except in the ineffectual manner they have chosen. Some are chronically afraid but unable directly to face their fears or to recognize or analyse their causes.

But it is questionable whether most 'hypochondriacs' can be acquitted of the responsibility for their state. One feature common to many people with this disorder is that they have become much more interested in themselves and their problems than in the outside world. This is harmful to the happiness of those who have to relate to them and to come to terms with their unremitting self-absorption. The emotional needs of partners are often neglected.

Any activity which helps to turn the attention outward is helpful but, at the same time, attempts should be made to understand the possible significance of complaints which seem to be of central interest. This is especially true of persistent physical complaints, which seem to be without foundation, and an attempt should always be made to discover the origins of such fears. Did a parent or close relative die of cancer? Is there, perhaps, a concealed symptom which is causing secret worry? Neurotic people are as liable to develop organic disease as anyone else and many people who have been branded as neurotics have been found, on closer investigation, to have an organic disease.

A mild tendency to be unjustifiably convinced of illness (hypochondriasis) is one thing. Real neurotic illness is quite another. It would be naïve to suppose that severe neurosis can be cured by even the most sympathetic and supportive help. The condition is a fundamental personality defect and can be considered a failure to develop the normal degree of fortitude and resistance to the daily stresses of life. True neurotics require a great deal of support and protection, and quite exceptional patience and understanding is required of those who live with them.

Censoriousness and self preoccupation

A common feature of psycho-social disorder is the habit of criticism and fault-finding. The springs of this trend are obvious – each censorious comment contains the implicit statement 'Of course, I'm not like that!' and this brings gratification. But the habit is liable to be seriously damaging to personal relationships and has been the cause of an immense amount of disruption of friendship and marriage. Blaming others is undoubtedly comforting, but it is a comfort purchased at a heavy price, a transaction to be carefully avoided. Silence, when criticism is obvious, can earn respect, especially from the discriminating. Criticism of an absent third person is unendearing, for it invites the hearer to participate whether he or she agrees or not. Breaking the habit of gratuitous censoriousness is a major step in the pursuit of happiness.

This is not to imply that adverse criticism is never justified. The bad behaviour of those close to us may have to be criticized. But we should first be careful to recognize our own relevant faults and should always try to see things from the other person's point of view before commenting. And criticism, if applied, must always be strictly relevant, accurate and specific. Too often, our response to the behaviour of others is merely one of general condemnation, which only has the effect of provoking aggression.

Be as honest as you can with yourself and with others, especially in any close relationship. This is not always easy. Love and affection can vary with the changing circumstances of a relationship and open discussion is necessary. Honesty and the expression of affection can turn dislike into love. Never feign affection. Some people do so simply out of kindness and a disinclination to hurt feelings; some find it impossible to reject the advances of others, and allow themselves to be drawn into a false position. Perhaps the worst reason for feigning affection is to gain sexual access. This kind of dishonesty is mutually destructive. Good relationships are among the greatest sources of happiness and should be cherished as precious.

Cheerfulness

Strive to be cheerful. This may not always be easy, but it is important, for the morose old person is universally disliked. However great your justification for churlishness and ill temper, however badly you think life has treated you, you will only do yourself harm if you give way to the temptation. Whether a general cheerfulness of outlook can be easily acquired is not obvious, but sustained ill humour certainly can.

When the characteristics of those who live long active lives are studied, it is found that a high proportion of them have managed to maintain a cheerful disposition. This is associated with sustained optimism, a sense of humour and enjoyment of life. It would be ridiculous to suggest that all these people have suffered no hardship, have led trouble-free lives and have never had occasion for resentment or unhappiness. The critical point is how they react to them. They have learned to take the rough with the smooth and, in Kipling's words '. . . meet with Triumph and Disaster and treat these two impostors just the same.'

Cheerfulness does not imply having a constant inane grin on your face. It means reacting to others in a positive, friendly way and with optimistic rather than pessimistic responses. If you can introduce an occasional flash of humour, so much the better, but don't force it or work it up in advance. Cheerfulness is a habit of mind; a determination to resist the temptation to reflect in your personality all the mountain of painful experience you and every other older person has suffered. Mature people don't need to call for sympathy by bemoaning their fate.

Leisure and old age

People in boring, tiring or otherwise unpleasant occupations often long for retirement and indulge in dreams of leisure. 'I'm never going to do another day's work in my life. I'm going to lie on a beach and bask in the sun, drinking

beer (or cocktails) and watching the pretty girls (or bronzed young men) . . .'
Such people imagine that as soon the great day dawns, they will be happy for
the rest of their lives. This is nonsense and it is time that permanent leisure was
recognized for what it is – an unmitigated disaster.

Leisure should imply a short break from work – a brief, refreshing change
after which you return to your occupation with renewed vigour. So the phrase
'permanent leisure' – which may mean 20 years of doing nothing, from the age
of 65 onward – is a contradiction in terms.

Someone has described retirement as 'compulsory unemployment' but to
treat it as such is seldom necessary. Retirement should be regarded as a change
of working direction, perhaps as a move to more congenial employment,
selected by yourself rather than imposed by economic necessity. Once this view
is accepted and acted on, leisure will immediately reacquire its full status and
value as a break from work.

Using leisure well

Some time spent in wholly passive relaxation – lying on the beach and looking
at girls or boys – is, of course, pleasant and sometimes necessary. But the
natural counterpoise to hard work should be an engrossing leisure activity that
affords refreshment and contrast and provides, if possible, as real a challenge as
employment. And the day should be so filled that you look forward with
pleasure to sleep – the refreshing, deep sleep of the justifiably tired – in which
mind and body are restored.

Well-motivated people adopt the same attitude to leisure activities as to their
occupation and work equally hard at both. Non-participatory purveyed
'entertainment', such as uncritical TV viewing, is a poor substitute for the
lively and refreshing leisure use of mind or body. Ideally, spend comparatively
little time watching TV and make your viewing highly selective. Reading is more
satisfying since it is a participatory, even creative, activity.

Making a virtue of necessity

The most positive way to view the final years of life is how best to make a virtue
of necessity. The aim must be to live life to the full and achieve more than you
expected before you became aware that you had reached old age. This may
seem paradoxical but the fact is that the great majority of healthy people waste
much of their lives and never realize a fraction of their potential.

The change of lifestyle, the more sedentary and restricted life imposed by old
age may, if you are sufficiently determined, concentrate your attention and
unrealized abilities into new and more productive channels, and the result may
be surprising. The worst thing to do is to allow the disadvantages of old age to
make you aggrieved. Turn and look outward, cultivate appropriate new and

absorbing interests and drive them to the limit. You must learn to work harder than ever and get absorbed in something new, creative and fascinating. Something like running an accountancy business; managing an agency; taking a degree; writing new computer software; engaging in Internet communication with the rest of the world; working to qualify for an amateur radio licence or getting into CB radio; taking up oil, watercolour or acrylic painting; mosaic creation; stained glass window construction; writing biographies, fiction, specialized non-fiction, magazine articles.

Perhaps none of these things is appealing. Or perhaps you have done nothing about your hankering to be a writer or a painter or computer programmer because of lack of spare time. It makes no difference. The reasons for taking up an absorbing new occupation now are too serious to be brushed casually aside because of mere disinclination or apparent lack of interest. Interest is priceless and it will come only with the deliberate intent to engage in new activity, growing knowledge and experience. Interest can quickly grow to fascination. Interest displaces misery, self-preoccupation, boredom, depression. Contentment is a matter of filling the mind with a concern that constantly prompts curiosity.

You are going to have a great deal of free time, and that can be a curse or a blessing depending on whether or not you have something to do with it. Fill your mind with interests so that there are simply not enough hours in the day.

In addition to the sudden access of leisure time, a decrease in mobility – perhaps by having to give up driving or because of a move to a smaller house – may make it more difficult to keep up with many old friends. You may have to find new friends and the way to do this is to establish real interests and then proceed to seek out those who share them. Some of the activities mentioned have the means of doing this built in. The development of cheap computer technology has brought communication possibilities of unprecedented scope within reach, allowing extension of personal range of contact. Writing, too, both private and public, has been made very much easier. Again, people who attend evening or day adult education classes have a common interest. In most areas, classes are available in an extremely wide range of subjects.

Activity in old age does not, of course, have to be sedentary. People who have been accustomed to sporting activities should do everything they can to keep them up, possibly with an appropriate change of activity. There are plenty of examples of sustained participation in games such as golf and tennis well into old age; octogenarian marathon runners are by no means unknown. There are many inspiring examples of what can be done to maintain enough fitness in old age to engage in sport. Ask about classes and courses geared to the over-50s at your local leisure centre. Even participation as a spectator in sports once indulged in personally can provide a source of interest. If your family lives close, consider taking your grandchildren along to spectator sports with you. Or get involved with a weekend league – few ever have enough helpers.

There is, of course, a place for unchallenging games and passive entertainment. But it is a mistake for mentally active people to think that time can be satisfactorily filled by such means. Time is not something to be disposed of. Choose instead games, such as chess or bridge, which challenge your mental resources to the limit. These may be, or may become, an absorbing part-time activity. (Some schools have chess clubs and actively invite the participation of parents, grandparents and others from the local community.)

Finding new interests

Motivation for activity is greatly helped if that activity is also a source of income. Those who have developed an interest that can be pursued right to the end of life and which also earns money on which they are not absolutely dependent are very fortunate. There are many interests of this kind that can be followed indefinitely, and some are highly creative, gratifying and rewarding.

But for many people, the end of the formal professional career means that the occupation that has sustained and interested them for many years must now be abandoned. It is extremely important in such a case to find a substitute interest. Ideally, major interests – those that may reasonably be expected to last for the rest of a person's life – should be formed prior to the end of gainful employment. Some experimentation may be required and this may take time. False avenues may have to be explored and it may be weeks or months before they are recognized as such.

A great many people feel that they would like to write a book, and the old saying that everyone has at least one book in him or her is probably true. Old age is certainly the right time to do this and there can be few more absorbing or rewarding pursuits. Elderly people have at least one substantial resource in this context: a unique and detailed insight into the history and sociology of a period of at least half a century. There is a great deal of interest in recent history and older people are the ideal persons to write it.

Many, contemplating the daunting prospect of getting 80,000 words down on paper simply give up: 'I wouldn't know where to start or what to put'. Very few realize that the actual process of creative writing is, for the most part, self-perpetuating. The act of putting something down on paper or a word processor screen, actually stimulates the unconscious mind into bringing up something else relevant to what has been written. This is how the mind works and the process can be cultivated so that there need never be any shortage of raw material. The secret is to 'get something down' without too much concern initially about quality, content, grammar or spelling.

Be warned, however: the exploration of the unconscious mind can bring up some surprising material. You may find out things about yourself that you had never suspected. It is damaging to creativity to inhibit the flow for reasons of prudery, embarrassment or even regard for the feelings of others. Remember that you will not use everything that comes to mind – you are in for a massive editing job before you can even consider that your book is beginning to take shape.

Writing, especially when you have decided on a major aim such as the production of a book, can become completely engrossing. Whether you are working on a novel or a piece of non-fiction, you will find that once the book is under way, it will live with you always, providing you with a succession of intriguing problems to solve and a perpetual source of interest. Writing a work of fiction is especially engrossing and you may well find that your characters become more real to you than anyone you know.

Computers in life enhancement

The personal computer can be used to enhance and expand communication with friends and others. E-mail communication with anyone in any part of the world is quicker than sending letters by post and much cheaper. Regardless of the location of your correspondents each communication costs no more than a local telephone call. You can save both your outgoing and incoming letters for future reference.

Surfing the Internet can waste a lot of time, but once you know where to look and how to find the kind of subjects that interest you, the possibilities are limitless. There are Web pages for every conceivable subject and you can learn a great deal so long as you are reasonably sceptical about the authority of what you are reading. Contact an on-line provider, if you think this might interest you.

You don't need a technical background to make full use of computers. Think of them as boxes in which something useful happens when you touch certain keys. By doing this you can produce text, numbers, questions, instructions and so on. These will appear on the screen and can be edited and then printed. Pressing a few keys can cause something to happen on the other side of the world. Pressing the wrong keys may cause problems but cannot damage the computer hardware.

Word processing

A word processor is easier to use than a typewriter, especially for older or disabled people, because no force is required on the keyboard, just a gentle downward pressure. With a word processor, nearly all the physical difficulties of typing are eliminated.

Everything typed on the keyboard appears first on a screen and the effect of any additions, deletions or alterations is immediately visible there. The text moves down automatically at the end of each line with no action required by the user; margins can be set from the keyboard; type can be justified or not; mistakes are corrected on the screen either by overtyping or by deleting and inserting new letters or words; and the most detailed editing can be done at the touch of a few keys. Words, sentences, paragraphs, or even pages of type can be shifted around until everything is exactly right. Only then need the printing be done, by a simple keyboard command. Because corrections are so easy, bold working is encouraged and good speeds can soon be achieved.

At any time, the work can be saved to be added to or printed later. A whole book can be stored on a single floppy disk, which can be kept for years for future reference or revision. Any word processing personal computer can be connected to a printer that will produce typescript to rival that of commercial printing.

Any PC is also capable of 'desk-top publishing' by means of which it is now feasible to produce complete books – to carry out all the functions of the writer, illustrator, editor, proofreader, designer – indeed the whole writing and publishing function, except for distribution, in the privacy of home. With good ideas, writing, artistic and design ability, anybody can in theory produce a money-making magazine.

For the visually impaired

If you, or someone you know, is visually impaired, you should be aware that most word-processing programs on the market can increase the type size of what you see on the screen enormously (up to perhaps three or four characters across an average screen). For anyone who has at least some vision, this is certainly worth considering, as it allows the affected person to continue such activities as letter writing and basic accounts, as well as creative writing.

For those who have no vision at all, a voice-activated program – which tells you what you have typed – may be the answer.

Obviously to use either of these effectively it is an advantage – but by no means essential – to be able to touch type. Again, simple programs to help you learn this skill are available.

Computer graphics

Personal computers allow you to engage in a wide range of graphics activities, from the production of original 'paintings' on the computer to the most subtle or radical amendment and adjustment of existing images. Modern graphics software works to a high degree of resolution with an almost infinite range of colours, and offers the artistically inclined astonishing control and scope for imagination. It allows complex manipulation of shapes and areas, with controlled distortion and rotation into any plane, automatic colouring, and enlargement or reduction.

A whole new, and perhaps highly paid, career may be opened up to people with the appropriate artistic and design abilities. These are the talents you need, not technical know-how.

The on-line office

A growing number of firms – accountancy, sales, estate agencies, public relations, advertising, publishing – have realized that it is extremely cost effective for as many employees as possible to work in their own homes. Using computer communications, the functional link with employees can be almost as complete as if they were physically present in the office. If your business life has been cut short by 'retirement', perhaps against your will, this could be an avenue for you to investigate.

There is no need to be put off by the seemingly alarming technology involved. It is not necessary to be an electronic engineer to use a TV set or a video tape recorder. Operating a computer terminal is easier than setting up a video recorder to capture a film next week, and has been mastered by many thousands of people. It is simply a matter of practice. What really counts is business experience, judgement and capacity for hard work.

Other computer applications

The literature on computer applications is enormous if you have enough interest. Those with business and accounting skills are probably already familiar with computer applications, but can now investigate applying their experience more effectively by means of modern accounting software. Suites of programs covering all aspects of business management and offering ways of improving efficiency, cash flow and profitability are now available very cheaply from scores of different software houses, for all personal computers.

An important development is the growth of database management systems – programs which enable the user, after accumulating data, to access items in almost any way desired. A number of major programs of this type, designed to allow custom building of a system for special requirements, have been produced.

Safety with VDUs

Computers can be life enhancing, but a few safety precautions are necessary for maximum benefit.

◆ The eyes can easily become tired if you focus at the same distance for long periods of time. Every 10 minutes or so take a break from the screen, and look somewhere else for a minute or so. Check that your screen is set at a suitable brightness level.

◆ Sitting at a computer can strain your lower back and cause you to hunch your shoulders. Make sure your chair gives adequate support to your lower back and that you can sit with both feet flat on the floor. Your knees and elbows should be bent at 90°.

◆ Make sure your hands are flat and relaxed when you type. Hours spent at a computer with poor wrist posture can lead to repetitive strain injury, characterized by arthritic-type pain in the fingers, hands and arms.

◆ Take a 10-minute break at least once an hour to rest your eyes and body.

Spreadsheets, report generators, statistics programs, stock market programs, money managers, general ledgers, tax accounting programs, management system, desk organizers, decision-makers, computer-aided design systems, educational programs of all kinds, programming languages for visual programming . . . the list is endless and the variety in each category remarkable. Begin carefully and start by checking exactly what an apparently suitable piece of software will do; confirm that it is exactly what you need. Having settled on the software, think about which computer to buy, comparing prices and ensuring that the software will run on the machine you are considering.

Computer applications can be creative and, since computers can do so much for older people, it is a pity that so many of them find computers unattractive. But a PC can, to a remarkable extent, compensate for failing human memory, for example. There have even been cases in which people with Alzheimer's disease have been able, for a time, to maintain a relatively normal standard of performance by means of a PC and a printed card containing an aide memoire to remind them which keys to press to bring up any particular set of mementos.

Artistic pursuits

Many people gain enormous satisfaction from artistic pursuits such as sketching, watercolour, oil and acrylic painting, tile making, crockery decoration, tapestry, fine sewing and embroidery, knitting and weaving.

Various organizations exist to encourage older people, and those with physical handicaps to take up or continue with creative artistic pursuits.

Age-related muscle weakness can be a problem but should not be a bar, and various mechanical supports are available that can be attached to work tables, benches and wheelchairs. There is a range of adjustable clamps, grips, vices and mobile arm supports, which can be attached to almost anything. These give the necessary positioning for the use of weak arms and hands, while appropriately locating the boards or canvas for painting or sketching, or frames for embroidery. Some systems also includes scissors attachments, which can be operated by hand or foot, glass holders, mirrors, adjustable magnifying glasses and lecterns. Writers who feel happier with the traditional pen or pencil rather than with a word processor can also benefit from these systems.

Gardening

Immensely popular, gardening is a great source of satisfaction to older people and to the disabled. Whether or not you can sustain your former level of activity depends on your state of health and bodily strength but, at worst, and with the assistance of advice and support from one of the organizations concerned with gardening for the disabled, it should be possible to maintain some interest and pleasure. Perhaps the size of the garden or allotment will have to be limited or interests changed to the cultivation of more exotic conservatory or greenhouse flora. You may even have to limit your ambitions to large windowboxes or simply indoor plants, but it is unlikely that you will have to give up the interest altogether.

Gardening on a reasonably large scale may be ambitious but is certainly better than unnecessary limitation. Heavy work may seem impossible but, again, technology can assist. This is not because of the existence of any special gardening aids for the disabled, but simply because gardening has become such big business that many tools and gadgets have been developed to make the work easier for ordinary, able-bodied people. Working from a wheelchair calls for tools to extend the reach. Items intended for one job can, with imagination, be adapted for another. Fruit pickers and long tongs can considerably extend the range of activities. These are available in lengths from 1.2 to 4 m (4 to 10ft) and some can be operated by one hand.

There are branch cutters with considerable leverage and a ratchet action which require remarkably little strength; various grabbers and long-handled weeders, capable of one-handed use, some designed to grip and pull out the most stubborn weeds; wheelrakes which do not have to be lifted in use; ingenious hoes which can perform a variety of operations very easily; light-weight lawn shears with long handles for edging and general grass cutting; lightweight wheelbarrows; electric trimmers and hedge cutters, vacuum leaf collectors and many other useful gadgets. A visit to a large garden centre and a study of the garden tool section should pay dividends.

People confined to a wheelchair might consider a garden in raised pots or complete raised beds. The latter are available in reinforced concrete, galvanized steel or fibreglass and come in a wide range of sizes, some with preserved timber exteriors. Seating can be arranged around these raised beds. A herb garden is another of the many possibilities.

Getting help

For many people, asking others for help is anathema. But there are occasions when help can be the difference between allowing you to pursue a hobby and not. This is especially true with gardening. If asking a more able-bodied friend or family member to do heavy digging for you a couple of times a year means that you can continue gardening, it is worth doing so. If you have no one to ask, consider advertising for someone and pay him or her. Many frustrated gardeners have far smaller plots than they would wish and relish the chance to help with something bigger.

chapter eight

Philosophy and Ageing

Philosophy is not the prerogative of professional philosophers; countless ordinary people have found that awareness of advancing age concentrates the mind on serious questions. Those who have put down their thoughts in writing, however, have mostly been people of note.

The choice is wide and it would be easy to make points by biased selection but the aim here is to represent a reasonable cross-section of opinion, expressed by the most notable thinkers of the past, on the subject of ageing. Not all are professional philosophers; some are writers whose ideas and comments on the subject deserve as much respect as those of the academics.

Probably the most celebrated statement on the subject of old age by a classical writer is that of Marcus Cicero, the great Roman orator. Cicero put down his ideas about old age in the form of the dialogue, *De senectute*. A year after he wrote this work, Cicero was murdered by assassins hired by his political enemy Mark Antony, whom he had annoyed by making speeches against him. Cicero faced death with calm courage, bidding the murderers to strike.

Cicero's lengthy irrelevancies are better suited to a more leisurely age than ours (the following version is highly edited). But in essence he suggests that when people refer to the disadvantages of old age, their argument may be reduced to four headings. It is said that old age stops people from engaging in worldly affairs; that it weakens their bodies; that it deprives them of the enjoyment of sex and the other sensual pleasures; and that it brings them close to death. He proceeds to consider these in turn to see whether they are true.

Incapacity for affairs

Old age, it seems, disqualifies us from taking an active part in the great scenes of public affairs. But in what scenes? If we are thinking of those which require the strength and energy of youth, I must of course admit the charge. But are these the most important? Are there no others? Aren't there some which are peculiarly appropriate to old age, and which, being carried out by the power of the mind, are consistent with a less vigorous state of body? Of course there are. Nothing can be more foolish than to insist that old age necessarily disqualifies a man for the great affairs of the world. One might as well suggest that the pilot is totally useless and uninvolved in the business of the ship, because while the rest of the crew are rushing about hoisting sails and swabbing the decks he just sits quietly at the helm and does nothing but steer.

No one suggests that in the great scenes of public administration an old man can play a part which requires the force and energy of youth. The point is that he can, and commonly does, perform a finer and more important function. The momentous affairs of state are not conducted by physical strength and rushing about, but by cool deliberation, prudent counsel and the authoritative influence of men of long experience and high public regard. These qualifications are strengthened, not impaired, by an increase in age. If abilities of this kind were not the peculiar attributes of old age, do you imagine that our wise ancestors would have decided to call the supreme council of the state by the term *Senate* – a word derived, of course, from our word for an old man. The Senate is the Council of Elders.

If you study the history of foreign nations you will find frequent instances of flourishing communities which, after having been practically ruined by the impetuous acts of young and inexperienced statesmen, have been restored to their former glory by the prudent administration of men of more discreet years. Foolhardiness, indeed, is the usual characteristic of youth, as prudence is of old age.

Many critics will suggest that old age impairs the memory. This may be true of memories which were originally feeble, or which have not been kept up to scratch by proper use and exercise. But there are plenty of examples to the contrary. For my own part, I still perfectly well remember the names, not only of all our principal citizens now living, but of their ancestors also. Incidentally, I never yet heard of any old man whose memory was so weakened by time that he forget where he had buried his treasure. Old people have no difficulty in remembering the things that interest them most, and there are few at that period of life who can't readily call to mind the legal agreements they have entered into, or those with whom they have had any financial transactions. I could cite innumerable instances of strong memory in advanced years from among our celebrated lawyers, pontiffs and philosophers. Take it from me, all the faculties of the mind will preserve their powers in old age, unless they are allowed to become feeble by disuse.

The truth of this can be confirmed not only by the examples I have mentioned from the more active and prominent situations of the world, but also from numerous instances in academic and private lives. Sophocles continued to write tragedies in extreme old age. There is an interesting story here. As he obviously considered his writing more important than domestic matters, he was inclined to neglect his family affairs while concentrating on writing his plays. So, to get control of his affairs, his sons brought a lawsuit against him, suggesting that his mind was impaired, and demanding that he should no longer be allowed to manage his estate. There is a legal principle by which, if a father of a family is ruining his fortunes by neglect or foolish conduct, the magistrate may intervene and take the administration out of his hands. Apparently, when the old playwright appeared in court he asked to be allowed to read a play which he had just finished, the manuscript of which he happened to have in his hand. It was his *Oedipus in Colonos*. His request was granted. After he had finished the recital he appealed to the judges whether they could discover in his performance any indication of mental defect. The result, of course, was that the court unanimously dismissed the complainants' petition.

Did old age weaken the powers of Homer? Did old age interrupt the studies of those most distinguished Greek philosophers, Pythagoras, Democritus, Plato or Xenocrates? Or, to turn to more recent times, did grey hairs prove an obstacle to the philosophic pursuits of Zeno, Cleanthes or that famous stoic who lived in a barrel in Rome, the aged Diogenes? On the contrary; all these eminent people persevered in their studies with undiminished enthusiasm to the last moment of their long lives.

There are those who insist that a long life is to be deplored because it brings us much pain and distress. This really is nonsense. For if long life lets us witness many calamities which an earlier death would have concealed, it may equally afford us the satisfaction of seeing many happy events which we would otherwise have missed. And, of course, disagreeable events affect young people no less than old.

To deal with the next point: why should anyone suppose that old age necessarily lays us open to the neglect, or even the scorn or hate, of the young? Elderly people of good sense are generally fond of associating with younger people and, when they find them amiable, enjoy great satisfaction in winning their affection and esteem. So, too, well-inclined young people think themselves equally fortunate to have the guidance and instruction of men of great experience.

Old age, far from being necessarily a state of idleness and inactivity, is commonly devoted to the kind of occupation which the person favoured in earlier and more vigorous years. But it often happens that elderly people successfully take up some entirely new activity. Thus Solon, in one of his poems written at an advanced age, glories that 'he learned something every day he lived'. And old as I myself am, I have only recently acquired a knowledge of Greek. I worked at this with more than usual enthusiasm because I had long wanted to get to know the writings and characters of those outstanding men whose examples I have admired. Socrates, in his old age, actually learned to play the lyre, an art greatly approved of by the ancients. If I haven't followed the philosopher's musical example – which, indeed, I rather regret – I have, however, spared myself no pains to master the Greek language and literature.

Loss of strength

The next defect attributed to old age is that it impairs our strength. And it must be acknowledged that there is something in this charge. But there is a little more to be said about it than that. For my part, I no more regret the want of the physical power I possessed in my youth than I lamented in my youth that I didn't have the strength of a bull or an elephant. It is sufficient if we exert with spirit, on every proper occasion, the amount of strength which we still possess. Nothing could be more contemptible than the case of the once-famous Milo of Crotona. Milo once showed off by staggering the whole length of the Olympic games stadium carrying an ox across his shoulders. But when he was old, and was watching a set of athletes in combat in the public circus, he broke down and started crying bitterly: 'Alas!' he said, stretching forth his flabby arm, 'These muscles are wasted and powerless.'

What a frivolous old man! It wasn't debility of body but weakness of mind he had reason to lament. It was by the force of mere animal strength, and not by those superior qualities which ennoble man, that Milo became famous. Now tell me which would you prefer to have – this man's strength of body or the mental genius of Pythagoras?

I have to admit, however, that so far as public speaking is concerned, the power of the orator must necessarily, to some extent, become weakened by age. But there is a certain sweetness of utterance which isn't impaired by old age, and although, as you can see, I am now very old, I may venture to suggest that I haven't yet entirely lost it. There is a kind of graceful, calm and composed way of speaking that is well suited to advanced years, and I have often observed an eloquent old man captivate the attention of his audience by the charms of this soft and milder tone of delivery.

But even if age should make a man unfit for any kind of oratory, his powers of mind may still be usefully employed in coaching young men of genius to produce a brisk and manly eloquence. And can there be a greater satisfaction to an old man, than to find himself surrounded by a circle of admiring youths and in this way to win over their esteem and affection? You will not deny, I suppose, that old age has at least enough strength remaining to train the rising generation and instruct them in every duty to which they may later be called. Can there be a more important or a more honourable occupation? There is a considerable satisfaction in passing on useful knowledge of every kind. Happy is the man who employs the talents of his mind to so fine and beneficial a purpose.

But let's not forget that bodily weakness is more often the result of youthful irregularities than the natural and unavoidable consequences of long life. A debauched and intemperate young man will undoubtedly, if he lives, suffer for it in old age. If I may modestly mention myself as an instance of the same kind, I can truthfully state that old age hasn't totally relaxed my nerves and subdued my native vigour. My strength hasn't yet been found to fail me, either in the Senate or any other assembly of the people, when my country or my friends, my clients or my hosts, needed me. I have never tried to avoid work and have always made myself accessible whenever anyone wanted my advice or assistance in his affairs.

In a word, make a good use of your youthful vigour so long as it remains, but don't let it cost you even a sigh when age has deprived you of it. That would be as stupid as for a youth to regret the loss of infancy or for a man to regret the loss of youth. Nature conducts us by a regular and imperceptible progression through the different stages of human life; and to each of these she has allotted its proper and distinguishing characteristic. As foolishness is the attribute of infancy, enthusiasm of youth and gravity of manhood, so declining age has its essential properties, which gradually disclose themselves as the years add up.

By temperance and exercise, a man may retain into his old age much of his former spirit and activity. Certainly time weakens us, but in old age we don't need great vigour. Accordingly, by the laws and institutions of our country, we who are advanced to a certain age are excused from those jobs which require physical strength. Far from being compelled to undertake what is beyond our powers, we are not even called upon to exert our strength to its full extent.

No doubt you will point out that there are plenty of old men so totally worn out and decayed, that they can't do anything. I have to agree. But why are they like this? May not this debility have affected them all their lives? This is a misfortune by no means peculiar to old age, but common to every period of human life. Why should we be surprised then if old age is sometimes troubled by the same infirmities that may afflict the young?

As to those evil effects considered to be the natural features of old age, it must always be our first concern to fight constantly and resolutely against their progress. We must make it our business to combat the infirmities of old age as we would resist the approaches of a disease. We must do all we can to maintain health – taking moderate exercise, and neither eating nor drinking more than is necessary to keep up our strength. Nor is this all: the intellectual faculties must receive the same care as we give the body. For the powers of the mind, like the flame in the lamp, will eventually flicker and go out if not duly exercised by regular use. Both mind and body thrive by a suitable exertion of their powers. But there is a difference: bodily exercise ends in fatigue, whereas the mind is never wearied by its activity. Dotage isn't a feature of every old man, but only of those who have trifled away their frivolous days in idleness and folly.

As I love to see the fire of youth tempered by the gravity of age, so I am equally pleased when I observe the boredom of age enlivened by the vivacity of youth. And whoever has both fire and gravity in his character, while he may certainly bear the marks of years on his body, he will never show the same signs of deterioration in his mind. In my own case, my enthusiasm is now driving me to add a seventh book of history to those I have already written. I am collecting all the ancient records I can find that relate to my subject; finishing a revision of the speeches I made in the several important causes in which I have been engaged; and drawing up some observations concerning all aspects of the law. And to exercise my memory, I practise the advice of the Pythagorean philosophers, by recalling to my mind every night all that I have said, or done, or heard, on the preceding day. These are the employments by which I keep my mental faculties active, and preserve them in due vigour; employments in which I have little reason surely to lament the want of mere bodily strength.

Nor are my occupations wholly sedentary. On the contrary, I not only assist my friends in the courts of judicature, but frequently attend the Senate, where I propose such measures for the consideration of that assembly as I have previously weighed and duly matured in my own thoughts. But even if I were so worn down by age as to be incapable of exerting myself in the manner I have mentioned, yet one satisfaction nevertheless would still remain to me; the satisfaction of meditating on these subjects as I lie on my couch, and of performing in imagination what I can no longer execute in reality.

Thanks, however, to that regular and temperate course of life I have always led, I am still capable of taking an active part in public affairs. I am convinced that anyone who fills up every hour in such labours and pursuits as those I have mentioned, will slide imperceptibly into old age without perceiving its arrival; and his powers, instead of being suddenly and prematurely extinguished, will gradually decline by the gentle and natural effect of increasing age.

Deprivation of sensual pleasure

Let us now take a look at the third article of complaint against old age – that it deprives us of the sensual gratifications. Well, this would be a happy effect indeed, if it delivers us from those snares which allure youth into some of the worst vices to which they can be addicted.

Nature has conferred on humankind no more dangerous present than sensual pleasure. The passions excited by sensuality will brush reason aside, in an unbridled and lawless pursuit of enjoyment. To gratify such desires, men may be tempted to correspond secretly with the enemies of the state, to subvert governments and to turn traitors to their country. There is no sort of crime against the public welfare to which love of sensual pleasures may not directly lead. And as to crimes of a more private nature – rape, adultery and every other shameful moral violation – aren't they committed solely from this single motive?

Reason, on the other hand, is the finest gift which God has bestowed. But nothing is so great an enemy to reason as the pleasures of sexual indulgence. For neither temperance, nor any other fine virtue, count for anything in the minds of people who are carried away by this passion. Imagine a man in the actual enjoyment of sex – the highest pleasure that his animal nature is capable of. Can he then exert any of his rational powers?

If the principles of reason and virtue are not enough to inspire us with contempt for the sensual pleasures, we can at least be grateful to old age for weakening those appetites which it would ill become us to gratify. Seven years after Flamininus became Consul, I had to have him thrown out of the Senate because during his consulship, when he commanded our army in Gaul, this unworthy man was persuaded by his homosexual boyfriend, simply for the purposes of amusement, to murder one of the prisoners. And, of course, because his brother Titus was Censor, he got away with it. But when I succeeded him as Consul, I decided that so wanton and outrageous an act of cruelty and lewdness ought not to be allowed to pass without severe and public censure. Such behaviour reflected dishonour, not only on him, but in some measure too on the high office which he held.

There was a self-styled philosopher at Athens who maintained that the love of pleasure was the leading motive for all human actions. When the ambassador at the court of Pyrrhus related this extraordinary idea to his colleagues they immediately expressed the wish that Pyrrhus and the whole Samnite nation might become converts to this doctrine, as the people who were infected with such unmanly principles could hardly fail to prove an easy conquest to their enemies.

I have gone on a bit about this to show that if old people have lost much of their relish for sensual enjoyments, far from this being a criticism of this period of life, it actually raises its value. If age renders us incapable of taking an equal share in the flowing cups and luxuriant dishes of splendid tables, it secures us too from their immediate unfortunate consequences – painful indigestion, restless nights and disordered reason. Plato justly represents pleasure as the bait by which vice ensnares and captivates her deluded devotees. But although old age guards us from excess, it by no means prevents us from enjoying, in a moderate degree, the convivial gratifications.

If it should be further objected that the pleasures of the senses are less sharp in old age than in youth, my answer is that the wish for them is also weaker. There can be no loss where there is no desire. Sophocles, when he was old, on being asked if he still engaged in sexual intercourse with women replied: 'Heaven forbid! And I'm very glad to have escaped from the tyranny of so compelling a passion.'

To be deprived of enjoyments of this kind may be distressing to those whose desires are still warm; but where the passion is sufficiently subdued, the deprivation is better than the indulgence – if, indeed, one can properly be said to be deprived of a pleasure for which there is no remaining wish. There is more satisfaction in being delivered from the dominion of this passion than there is in its most frenzied gratification.

I admit that in the prime of life the pleasures of the senses can be exquisite and extreme. But I would say two things further: first that these pleasures are in themselves of little value; and second, that although old people can't enjoy them to the utmost, yet they aren't absolutely deprived of them. An old man will usually feel at least as much relish of them as is necessary to satisfy his more subdued desires. But whatever the case, surely the advantages of old age are inestimable if we consider it as delivering us from the tyranny of lust and ambition, from the angry and contentious passions, from every inordinate and irrational desire – if, in a word, it teaches us to retire within ourselves and look for happiness in our own hearts.

To these moral benefits naturally resulting from old age we must add the pleasures of the mind which are to be found in the fields of study and science. I don't know any season of life that is passed more agreeably than the learned leisure of a virtuous old age. Can the gay amusements of the theatre, the splendid luxuries of the table, or the soft blandishments of a mistress compare with the calm delights of the intellectual pleasures – pleasures which, in a well-stocked mind, never fail to improve and gather strength with years? What Solon, therefore, declared – that he learned something in his old age every day he lived – is much to his honour. Indeed, to be continually advancing in the paths of knowledge is one of the most pleasing satisfactions of the human mind.

The crown and glory of grey hairs is, indeed, that kind of authority which thus arises from a respectable old age. But never forget that when I speak of the advantages of old age, I mean only that respectable old age which stands supported on the firm foundation of a well-spent youth. Only he whose former years have been distinguished by an uniform series of laudable and meritorious actions shall taste this sweet fruit of revered age.

But besides those more important advantages of an honourable old age, there is a customary deference and attention which, although it may be thought routine courtesy, is still an honourable mark of general respect. Observances of this kind are strictly practised in our own country, as indeed they likewise are in every other, to the extent that they are civilised. It is said that Lacedaemon is the best place for an old man to live in. And it must be acknowledged that there is no place in the world where age is treated with so much civility and regard. It is reported that when a certain Athenian, far advanced in years, entered the crowded theatre at Athens, not one of his countrymen had the good manners to make room for him. But when he approached that part of the theatre reserved for the Lacedaemonian ambassadors, every one of them rose up and offered him a place among them. Immediately the whole assembly applauded, upon which one of the spectators remarked: 'The Athenians understand politeness much better than they practise it.'

You will tell me, perhaps, that many old people are petulant, morose and even avaricious. But these moral diseases of the mind are the constitutional imperfections of the man in whom they reside, rather than intrinsic features of old age. Indeed, some peevishness of temper may be – I will not say justified – but certainly at least to some extent excused by that suspicion, which old men too often have, that they are generally regarded by the young as objects of scorn and derision. Add to this, that when the bodily constitution is broken and worn out, the mind becomes the more sensitive to every little offence, and is inclined to magnify unintentional slights into real and intended insults.

But this fault-finding and irritable disposition, often found in the elderly, may be much softened and subdued by the practice of good manners and improved by a liberal education. The fact is plainly this: as with wine, so with temper – it isn't every kind that is turned sour by age. There is a certain gravity of deportment extremely becoming in advanced years, of which, as in other virtues, when it preserves its proper bounds, and doesn't degenerate into bad temper, I very much approve. As to avarice, I can't for the life of me conceive for what purpose that particular passion is admitted into an old man's mind. For surely nothing can be more irrational and absurd than to increase our provision for the road, the nearer we come to our journey's end.

The approach of death

It now remains only to consider the fourth and last criticism of that period of life at which I am arrived. Old age, it is alleged, must necessarily be a state of anxiety and disquietude from the near approach of death. That the hour of departure can't possibly be far distant from an old man is true. But how extraordinary that after so many years, anyone should still have to learn that there is nothing in that fact to cause alarm! Look at it this way: death either extinguishes the mind so that we have no further awareness of any kind; or it conveys our awareness to some region where it shall continue to exist for ever. In the first event there can be no cause for fear, so it is to be utterly disregarded; in the second event, the outcome is much to be wished. One or other of those two consequences must necessarily follow death. There is no other possible alternative. What then have I to fear, if after death I shall either not be aware of misery or any other feeling, or shall certainly be happy?

Why should death be deemed an evil peculiarly impending on old age, when daily experience proves that it is common to every other period of human life? It will be replied, perhaps, that youth may at least hope to enjoy many additional years; whereas an old man can't. But isn't it a mark of weakness to rely on precarious contingencies, as the young usually do, and to consider an event as bound to take place, which is, in fact, altogether doubtful and uncertain? But admitting that the young may reasonably indulge this expectation, still the advantage evidently lies on the side of the old – as the latter are already in possession of that length of life which the former can only hope to attain.

'Length of life,' did I say? In my own opinion, no portion of time can justly be deemed long that will necessarily have an end, since the longest, when once it is elapsed, leaves not a trace behind, and nothing valuable remains with us but the conscious satisfaction of having employed it well. Thus, hours and days, months and years glide imperceptibly away – the past never to return, the future impenetrably obscure.

But whatever may prove to be the extent of our present duration, a wise and good man ought to be contented with the allotted measure. He should remember that in life as on the stage, it isn't necessary, in order to be approved, that the actor's part should continue right to the end of the drama. It is enough, in whatever scene he makes his final exit, that he supports the character assigned him with deserved applause. The truth is, a small portion of time is abundantly adequate to the purposes of honour and virtue. But should our years continue to be multiplied, a wise man will no more lament his entrance into old age than the farmer regrets, when the bloom and fragrance of the spring is passed away, that summer or autumn is arrived. Youth is the vernal season of life, and the blossoms it then puts forth are indications of those future fruits which are to be gathered in the succeeding periods. Now the proper fruit to be gathered in the winter of our days is, as I have repeatedly observed, to be able to look back with self-approving satisfaction on the happy and abundant produce of more active years.

Every event agreeable to the course of nature ought to be looked upon as a real good, and surely none can be more natural than for an old man to die. It is true that youth likewise stands exposed to the same risk of death, but death in youth is contrary to nature's evident intentions, and is in direct opposition to her strongest efforts. In the latter instance, the loss of life may be compared to a fire forcibly extinguished by a deluge of water; in the former, to a fire gradually going out from a total consumption of its fuel. Or, to use another example, as fruit before it is ripe can't, without some degree of force, be separated from the stalk, but drops of itself when perfectly mature, so the separation of the soul and body is effected in the young by violence, but is wrought in the old by a mere fullness and completion of years.

This ripeness for death I perceive in myself, with much satisfaction. And I look forward to my death as to a secure haven, where I shall at length find a happy repose from the fatigues of a long voyage. Every stage of human life, except the last, is marked out by certain defined limits; old age alone has no precise and determinate boundary. It may well therefore be tolerated and enjoyed however far it may be extended, provided a man is capable of performing those offices which are suited to this season of life, and preserves at the same time complete indifference as to whether or not it continues.

Old age under these circumstances, and with these sentiments, may be animated with more courage and fortitude than is usually found even in the prime of life. Solon, being asked by the tyrant Pisistratus, what gave him the courage and boldness to oppose him, bravely replied, 'My old age.' Nevertheless, the most desirable manner of yielding up our lives is when nature herself thinks proper to destroy the work of her own hand while our understanding and our other senses still remain unimpaired. An old person should neither be anxious to preserve the small portion of life which remains, nor should wish to resign it without a just cause.

Death is a change which, sooner or later, perhaps even at this very moment, we must inevitably undergo. So how can anyone who lives in perpetual dread of an event with which he is constantly threatened, enjoy undisturbed rest and serenity of mind? The relief with which, in passing through the stages of our present being, we leave behind us the enjoyments peculiar to each, must necessarily, in the close of its last period, render life itself no longer desirable. Infancy and youth, manhood and old age, have each of them their peculiar and appropriated pursuits. But adolescents don't regret the toys of infancy, nor adults lament that they no longer have a taste for the amusements of youth. The season of adulthood has also its suitable objects, that are exchanged for others in old age; and these, too, like all the preceding, become languid and insipid in their turn. Now when this state of absolute satiety is at length arrived, when we have enjoyed the satisfactions peculiar to old age, till we have no longer any relish remaining for them, it is then that death may justly be considered as a mature and seasonable event.

And now, among the different opinions of the philosophers concerning the consequence of our final disintegration, may I venture to declare my own? The nearer death advances towards me, the more clearly I seem to discern its real nature. I am convinced, then, that after my departure, far from having ceased to live, I will enjoy a state that can alone properly be called life. The soul, during its confinement within this prison of the body, is doomed by fate to undergo a severe penance. For its native seat is in heaven; and it is with reluctance that it is forced down from those celestial mansions into these lower regions, where all is foreign and repugnant to its divine nature.

I am convinced of this opinion not only because it conforms to reason but also on the authority of the finest and most distinguished philosophers. Pythagoras and his followers firmly maintained that the human soul is a detached part, or emanation, from the great universal soul of the world. I am further confirmed in my belief of the soul's immortality, by the discourse which Socrates – the wisest of men – held upon this subject just before his death.

When I consider the faculties with which the human mind is endowed – its amazing speed; its wonderful power of remembering past events, and wisdom in discerning the future; and its numberless discoveries in the several arts and sciences – I am convinced that this principle can't possibly be of a mortal nature. And as this unceasing activity of the soul derives its energy from its own intrinsic and essential powers, without receiving it from any foreign or external impulse, it necessarily follows (as it is absurd to suppose the soul would desert itself) that its activity must continue for ever. I might add that the ease and speed with which young people are taught to acquire numerous difficult arts, strongly suggests that the soul possesses a considerable portion of knowledge *before* it enters into the human form; and that what seems to be obtained from teaching is in fact a recollection of its former ideas.

I have never believed that the soul could properly be said to live while it remained in this mortal body, or that it ceased to live when death had dissolved the vital union. I never could believe either that it became void of sense when it escaped from its connection with senseless matter, or that its intellectual powers were not enlarged and improved when it was discharged and refined from all bodily contact. When death has disunited the human frame, we clearly see what becomes of its material parts, as they apparently return to the elements out of which they were originally composed; but the soul continues to remain invisible, both when it is present in the body, and when it departs out of it.

Nothing so nearly resembles death as sleep, and nothing so strongly intimates the divinity of the soul as what passes in the mind upon that occasion. For the intellectual principle in man, during this state of relaxation and freedom from external impressions, frequently looks forward into the future, and discerns events before time has yet brought them forth – a plain indication of what the powers of the soul will hereafter be, when it is delivered from the restraints of its present bondage.

Why is it that those men who have made the greatest advances in true wisdom and genuine philosophy are observed to meet death with the most perfect equanimity, while ignorant and unimproved people generally see its approach with fear and reluctance? Isn't it because the more enlightened the mind is, and the further it extends its view, the more clearly it discerns in the hour of death – what narrow and vulgar souls are too short-sighted to discover – that it is taking its flight into some happier region? For my own part, I feel a most ardent impatience to join the society of my departed friends, whose characters I greatly respected, and whose persons I sincerely loved. Nor is this earnest desire limited to those excellent persons with whom I was formerly connected; I ardently wish also to meet those great men of whose honourable conduct I have heard and read much, or whose virtues I have myself commemorated in some of my writings.

To this glorious assembly I am speedily advancing; and I wouldn't be turned back in my journey, even to be young again. If some divinity proposed to confer on me a new grant of my life, and replace me once more in the cradle, I would without hesitation reject the offer. Having well-nigh finished my race, I have no inclination to return to the starting line. I am far from regretting that I have lived, as I have the satisfaction of believing that my achievements indicate that I haven't lived in vain. But I don't consider this world as a place which nature designed for my permanent abode, and I look upon my departure out of it, not as being driven from my habitation, but as no more than leaving a temporary lodging. These beliefs have enabled me to bear up under a load of years with ease and complacency. So, too, have they rendered my old age not only no inconvenient state to me, but even an agreeable one.

And after all, should my firm persuasion of the soul's immortality prove to be a mere delusion, it is at least a pleasing delusion, and I will cherish it to my last breath. I have the satisfaction in the meantime to be assured that if death should utterly extinguish my existence, as some philosophers assert, I shall not be exposed to the derision of these clever fellows over the groundless hope I entertained of an after-life in some better state.

In all events, and even admitting the possibility that our expectations of immortality are utterly vain, there comes a time nevertheless when death is a consummation most devoutly to be wished. For nature has appointed to the days of man, as to all things else, their proper limits, beyond which they are no longer of any value. Old age may be considered as the last scene in the great drama of life, and no one would wish, surely, to lengthen his part till he sank down sick with repetition and exhausted with fatigue.

These are the reflections I had to lay before you on the subject of old age, a period in which I hope you will prove, by your own experience, the truth of what I have asserted to you, by mine.

Selections from philosophers and writers

As in the case of *de Senectute*, nearly all the references in the quotations that follow are to men. Until recently, very few women had the opportunities either to show what they could do or to express their opinions.

Seneca

The Roman stoic philosopher Lucius Seneca (c.4 BC–c.65 AD) asks 'Of what use are 80 years to a man who has done nothing with them? Such a man has not lived, merely passed through life and has been dead for a long time. It is by action and achievements rather than by duration that a life is to be judged. An old person will make more vigorous use of life when he or she knows that it is agreeable, useful and desirable to someone else. No one who speaks ill of death has ever tried it.'

Seneca aptly reminded us that poverty consists in desiring much rather than in having little and that richness lies in becoming accustomed to poverty. This applies to the effects of old age as much as it does to material things. There remain, he thinks, pleasures and satisfactions even on the edge of the grave, but there is much satisfaction in no longer needing certain pleasures. Commending study, he remarks that we should do so not to know more but to know better and to lay up treasure in our youth so that we can enjoy it in old age. Just as we must be awake to tell someone our dreams, so we must be cured of our vices to acknowledge them. This, he implies, is another blessing of old age. The time of life best fitted for virtue is when experience and changes of fortune have enlightened a person, and when passion is spent. One who becomes wise in old age becomes so only through old age. We are born unequal, but we all die equal.

People to whom the business of public affairs is everything take badly to enforced retirement and are not readily consoled for the loss of the pleasures of being occupied. To be confined to the house and to solitude is like a prison. From this springs weariness, dissatisfaction and the constant turning over of a mind that cannot settle on anything. But the worst misfortune of all is to be too ashamed to be able to acknowledge the wrong done. So the cultivation of the mind and the pursuit of virtuous ways are the best preparation for old age.

Dean Swift

The satirist Dean Swift (1667–1745) wrote a pamphlet on making resolutions for old age. He advised not to marry a young woman; not to be sour, morose or suspicious; not to despise the manners, styles, wit or fashion of the present; not to be covetous; and never to repeat the same stories over and over again to young people. It was, however, said of the embittered Swift that no writer had appreciated as well as he did 'the sad condition of old age, of feebleness humiliated, of an isolation which leaves an old man who has come to decrepitude hardly able to think, living only a vegetable life, indifferent to everything around him, and well-nigh cut off from the rest of mankind.'

La Bruyère

The principal work of the French social critic and philosopher La Bruyère (1645–96), *Characters* is worth reading. He wittily remarks that our regret over our wasted lives seldom leads us to make the best of the time that is left to us. We all fear old age but we all still hope to attain it. If life is miserable it is painful to bear; if it is happy, it is painful to lose it; either way, you can't win. Children and their fathers would get on better if they had no claims as heirs. How sad it is to have to bow and scrape and, in the end, to depend on the death of a parent to get a scanty living by an inheritance. There are fathers whose chief concern in life seems to be to prepare the minds of their children to be easily consoled over their deaths. Life is short and wearisome; it is all passed in desire; we put off to the future our repose and enjoyments, to that age at which the greatest blessings – those of health and youth – have departed.

La Rochefoucauld

The French writer of maxims François Duc de la Rochefoucauld (1613–80) had some acute and amusing things to say of old age. Old people, he wrote, love to give out with wise precepts so as to console themselves for no longer being in a position to set a bad example. When our vices finally leave us, we try to flatter ourselves that it is we who have left them. We often pardon those who bore us; but we can never pardon those whom we bore. The worst silliness of old age in people who were once amusing is to forget that they are amusing no longer. Young women who do not want to seem frivolous and old men who do not want to seem ridiculous should never talk of love for each other. In growing old a man becomes more foolish and more wise. Old age is a tyrant who forbids, under pain of death, all the pleasures of youth.

Francis Bacon

Lord Verulam of Verulam (1561–1626), Francis Bacon was one of the earliest and most distinguished English essayists. This is a freely edited version of Bacon's *Essay on Youth and Age* rendered into more modern English and with the Latin quotations translated.

> A man that is young in years, may be old in experience, if he has not wasted his time. But that happens rarely. Generally, youth is like the first thoughts – not so wise as the second. For there is a youth in ideas, as well as in years. And yet the imagination of young men is more lively than that of old; and new ideas stream into their minds better, and with more inspiration. Impulsive natures, prone to strong, violent and ever-changing desires, are not ripe for action, till they have passed middle age; it was thus with Julius Caesar and Septimius Severus. Of the latter it was said 'He was a mad youth, always in trouble.' But quiet natures may do well in youth. As it is seen in Augustus Caesar, Cosmus Duke of Florence, Gaston de Foix, and others.
>
> By contrast, impulsiveness in old age is an excellent recipe for success in business. Young men are better at inventing, than showing

judgement; fitter to act than to advise; and better suited to new projects, than for settled affairs. For in matters appropriate to the old their experience directs them; but in new things, this experience holds them back.

The errors of young men are the ruin of business; but aged men err in that they might have done more, or acted sooner. Young men, in the conduct and management of affairs, bite off more than they can chew; stir up more trouble than they can quieten; rush to the end, without considering the means and stages; concentrate on some few principles which they have chanced on arbitrarily; don't bother to innovate, and thus encounter all kinds of problems. They hurry into extreme remedies – of a kind that multiply their problems – and will not admit or retract their errors; they are like an unbroken horse, that will neither stop nor turn.

Old men object too much, consult too long, adventure too little, repent too soon, and seldom drive business home to its full potential, but content themselves with a feeble and partial success. The best is to be achieved only by combining the virtues of both youth and age. It is right and proper that young men should be learners, while old men should act. In moral matters it may be that the young have the edge over the old. A certain rabbi, pondering on the text 'Your young men shall see visions, and your old men shall dream dreams' decided that it meant that young men are nearer to God than old men, because a vision is a clearer revelation than a dream. And certainly, the more a man drinks of the world, the more it intoxicates; and with age comes an increase in the power of understanding rather than in the virtues of the will and the affections.

Some people mature too early and then fade early. Of this sort there are three kinds. The first is those that have brittle wits, the sharp edge of which is soon turned; such as was Hermogenes the rhetorician, whose books are exceeding subtle; but who afterward became stupid. A second sort, is of those whose natural dispositions – such as fluent and luxuriant speech – are better suited to youth than to age. The third is of those who are so brilliant in youth that they burn themselves out too early. Such was Scipio Africanus, of whom Livy said: 'There was great promise in the beginning, but it was not fulfilled in the close.'

Michel de Montaigne

The essays of Michel de Montaigne (1533–92) have been read with pleasure since the middle of the 16th century. Here is his essay entitled *Of Age* freely adapted from the 1927 translation of E. J. Trenchermann. This essay is uncharacteristically pessimistic and sombre for Montaigne. But in the 16th century the expectation of life was much shorter than it is today. This essay, however, also contains much good advice, and may help us to appreciate the better chances we have today of living long and well.

> When the younger Cato wanted to kill himself and his friends tried to stop him, he said: 'Am I so young that you should reproach me for giving up life too soon?' He was only 48. As far as Cato was concerned, this was a ripe old age. People who expect to live for a certain number of years – which they call the natural duration of life – tend to forget that they are not exempt from the numerous accidents to which each of us, by the natural course of things, is exposed. Unfortunately, these things are likely to cut short the term these people promise themselves.
>
> What an idle fancy it is to expect to wear out and die of old age and to propose that as the proper span of our life! In fact, that kind of death is actually the rarest of all. What nonsense to consider death from old age the only natural kind of death! Is it contrary to nature to see a man break his neck by falling out of a window, drowning in a shipwreck or suddenly snatched away by the plague or pneumonia? Isn't it our normal condition to be exposed to all such calamities? Let's not flatter ourselves with such fine words. It is these disasters that we ought to call natural, for they are general, common and pretty well universal.
>
> To die of old age is rare, singular and out of the ordinary, and hence much less natural than other deaths; in the list of all the ways we can die it is the last and the most extreme. The further it is from us, the less we can expect it. It is indeed the boundary beyond which we shall not go, and which nature has prescribed as a limit not to be overstepped; and it is a rare privilege if we are allowed to live so long. This is an exemption nature gives by special favour to one man in a thousand, by sparing him the fatal events almost everyone else has to suffer and that make such a long career so rare.
>
> I have now reached an age few people attain. Since in the ordinary course of things men do not reach that stage, it is a sign that I am well advanced. And since I have passed the usual limits, which are the true measure of our life, I must not hope to go much beyond. Having escaped so many occasions of death into which we see humankind stumbling, I must acknowledge that the

extraordinary and uncommon fortune which has kept me alive, is not likely to continue much longer.

From this vantage point, let me look back. I find that I am very much against the idea – on which our laws are based – that a man is assumed to be incapable of managing his own affairs till he is 25, and that he will barely be able to manage his life till then. Augustus declared that a man was old enough at 30 to become a judge. Servius Tullius decreed that knights need not go to war after the age of 47; Augustus exempted them at 45. It seems to me ridiculous to send men into retirement before they are 55 or 60. In my opinion we should continue our professions and occupations as long as possible, for the public good. I also see a fault in the other direction, in that we are not set to work early enough. Augustus, first Roman Emperor and the most powerful man in the world at the age of 19, was insisting that a man must be 30 before he can give a judgement about the position of the spout on a kettle!

For my part, I consider that our minds are developed as far as they are likely to be at 20 and as promising as they can ever be. If a mind has not shown what it can do at that age, it will never do so. Of all the great human deeds, both ancient and modern and of whatever kind, that have come to my knowledge, the list of those that have been performed by people under 30 is very much longer than that performed by older people. Think of Hannibal and of his great adversary Scipio. The better half of their lives was lived on the fame they acquired in their youth. Certainly they were great men afterward compared with all others, but by no means so in comparison with their own early achievements.

As far as I am concerned, I am quite sure that after I was 30 both my mind and my body lost rather than gained, and went back rather than forward. It is possible that people who spend their time well, gain in knowledge and experience as they get older; but even they lose in vivacity, quickness, firmness and in other personal qualities. Sometimes it is the body that first surrenders to old age, sometimes the mind; and I have seen a fair number of people whose brains were enfeebled before their stomach and legs. This misfortune is the more dangerous, as it is an infirmity the sufferer is unaware of.

So this is the main objection I have to the laws: not that they keep us working too late in life but that they start us working too late. When you consider the frailty of our life, and remember how many dangers it is exposed to, we should not, in my opinion, allot so large a share at the beginning of it to idleness and to preparation.

Isaac d'Israeli

Isaac d'Israeli (1776–1848), the English man of letters and father of the more celebrated Benjamin Disraeli, said of old age in his *Curiosities of Literature*: 'Of the pleasures derivable from the cultivation of the arts, sciences, and literature, time will not abate the growing passion; for old men still cherish as affection and feel a youthful enthusiasm in those pursuits, when all others have ceased to interest.'

Bertrand Russell

The English philosopher and mathematician Bertrand Russell (1872–1970) had a very positive attitude to old age.

> Psychologically there are two dangers to be guarded against in old age. One of these is undue absorption with the past. It does not do to live in memories, in regrets for the good old days, or in sadness about friends who are dead. One's thoughts must be directed to the future and to things about which there is something to be done. . . The best way to overcome it – so at least it seems to me – is to make your interests gradually wider and more impersonal, until bit by bit the walls of the ego recede, and your life becomes increasingly merged in the universal life. An individual human existence should be like a river – small at first, narrowly contained within its banks, and rushing passionately past boulders and over waterfalls. Gradually the river grows wider, the banks recede, the waters flow more quietly, and in the end, without any visible break, they become merged in the sea and lose their individual being.

Karl Jaspers

The German-born Swiss existentialist philosopher Karl Theodor Jaspers (1893–1969) said of old age:

> In my mind I am still very young. It is only when you are old that you know what life is about. It is splendid to be old because I have seen so much. I feel that I have witnessed 1000 years of history. I have seen the world undergo many changes. I have a Utopian theory about life. Most people think they cannot influence world history. I believe they can. Every person is important and should influence history – by living fully, and by being sincere, faithful and true. Follow your conscience and instincts. Feel everything you do has a definite purpose. Always have that in mind in daily decisions. Wisdom is never fully attainable but there are ways of getting at it. Do what is important. Avoid trivial

daily tasks. Mere industriousness is not enough. It is particularly important to have regular hours, regular study, regular sleep, proper exercise and avoid trivia.

Jeanette Kupfermann

In her book *The MsTaken Body*, the social anthropologist and broadcaster Jeanette Kupfermann draws attention to society's mistaken concept of the ageing female body – and, by extension, its concept of women generally. She points out that two causes are at the heart of the general damaging view of the ageing body – the almost universal 'machine paradigm' and the decline in belief in an afterlife. By the machine paradigm she means the unthinking acceptance that the body is to be regarded in much the same way as we regard a car. If it is damaged it must immediately be repaired. The older and more worn out it becomes, the less it is valued and the more it is despised. Ageing is to be concealed by a paint job and new parts in the one case and cosmetics, wigs, breast implants, hormone replacement therapy and so on, in the other.

The machine paradigm in Western societies is in striking contrast to the attitudes in earlier, traditional societies in which older people are given increasing status and responsibility. The decline in the belief in life after death influences the machine paradigm and forces the view that death must be postponed by every possible means available to us. The physical deterioration of the body, with its intimation of mortality, has become too horrible for many to contemplate. Society's image of death defines its concept of health and this concept, she believes, is conditioned by these factors.

She also makes some interesting points about how attitudes to old women are modulated by the – only partly unconscious – tendency to equate them with witches. Older women often wield considerable economic power; they live longer than old men; and their position in society is ambiguous. For these reasons, Kupfermann believes, they may attract the fear and dislike of others. The accusation of witchiness, implicit or otherwise, is the only way society can exert some control over them.

Simone de Beauvoir

The French existentialist novelist and feminist, Simone de Beauvoir has many important things to say about old age from the feminist point of view. Her general ideas on the subject are, however, encapsulated in the proposition that the whole of a society is to be judged by the attitude it takes to old age. It is this attitude, she believes, that reveals whether or not a society has a healthy view of the meaning of life. The attitude of society to old people is a clear indication of the values of that society.

De Beauvoir, who was strikingly ahead of her time in her outspokenness on the subject of female sexuality, was noted for her diatribes against those moralists who saw old age as a release from the sinful passions. She was distressed that this stereotype had been imprinted on the minds of young and even middle-aged people and that it was responsible for their tendency to be shocked by any manifestation of sexuality in older people.

chapter nine

The Science of Dying: Dispelling the Fear of Death

The last three parts of this book, although relatively short, concern a matter of great importance to many older people. Since health means 'wholeness' such an important matter cannot be neglected.

The subject of death ought not to be a constant preoccupation; that is unhealthy and damaging to the quality of life. But, equally, it ought not to be a subject from which we shrink in horror. Some older people deliberately try to avoid thinking about death; some have persuaded themselves that to do so is morbid; some are fascinated by the subject. None of these responses is ideal. The awareness of the inevitability, within a comparatively short time, of our own deaths and those of people who are dear to us is an inescapable consequence of reaching old age. It is certainly a matter that should concern us. But the best way to avoid becoming obsessed with death is to understand some of the basic facts about it.

The experience of dying

Human experience of the last stages of life has traditionally described them as the 'death agonies'. The truth is that the idea of 'death agonies' is a fiction, convenient for writers of gothic romances or sentimental biography, but entirely without foundation. The idea probably arose partly from the occasional observation of convulsive body movement and contraction of the face muscles at the moment of death, but mainly from the emotional response of people to the idea of dying and especially to the deaths of those they love. To most people, the thought of parting from life is so horrifying that they cannot imagine it could happen without a desperate struggle and profound agony of body and mind.

The truth is quite different: we have a great deal of evidence that the last stage of dying is, in fact, one of the easiest and least disturbing experiences of all. Numerous records of the statements of dying people have testified to this. Most of these statements made by dying people are necessarily short, but this account of a relevant experience may help you to put aside at least this element in your concern.

The blunted brain

About 40 years ago a young army doctor, serving with a battalion in Malaya, had an experience which he remembers in detail to this day and which has had a profound effect on his attitude to the experience of dying. The things he learned at that time have remained with him, and nothing that he has since observed or experienced, in the course of a varied clinical career, has caused him to modify the conviction he formed at that time.

Battalion headquarters was in an isolated area and, because the army was engaged in a war against guerrillas, there were severe restrictions on movement. So when he was accidentally poisoned by an overdose of tetrachloroethylene, there was not much to be done. For three days he lay on his narrow bed in the officers' mess, visited at intervals by a very anxious sergeant.

His room was in an *atap bashah* – the walls and roof made of dusty woven nipa palm leaf thatching, and as he lay in that crude room, with gecko lizards rustling in the ceiling and mosquitos whining round his net, he knew that he was dying. It was not a matter of thinking that he might die or that, in his medical judgement based on his symptoms, he thought he was likely to die. He knew with clear, unequivocal, conviction that he was dying.

Many times during the course of these three days, he lapsed into unconsciousness and between the periods of coma he had a series of amazing hallucinations with grotesque distortion of space and time. But the important thing about this extraordinary preview of dying was that, although he was a perfectly ordinary person so far as moral courage or general bravery were concerned, he accepted the fact with perfect composure. Each time he felt himself slipping into coma he believed that this was the end, and he accepted it easily. There was no struggle. No attempt to hang on to life. No horror. No pain or sense of loss. No regret for the loss of his life. Just complete acceptance.

He thought of his young wife and recently born child back in England and was sorry that he would not see them again, but even this regret was mild and passing. He was 25 years old, just at the beginning of his medical career. But there was no bitterness or resentment at having to die so young. Just calm and easy acceptance.

Later, of course, when he was recovering, he saw to his intense surprise that he had been mistaken – that the conviction was the result of an abnormal state of brain function, brought on by the depressant effect of the poison. Nevertheless, his response to that conviction at the time has ever since been a source of great consolation to him and he is convinced that, when he comes to die, his last moments of consciousness will be as easy and as accepting. He believes this because he knows, from this and much other evidence, that when brain function is dangerously dampened – as it is just before death, or as it is by a variety of poisons and drugs – there is a clear conviction of dying and no distress.

Since then this conviction has been fortified by much that he has learned about the physiology of brain function and by his studies of the changes occurring during the final approach of death. He now knows the reasons for the acceptance and easy resignation. But academic knowledge is one thing and direct experience is another and he believes that he has been unusually fortunate to have had prior personal experience of dying.

This effect on the brain, and hence on the consciousness of the individual's state, is one of nature's provisions and we should consider it as normal. And it is a truth which should be of comfort to those feeling that death is approaching, as well as to those who must watch their loved ones approaching death. This is not, of course, to suggest that the whole process of dying is easy, and particularly not in young people. If there is early knowledge that death is coming soon, there is inevitably a great deal of suffering. Nor is it to suggest that this alteration in brain function occurs a long time before the actual moment of death. That may often be so, depending on the type of illness from which the person is dying, and especially in old people. When it does, there is peace of mind for days or even weeks before death.

Science and the experience of dying

Many people who have come very close to death, but have been saved at the last moment, have recorded their experience and the most interesting thing about this is how closely their experiences correspond. Common to nearly all of them is a strong sense of peace, contentment and acceptance. About 40 per cent had a feeling of spiritual detachment from the body and about one quarter felt they were moving into an area of darkness. About 10 per cent were then convinced that they were passing on into an area of bright light.

Medical science is now able to give clear explanations for these experiences. The sense of tranquillity comes from a decrease in the rate of neural activity in the brain – the same sort of thing that happens with tranquillizers, or when we are falling asleep – and this results from decreased blood supply to the brain. Next, natural substances called endorphins – morphine-like chemicals pro- duced by the body – act increasingly on a part of the brain called the 'limbic system' to produce a feeling of happiness and of separation from the physical body. As the blood supply to the brain declines further, the part at the back responsible for vision is damped down and we 'enter the darkness'. Before this visual area ceases to function altogether, it may have a burst of abnormal activity causing a sensation of bright light. And, briefly, just before the brain blacks out altogether, abnormal activity in other areas may produce a strong sense – actually a hallucination – of bodily movement. Such activity in the motor area might well produce the conviction that an individual is walking.

This kind of experience must, in the past, have caused many people to attribute some religious or spiritual significance to what they have gone through, perhaps even to take it as proof of life after death. When, for any reason, we pass into coma (or even when we fall asleep), we are not aware of the moment of passage. The idea that we 'black out', in any literal sense, while actually becoming unconscious is not true. The awareness of blackness is a conscious phenomenon and occurs a significant time before we lose consciousness. We are never aware of the moment of loss of consciousness, and every night of our lives our experience proves it. So, if the brain is undergoing these progressive reductions in function, and has reached the stage of hallucination of bright light, if we are actually going to die, we would then pass without any awareness at all into whatever follows. And there is no way we can ever know, in any scientific sense of the word, what does follow.

It is not in the nature of religion to reveal its secrets in this or any other way. If it could, these 'secrets' would be known to all and would be incorporated into science. Religion is, and must always be, based on faith in matters which can never be proved.

Death and the medical profession

Critics of the medical profession sometimes wonder how many doctors ever seriously consider what medicine is really all about. But it is hard for doctors to do this because they are intensely preoccupied with the purely technical difficulties of the job. With many doctors, the central concern is the state of their knowledge. This concern is often competitive, so they spend long hours reading medical journals and new textbooks. With so much emphasis on physiology, biochemistry, pathology, immunology, genetics and so on, it is hardly surprising that there should be a tendency to neglect the human aspects of medicine and forget that the whole purpose of medicine is to promote the happiness of the human mind and to relieve its distress.

Doctors do sometimes forget that the practice of their profession is a means to this end, not an end in itself. If doctors are asked to define their function the response is usually: to know as much as possible so as to be able to diagnose and treat illness effectively. If pressed, any doctor would acknowledge that healing has a mental as well as a physical side and that the ultimate objective is the state of wellbeing of the mind of the patient. But in practice, this is often forgotten. Some doctors seem to consider death the final insult to their skill. Unable to accept the inevitable even when this stage is reached, they react to the situation by determining to do everything possible to promote recovery, at whatever cost, right to the end. This is why people die without dignity, in the apparent inhumanity and scientific coldness of intensive-care wards, with tubes and monitoring leads connected everywhere.

Mature and wise physicians know that, in every case, there is a time to recognize that it is no longer appropriate to persist in fruitless and demeaning attempts to cure.

Death with dignity

There are many records of patients who, at an extreme terminal stage have by intensive medical efforts been brought back temporarily to their former state of mind. Significantly, instead of being grateful, these patients are reported often to have resented these efforts.

In the early 1970s an article appeared in the *News Bulletin* of the American Association of Retired Persons, entitled 'Death with Dignity'. The article discussed whether people should be allowed to die in peace when there was no medical chance of recovery, or whether every medical resource should be tried to keep them alive at all costs. Of the 250 people who were prompted by the article to write in and express their views, 215 were in support of death with dignity. Only 35 wanted everything possible to be done to prolong life. Many who wrote had been deeply distressed by the sight of their loved ones being subjected to intensive care.

Doctors clearly sometimes go too far in their efforts to save life. But there was another aspect to this. Although such patients may certainly suffer pain and distress in the early stages of their illness, pain and distress are likely to be relieved almost from the moment they are in medical hands. It is easy for experienced doctors to see to this, and to ensure that even before nature takes over, pain and mental distress are prevented. So, at the times when the situation is most distressing to the onlooker – when all the medical equipment is most in evidence – that is the very time when the distress to the patient is likely to be least. For it is then that the illness has the greatest effect on the brain – blunting consciousness, promoting acceptance and making the prospect of death easiest.

Take comfort from this. If you have to go through the pain of seeing your loved one in intensive care, remember that the distress is likely to be all on your side and that, in all probability, he or she is suffering nothing at all.

chapter ten

The Sociology of Dying

T he final stage of dying is easy (see pp. 208–10). The natural processes occurring in the brain, at that time, ensure that all of us may confidently look forward to peace and acceptance at the end. But most dying people have to pass through a period of weeks or months during which they are clearly aware of what is happening and have to face up to, and come to terms with, the knowledge that their lives will shortly be over. It is during this period that you, or the person close to you, are going to experience the fear of death most strongly. If a loved one is dying, it is during this time that you can in spite of your distress be of most help.

To be able to do your best you need to know quite a lot about death and dying. The subject has been studied by a number of researchers and it is the fruits of their experience and learning that are distilled here.

The fear of death is natural but seldom apparent unless death is imminent. Healthy people of all ages, of course, suffer acute and intense fear when faced with sudden danger to life. At other times, the concern is so minor, especially with young people, that they often take terrible chances – with motorcycles, great heights, drugs and so on – often with tragic results. All hospital doctors have seen many young lives cut short, and many more shattered by permanent damage, through ignorance of the dangers of many of the things they do. Young people often lack imagination and experience, and this is one reason why the fear of death is more apparent in the mature than in the young.

Young people usually laugh when you put this point to them. They counter with statements like: 'Well, if it's going to happen, it's going to happen' or 'There's no use worrying about it, is there?' These illustrate that the young person is unable to address the question seriously, and this is probably natural and healthy. In a study of attitudes to death in college students, over 90 per cent reported that they hardly ever considered death in relation to themselves. By contrast, studies of older people showed that 60 to 70 per cent often do.

The situation is different when the person concerned knows that death is coming soon. In this case, the younger ones in general fear death more keenly than older people. The very fact that they have been unable to think through the problem of death, makes the prospect even more horrifying. For the young and middle-aged, the approach of death is the ultimate crisis, beside which everything else fades into insignificance.

Death in old age

Elderly people, especially the very old, are able to accept the fact of death much more readily than the young. This, too, is natural. In people who have lived out their natural lifespan, death is normal and right. We do not necessarily die from disease or injury, but simply from the gradual ebbing of the biological vitality within the cells. At such a time, people die easily, without struggle or resentment and with an easy and accepting mind. Officious medical intervention to try to prolong such life at all costs is inappropriate. If asked, the dying person would say, 'Just leave me to go quietly.'

Regrettably, we do not all die in this enviable way, and that is because many of us, whatever our age, are cut off prematurely often when life seems to be at its best. This may apply to the elderly as much as to the young.

The dying want to know

Many doctors and nurses, when asked whether the dying want to know, respond negatively: 'No! Patients don't want to know. It would be too upsetting. It would deprive them of hope and of the will to fight. And miracles do occasionally happen.'

This response may be as much for the protection of the doctor as the patient. For very good reasons, doctors wish to remain emotionally detached, and it is much more difficult for a doctor to maintain such detachment if he or she knows that the patient realizes that medical science has failed and that death is inevitable. Many doctors fear the painful emotional outburst which they expect their disclosure would cause. They fear the distress they too would experience, and the effect such a disclosure would have on their future relationship with the patient, however short. Doctors have enormous demands on their time, but most are sensitive enough to recognize that if there is one thing that cannot be hurried it is the association with a person on whom they have imposed a death sentence.

Major advances in medical science have meant that death has come to represent a defeat for the doctors. Many have become conditioned, throughout their training and clinical experience, to avoid serious consideration of it. Constant association with the dying would normally force doctors and nurses to consider the inevitable fact of their own deaths, so they have to find a way to avoid this. One way is by humour. Doubtless stockbrokers joke about a financial crash, and priests about hell and damnation. It is certainly true that doctors joke about death. And joking is, of course, a routine psychological ploy – a defence mechanism – to avoid facing up to something.

Medical people have other ways of insulating themselves from these regular intimations of their own mortality, and doctors – especially hospital doctors – often manage this skilfully. A male physician dresses and acts in such a way as to lend him distance from, and authority over, his patient. He uses language which he knows the patient will often fail to understand. He is master of the patient's environment and has complete control while the patient has little or none. All these elements make it almost impossible for any sort of real human relationship to exist between a patient and the average doctor.

Worst of all, in their determination to avoid facing up to their own mortality, many doctors think of their patients not as people, but as 'cases': 'Sister, the colostomy in bed 3 is getting a bit dehydrated. Press fluids, please. Oh, and the stroke in 7 needs turning more often. Watch out for pressure sores.' Such inhuman detachment is common and does not, as it seems to, denote complete coldness of heart. It is an indication of a deep need for insulation from the emotional effects of identification with patients, without which the doctor would have difficulty in doing the job.

It is an ironic commentary on the importance we place on money that the one argument that usually succeeds with doctors reluctant to agree to telling the patient, is that wills or inheritance are involved. Obviously it is important that people should be allowed to make provision for their relatives and enjoy the peace of mind of knowing that they have done so.

But there are many other matters, perhaps of less financial moment, which may be troubling dying people just as much. They may, for instance, wish to make up a quarrel or apologize for something they regret. They may wish to disclose a long-held secret, or there may be some unfinished business or professional duty to discharge. Ernst Kris, a well-known psychoanalyst, after suffering a heart attack, spent the last hours of his life dictating to his wife important details about his patients which would be necessary to those who were to take over their care.

There are all sorts of reasons why people want to know if they have developed a fatal disease. Doctors are aware of this and sometimes ask the relatives whether such factors exist. But you may take it that, as a general rule, doctors prefer that their patients should not be told the truth. A few even reject the suggestion that their patients have any rights in the matter. Doctors will, of course, tell you as a spouse or close relative that they believe that death is coming soon, but most will not be too pleased if you immediately inform the dying person.

The conspiracy of silence

It is certain that in thousands of cases everyone concerned, including the dying person, is well aware that death is approaching. Doctors and nurses, smiling confidently, calmly maintain the fiction that all is well; relatives and friends say 'Oh, you are looking better today!'; sometimes there is even a systematic pretence involving plans for the future. The patient, too, often participates in this conspiracy of silence, sometimes because it is believed, often because it is comforting (although recognized as a delusion), but frequently out of simple politeness. Dying patients, fully aware of the fact, join the conspiracy to avoid embarrassing others.

But surveys have shown that while about 80 per cent of doctors take the view that patients should not be told, about 80 per cent of patients actually want to know. Dying people, especially the elderly, often take a very realistic view of what is happening and, perhaps more often than we realize, fully accept that they are dying and want others to acknowledge this too. Perhaps they want to talk about it. Perhaps they have questions they want to ask about the actual process of dying. In many cases, there are important matters they want to attend to. But, for many, the pressing need is simply to talk openly and calmly about the coming event.

Shared knowledge

There is another important reason why denial of the truth can be dangerous. Human relationships must be based on honesty if they are to be secure and easy. Obviously we can, and should, turn a blind eye to minor and inconsequential matters, but to go on acting a systematic lie over something as fundamental as the future existence of one of the partners in the relationship is bound to have a damaging effect.

In a symposium on the care of the dying, Dr Cecily Saunders, then Medical Director of St Christopher's Hospice, London, recalled how a patient had told her that for 18 months after his first operation he was aware that something was wrong with his marriage but did not know what it was. When he had a recurrence of the disease, he asked for a direct statement from his doctor and was told the truth – which his wife had known all along. As a result, they were able to come together again and remained close thereafter.

Now Dame Cecily, and Chair of the Board of St Christopher's Hospice, Dr Saunders emphasizes the importance of the whole family, including children, visiting the dying person, so that the sense of family involvement is preserved. Children should be spared the sight of any pain and distress, and medical cooperation is essential. But she has found that in the presence of death, long-standing family quarrels are often seen in their proper perspective and resolved.

Acknowledging the truth

If a loved one is approaching death, one of the most difficult things you have to do at the proper time is to decide whether or not to break the conspiracy of silence and acknowledge openly that you know that he or she is dying. This act of courage and charity can, in appropriate cases, confer much-needed dignity and comfort on the dying person and open the way to honest discussion which can be deeply comforting. If it is to be done at all – and only you can decide – it must not of course be done too soon. Discuss the matter with the doctor and, preferably, get the doctor's permission. In most cases, nothing should be said or implied until active medical treatment, given in the hope of achieving recovery, has been abandoned.

But, although only those in medical charge can tell you whether there is any hope, and although they can advise you on the possible psychological effects on the dying person, the decision rests with you. You know, better than anyone, whether your loved one would want to know the truth. You may even know that the truth is already known, and just not being acknowledged. You may have guessed that your loved one is simply waiting for a word from you.

It may be necessary for you to take on yourself the responsibility for ignoring the doctor's advice. This is something you must consider carefully: you are going to have to make a judgement about the doctor's qualification to advise you. When you do, bear in mind that the whole of a doctor's concern, almost all of the time, is for the recovery of his patients and that to admit that a patient is dying is to admit failure. So you may also have to decide whether the doctor's judgement, in this matter, is as good as yours.

How to tell

Even when all agree that your decision is right, it is seldom easy to indicate to someone that you know they are soon to die. There are all sorts of reasons for this difficulty. At the beginning of an illness, and for some considerable time afterward, we are all – rightly – optimistic about the outcome. And even after optimism has faded, it is right and proper to keep up an attitude that suggests an expectation of recovery, and it is hard to abandon this attitude. Again, you may not be able to face the truth yourself, or may feel that to say anything would be unpardonable cruelty.

It is extremely important that you should never, under any circumstances, blurt out the bald truth of the matter. Never utter any such statement as, 'You have only a few days to live.' What is essential is that you should, carefully, allow the dying person to see that you know that the high probability is that death is near. Don't say anything that will crush all hope. 'I'm afraid it looks bad, my dear . . .' will often give the patient the chance to agree and to voice unspoken fears. Feel your way, gradually, so that you can assess what your loved one really wants. Some will be unable to face the prospect and deny that there is any question of a fatal illness. If this is the response, withhold your attempts, for the time is not yet right. Later the response is likely to change.

The reaction to the awareness that death is coming varies greatly according to the mind of the person concerned and with other circumstances. Age, for instance, is an important factor. Elderly people, and especially the very old, often take the reasonable view that they have had their time, lived a full life, and should not expect or demand much more. To them, the approach of death often seems natural and right and they may be much more concerned with the preservation of their dignity, calm and sense of orderliness, than with trying to prolong life.

To such people, an unwarranted and unwanted medical interference with the natural stage for which they are ready may seem an outrageous infringe-ment of their liberty. Very often they are old, patient and tolerant, and say nothing. But this does not mean that they would not welcome the chance to express their opinion of what is being done. Maybe it is your responsibility to give your loved one the chance to speak, even if to do so means breaking the barrier of silence and acknowledging that death is near.

Old people often value their dignity and privacy above all things. Many have said that they do not fear death but that they fear the process of dying with its attendant intrusion of others into their private affairs. This is one reason why it is nearly always better for an old person to die at home, in the presence of family members, rather than in hospital. The modern fragmentation of families makes this a much rarer event than it used to be.

If you are going to make the decision to tell the truth to your loved one, you should be aware of the probable consequences. You know that death is likely in the near future and will almost certainly occur eventually, whether you tell or not. It will not be your fault – but the emotional reaction of your loved one, especially if young, may make you think that you have caused it.

The mental acceptance of death

In 1965, Dr Elizabeth Kubler-Ross, an American psychiatrist working in Billings Hospital in Chicago, was approached by four theology students who asked her for help with a project on facing the crisis of death. They discussed the matter and decided that the best way to proceed was to interview dying patients. This was more easily said than done and doctor after doctor flatly refused to allow it. The response of the nurses, too, was antagonistic.

At last, Dr Kubler-Ross managed to get to a dying patient, an old man. He was obviously anxious to talk to her and asked her to sit down there and then and proceed. But she wanted to share the experience with her students and said she would come back the next day. When the little group arrived, the patient was having oxygen and was almost too weak to speak. He tried to lift his arm, whispered, 'Thank you for trying . . .' and died within the hour, unable to tell them what they so much wanted to hear.

In time Dr Kubler-Ross gained the confidence of the medical staff and, as they saw that no harm was being done and appreciated the serious reasons for the study, more and more terminally ill patients became available for conversation. Soon patients were actually being referred by medical staff and social workers and, as patients talked among themselves, volunteers came forward. Dr Kubler-Ross made a practice of telling the patients that she wanted to learn from them what it was like to be seriously ill or dying. Many told her that they were anxious to talk to her. It was often, she says, like opening the flood gates, and she learned much that she had not known before.

Among other things, she learned that gravely ill patients always knew when they were dying and often knew the day on which they were going to die. Many of the hundreds of patients she interviewed would, at the appropriate time, indicate that they knew they would not see her again. And usually they were right.

Interest in her activities grew and more and more students appeared to listen to the interviews and take part in the discussions which followed. In the end, these seminars evolved into an accredited course for medical and theological students, attended by up to 50 participants. From these hundreds of interviews she obtained much information and established some important basic principles. From this work, and that of others in the field, much is now known of the reactions of those told that they have a fatal disorder.

Dr Kubler-Ross found that, in most cases, the reaction came in five discernible stages. These reactions vary with the personality and especially with the age of the dying person. In young and middle-aged people they are particularly strongly marked. In the aged, who often accept death readily, they are much less apparent. These findings have now been widely confirmed by a great deal of observation and experience, and are universally accepted.

Denial

'I don't believe it! It's not true!' This first reaction occurs even when the person concerned has guessed the truth and has gone to much trouble to confirm it. Denial is understandable. It is not likely that the habit of a lifetime can be reversed in a moment. All our reactions are geared to continuation, to forming and carrying out plans, and it is very difficult to accept that this is no longer so.

The period of denial may be short or long. Some people have an amazing ability to weigh up evidence, to form firm conclusions and to face facts. For

these people, the stage of denial may be very short indeed. They may simply say
'Oh no!', remain silent for a moment, and then accept what has happened. But
for most, the denial stage lasts much longer, sometimes for months. In this
stage there is much thinking to be done, but thinking is difficult for the mind
stunned by such devastating news. Commonly there is a retreat into silence and
isolation and the patient may refuse to see anyone.

Don't assume that the end of the stage of denial means that the person
concerned has given up hope. Neither now nor during the later stages does this
ever really happen. No one ever completely abandons the hope that there may
have been some mistake, or that a cure will be found after all.

Anger

This is especially striking in the young who feel cheated of life and of their
reasonable expectations of experiences of all kinds. Older people can look
back on a life in which they may have fulfilled their ambitions and experienced
much, and may feel that they have had 'a fair innings'. The anger may be
directed at particular persons – often the doctors or nurses, or relatives or
friends who may seem to be getting an unfair advantage in life – or at
institutions such as the medical profession as a whole.

All doctors are familiar with this effect. Because the anger has to be directed,
it is quite common for a member of the medical staff to be accused of some
kind of neglect or action which has actually brought about the condition which
is going to cause death. A similar effect is possibly even more common in the
bereaved who also suffer powerful anger in proportion to the extent of the loss.
You will experience this, or may already have, and you should think it no more
unnatural in yourself than it is in the case of your loved one on learning of the
prospect of death.

This anger can be hard to take and it is as well to be ready for it. Furious, cup-
smashing anger cannot be kept up, but a slow, burning, intense hatred, directed
against someone or something can. You will know how your loved one tends to
react when angered, but you may be unprepared for systematic nastiness,
constant carping criticism of everything you do or say, dismissive ingratitude
and a total disregard for your feelings.

It is very difficult to understand and learn to live with this. Constantly remind
yourself that there is very little room in the mind of the sufferer for anything else
but the intense feeling of resentment. In the circumstances, only a saint could
consider other people's feelings. The anger has to be let out and you can help
to do this. Anger is like steam pressure rising in a closed vessel. If the patient is
not allowed even to talk about the cause of the anger, the pressure will have to
be released in some pointless, and perhaps more damaging, direction.
Although it may not be apparent at the time, you will get much appreciation

from the sufferer if you understand what is going on and actually encourage the direct expression of the bitterness and resentment.

Dr Kubler-Ross was not averse to taking a patient into her arms and saying, 'Why don't you just scream!' This would not always be appropriate, but there could hardly be more direct help with the release of anger.

Bargaining

'I will do anything, if only I don't have to die.' We have to be understanding about bargaining. It is an act of desperation involving a certain amount of intellectual dishonesty or childishness: 'I promise to be good, if you will let me off.'

People with religious convictions try to bargain with God, who clearly has the power to suspend the death sentence. Since we cannot live for ever, we bargain for a certain period of extension of life. 'Just let me have one more month and then I don't care what happens.' If such promises are followed by the desired extension they must, of course, at the end of the time be renewed. Patients promise religious observances, a life dedicated to a church, a complete change of conduct, large donations to a charity, anything. Some who have not had any religious faith for years, in this moment of extremity, turn again to belief, but this is often so that they can bargain with God, rather than to have the comfort that they may, in some form, survive death.

A kind of unspoken bargaining with the doctors is common. Patients promise their bodies for 'medical research' after death, or sign cards stating their wish to donate their corneas, kidneys or hearts for transplantation. It is sad, but understandable, that such valuable offers should be made for such reasons: 'You can have my eyes later, if you will do a better job and save me now.'

The form of the bargain can sometimes give a clue to hidden feelings of guilt, which may be causing additional distress, and it may be possible for you to understand these and perhaps help to relieve them. There was a dying patient who said, 'Just let me have a little longer and I will forget the wrong Madge did me, and make it up with her.' She had not spoken to Madge for over 20 years and knew in her heart that the fault was as much hers as Madge's. She died, easily and at peace, soon after Madge was persuaded to visit her in hospital.

Depression

This is the saddest stage of all, for it is the stage of mourning. Mourning is the response to loss of any kind and the greater the loss, the greater the mourning. However intense may be your sense of loss when your loved one dies, is this likely to be as great as the sense of loss for the remainder of your own life? For the loss of everything you hold dear and of every friend and associate you have. That is what this stage is about.

Depression starts when the stages of denial and anger are past and when bargaining is obviously not going to work. It is a perfectly normal reaction and, however intense, is not a mental disorder. It is called 'reactive depression' and occurs in all circumstances, as a response to loss, although seldom so powerfully as in this.

This depression is probably the worst point of the experience of the approach of death, and it is hard for others to take, too. Weeping, by men as well as women, is a major feature. As in all forms of mourning, grieving is an essential stage in the process and has to be worked through, preferably in company. This is another reason why the conspiracy of silence can be so damaging. A refusal to acknowledge that a person is dying makes it impossible for us to share that person's grief at the loss of his or her life, so the dying person grieves alone.

By courage and simple honesty, we do much to help our loved one to pass through this terrible stage and reach the final stage.

Acceptance

Acceptance is different from giving up. Hope is not lost until the very last stages when it becomes irrelevant and is forgotten. Acceptance is a serene state of readiness for death. The dying person no longer struggles against it, is ready to go and has lost all fear. This is the stage beyond words, in which human presence is wanted, but not for conversation. The stage of the quiet awareness of the presence of the beloved, the reassuring touch of the hand.

The pioneers

Dr Elizabeth Kubler-Ross's book *On Death and Dying* has become a classic and is required reading for anyone taking a professional interest in the subject. But she is by no means the only pioneer. In Britain, Dr Cecily Saunders' work to promote the hospice movement was recognized by the award of a title. Professor John Hinton, a noted psychiatrist, made a detailed study of the reactions of the dying and their relatives and, in 1967, published the scholarly book *Dying*, which has remained in print ever since as a major sourcebook for all concerned with the subject.

Dr Colin Murray Parkes, also a psychiatrist, conducted a great deal of research into all aspects of the subject, both at the British Medical Research Council's Social Psychiatry Unit at the Maudsley Hospital, London and at the Laboratory of Community Psychiatry at Harvard Medical School, Boston. Dr Parkes worked in association with Cecily Saunders at St Christopher's Hospice to develop a system of care for families, both before and after bereavement, and did much to develop the major British organization, CRUSE-Bereavement Care, for the support of the bereaved, which now has branches all over Britain.

Dr Parkes is now Chair of the governing body of CRUSE-Bereavement Care. His many article and books have brought him an international reputation. His book *Bereavement: Studies in Grief in Adult Life* is a scientific masterpiece.

The dying need us

In the studies and writings of all these devoted people, one central fact comes to the fore again and again. The dying need close human contact. Nothing can substitute for that. No one can buy what the dying need – only give it personally.

This increasing dependence does not always produce the kind of response it should. Dying people need us desperately. They need to matter to us. They still need to feel important and to maintain their dignity while they are struggling with the terrible questions facing them. So our presence is essential to them. But we, too, when we are with them, are also forced to face these questions and, because few of us are willing to do so, we tend to avoid the dying just when they need us most. It is only too easy for us to take the easy way when we think we can get away with it.

chapter eleven

Euthanasia

The word euthanasia literally means 'a good death' or 'a gentle and easy death'. In this sense, no one can possibly have any ethical objection to euthanasia. But the word has come to mean something fundamentally different and is now generally equated with 'mercy killing'. And in this sense there can be no unanimity of opinion on the matter. It is in this sense that the word is used here.

As the public of the Western world has become increasingly well-informed on medical matters, so attitudes to euthanasia have gradually changed. In 1992 in Britain considerable public interest and debate was aroused by the trial and conviction of a consultant rheumatologist, Nigel Cox, who had been indicted for attempted murder after giving a lethal injection of potassium chloride to a patient. This was a 70-year-old lady, a patient in hospital, whose condition was so desperate and whose pain so terrible that she screamed whenever she was touched. As matters worsened and her body became unable to absorb the doses of diamorphine needed to control the pain, she pleaded for her life to be ended. She had been Dr Cox's patient for 13 years and knew him to be a caring and dedicated doctor.

Five days before her death she begged for release and Dr Cox refused. He had promised her that she would not be allowed to suffer terrible pain during the last days of her life, but the failure of the diamorphine made it impossible for him to keep that promise. So he gave her the lethal injection at a time when she was not expected to live for another day. He made a clear entry in the case notes. His action was fully supported by the lady's two sons. She died peacefully a few minutes after the injection. Some time later, a nurse saw this entry in the notes and reported the matter to the hospital authorities. The police were called and Dr Cox was arrested.

By then, the body had been cremated and it was impossible for the prosecution to prove that the injection had caused her death. In accordance with the letter of the law, the jury was instructed to be guided by Dr Cox's intent rather than by his motives, and after eight hours' deliberation brought in a verdict of guilty. Dr Cox was convicted and sentenced to 12 months' imprisonment. The sentence was suspended.

This result caused great distress in the court room. Some of the jurors burst into tears. The judge, Mr Justice Ognall, was not unmoved. He said to the jury, 'There are times when, speaking for myself and, I strongly suspect, speaking for all of you, a criminal trial is an almost overwhelming burden.'

Dr Cox was immediately suspended from duty as a hospital consultant and faced what amounted to a further trial by the General Medical Council. The usual penalty for a doctor following such a conviction is that his name is erased from the Medical Register so that he is no longer legally qualified to practice. Toward the end of November Dr Cox's case was heard by the General Medical Council. The conclusion was that, although he was guilty of serious professional misconduct and would have to acknowledge this, he could, subject to certain conditions, return to work. The President of the GMC told Dr Cox that it was both unlawful and wholly outside a doctor's professional duty to a patient to give a lethal substance with no therapeutic value, whose only purpose was to shorten the patient's life. Dr Cox would have to accept a senior consultant as a 'mentor', and would have to attend a palliative care unit for a time to learn the full range of available techniques. The Wessex Regional Health authority, Dr Cox's employers, stated that they took an extremely serious view of his conduct and the effect it would have on the hospital. The authority wholly supported the action of the nursing sister in reporting the matter, as was her duty under her professional code of conduct.

Following this and the case of Tony Bland, who had been in a persistent vegetative state for three years following the Hillsborough football disaster, a select committee was set up by the House of Lords to consider euthanasia and published its report in February 1994. The committee concluded that new legislation was not required but that the medical colleges and faculties should develop a code of practice for doctors. Most of the people who gave evidence to the committee and who represented the views of bodies such as the Home Office, the Department of Health, the British Medical Association, and the Royal College of Nursing, were strongly against euthanasia. The principal voice dissenting from this opinion was that of the Voluntary Euthanasia Society. The representative of this organization suggested that general public opinion was very different from that of these official bodies. In May 1994 the Government endorsed the findings of the House of Lords committee.

Any consideration of euthanasia is likely to be fraught with emotion. This is illustrated by comparing the attitudes of lay people with those of doctors who might be personally involved, and with the attitudes of the official bodies who can be relatively detached about the matter. Comparable lay opinion polls in Britain were held in 1976 and 1989. In both of these, people were asked to say whether they agreed with the following statement: 'Some people say that the law should allow adults to receive medical help to assist them to an immediate peaceful death if they suffer from an incurable illness that is intolerable to them, provided they have previously requested such help in writing.' In 1976, 69 per cent of people agreed; in 1989, 75 per cent of people agreed.

In a research study recently reported in the *British Medical Journal*, 424 doctors, half of them GPs and half hospital consultants, were asked if patients had ever requested them to hasten death. The enquiry was carried out by post and with complete anonymity, so there was no question of legal repercussions. Of the 273 doctors who responded to the question, 163 said they had been asked to hasten death, 124 had been asked to take active steps to this end. Of these, 38 said they had complied with this request. Note that this was less than 10 per cent of all who had been asked the questions. There was a general agreement among doctors that the subject required further consideration and that it should be discussed more openly.

Clearly many lay people claim to be in favour of euthanasia; the number of doctors is much less; and, as we have seen, the attitude of official bodies – apart from those expressly in favour of euthanasia – is almost wholly against it. It would be wrong, however, to suggest that official attitudes are heartless. These authorities are composed of people with the same feelings and sympathies as anyone else, but they have the safeguard of knowing that they must not express opinions without preliminary consultation and internal discussion. The committee of the House of Lords considered in detail the provision of an adequate hospice service as an alternative to euthanasia. Many of the members visited hospices and were moved by the quality of care afforded. They recognized that there had been considerable development in the quality of palliative care in recent decades and that the number of hospices and palliative home care teams had increased steadily.

The meaning of euthanasia

It is essential to consider exactly what any particular person means when he or she uses the term euthanasia. One of the possible meanings – compulsory euthanasia – is a contradiction in terms and can be quickly dismissed. The idea of deliberately ending a person's life without his or her consent or against his or her wishes is abhorrent and, by any criterion, murder.

Voluntary euthanasia is considered by many, although by no means all, to be a basically different matter. But in this category we have to make a distinction between active euthanasia in which drugs are used, or other measures taken, deliberately to cause death, and passive enthanasia in which treatment that could prolong life is deliberately withheld. While some doctors hold rigidly to the view that their first duty is to preserve life at all costs, most doctors consider that there are circumstances in which this is not so. These doctors therefore consider the distinction between active and passive euthanasia to be very important. While most would hesitate to practice active euthanasia, they would be willing in appropriate cases and after thorough consideration – especially in cases of severe distress and pain – to stand aside and allow nature to take its course.

Passive euthanasia

A great many agree that there often comes a time when it is the doctor's first duty to look to the comfort of mind and body of his patient and assist in bringing about an 'easeful death'. There is a well-known rhyme in medical circles: 'Thou shalt not kill; but needst not strive officiously to keep alive.'

To many doctors such behaviour seems so obviously right that they would hardly agree that it should be classified under the heading of euthanasia. Passive euthanasia, in this sense, is in fact widely practised and can safely be left to the discretion and kindness of doctors. Nearly all official bodies, including the Roman Catholic church, agree that there is no moral imperative to prolong life at all costs. The problem becomes more difficult when a person has been kept alive artificially by a life-support system that, for instance, maintains breathing mechanically. To withdraw such a facility is seen by some as coming closer to deliberate killing.

There is a further distinction. When terminally ill patients are in great pain, the most important drugs for the relief of that pain are the powerful narcotic painkillers. These drugs not only relieve bodily pain but have a major beneficial effect on the state of mind of the patient. With continued use, the body becomes progressively habituated to these drugs and ever-larger doses are necessary to achieve the same effect. Sometimes, when this stage is prolonged, the doses rise to levels that would be fatal in a non-habituated person. Such large doses may shorten life and this raises the ethical question of whether they are justified.

Active euthanasia

Active voluntary euthanasia is opposed by most doctors. They point out that a doctor who engages in it breaks the Hippocratic oath. They believe that if legislation is passed to allow active voluntary euthanasia, there will inevitably be pressure on some old and seriously infirm people – who may be 'inconvenient' to their relatives – to agree. At present, such relatively helpless and vulnerable people enjoy the powerful protection of the law. If that protection were withdrawn, even under the most stringent regulations, there is no saying how matters might develop.

On the other hand, most doctors have encountered cases in which the emotional pressures on them to end a patient's suffering have been powerful. Many have given way to these pressures. But the debate does not resolve itself into opinions formed by emotional and humanitarian factors on the one hand, and opinions formed by reason on the other. Doctors who advocate some legal support for euthanasia – perhaps the legalization of suicide, for instance – also have strong reasonable grounds on their side. They point out that it is grossly unfair to apply broad legal and ethical principles to individual cases as if these were all the same. To do so brings the law and society into conflict with the doctor's compassion for his or her patient.

Euthanasia in other countries

There is a widespread belief that euthanasia is legal in Holland. This is not so. Euthanasia is still a criminal offence in the Netherlands. The difference there is that if doctors perform active euthanasia in accordance with certain legal guidelines they are not prosecuted.

It is important to be aware of the effect this has had. According to one correspondent in the *British Medical Journal*, over 1000 patients have their lives terminated each year in the Netherlands without their consent. This is happening in spite of attempts to control the situation by both the legal and medical professions. It seems, to quote this writer, that 'unrequested, non-voluntary euthanasia is creeping into Dutch medical practice – the "slippery slope" described by moral philosophers.'

Elsewhere in Europe

In Germany, as in Britain, passive euthanasia – the withholding of treatment to terminally ill patients – has long been regarded as a matter for the decision of doctors in consultation with their patients and, when necessary, with the relatives. Under the law, active euthanasia is a crime punishable by up to five years' imprisonment. Suicide, and assisting in suicide, are not expressly forbidden, but the Penal Code forbids 'killing on request'. The German Society for Humane Dying (Deutche Gesellschaft für Humanes Sterben) has existed for more than 20 years and can give advice on methods of committing suicide and can provide suitable drugs.

The French are wary of legislation on euthanasia. Their National Ethical Committee considered that a law allowing euthanasia would probably be abused and would give doctors an unreasonable degree of power over people's lives. In 1991 a cancer specialist was temporarily suspended from work after he had stated that he had helped some of his terminally ill patients to die. In spite of all this, it is reputedly quite common in France for terminally ill patients to be given a lethal dose of drugs.

The United States

In the United States, the euthanasia debate has in recent years been stimulated by the actions of a Michigan pathologist, Dr Jack Kevorkian, who has widely advocated voluntary euthanasia and openly assisted many patients to commit suicide. After the first occasion, Dr Kevorkian was charged with murder but the judge dismissed the case, ruling that Michigan has no law against assisted suicide. Subsequently, Dr Kevorkian helped two more patients to die, using a simple device for giving an intravenous infusion of potassium chloride. Legislators in Michigan then passed a law prohibiting assisted suicide, but by 1994 Dr Kevorkian had helped 20 terminally ill patients to kill themselves. He was indicted that year for the murder of a patient Thomas Hyde who had begged him for help. The jury deliberated for nine hours and then brought in a verdict of not guilty. In early 1996 Dr Kevorkian was again indicted under a Michigan law intended to stop assisted suicide. Again he was acquitted.

California and Washington states have attempted to pass laws allowing assisted suicide. In both cases, these were narrowly defeated. In 1992 and 1993 a study was made to determine the attitudes of American doctors in Washington to assisted suicide. The researchers sent out 1,355 questionnaires to randomly selected doctors asking many questions about themselves and enquiring specifically whether they would 'deliberately administer an overdose of medication to an ill patient at his or her request with the primary intent to end his or her life.' Of the 938 doctors who responded, 48 per cent agreed with the statement that euthanasia was never ethically justified, and 42 per cent disagreed; 54 per cent thought that there were some situations in which euthanasia should be made legal, but only 33 per cent agreed that they would be willing to perform euthanasia. Exactly half of the doctors agreed that doctor-assisted suicide was never ethically justified; half disagreed.

In November 1994, the State of Oregon legalized doctor-assisted suicide, the first time this had been done anywhere in the world. At present, an injunction effectively suspends the law but, if this is lifted, any general practitioner in the state will be entitled to prescribe a lethal dose of drugs to a resident of Oregon who requests it, who is competent and properly informed and who is expected to die within six months. The measure is hedged by all kinds of qualifications and restrictions but, even so, was opposed by the American Medical Association, which quickly censured the Oregon Medical Association for allowing such a thing to happen.

Australia

In Australia euthanasia is illegal but opinion seems to be veering in its favour. A survey of 2,000 doctors conducted in 1988 showed that almost half supported voluntary euthanasia. Most said they would practise it if it were legal. About a third had already been involved in voluntary euthanasia. There seems to be less unanimity on the question of withdrawing treatment; this is considered to be a major ethical issue.

General considerations

Because most legal systems have no specific provision for euthanasia and because the law cannot disregard a death brought about other than by natural means, euthanasia has to be regarded legally as either suicide, murder or manslaughter. There is general agreement that a doctor may legally decide, when there is extreme suffering, not to prolong life by medical treatment. It is also generally agreed that, in such cases, the law need not interfere if the doctor used powerful drugs to relieve pain even if this shortens life. Some European countries have included in their criminal codes, provision for taking extenuating circumstances into consideration when considering prosecutions for euthanasia, and for lenience in sentencing doctors and others convicted of euthanasia.

Demands for euthanasia have raised a number of difficult ethical and philosophical questions, the central question being whether life must be regarded as sacrosanct or whether there are ever circumstances in which deliberate killing is justified. Such questions have been hotly argued, usually on emotional rather than empirical grounds. The problem for those who claim that killing can never be justified is to say why human life should be singled out from all other forms of life. The Buddhists addressed this problem centuries ago and concluded that all life must be considered sacrosanct. Christian theology provides the answer that humans are made in the image of God and that they have an immortal soul. For those not subscribing to Christian dogma, it has proved hard to find a convincing secular alternative.

There are many who consider that voluntary euthanasia should be a right and that the law should not concern itself with the free, informed choice of citizens to behave in a manner important to them so long as no harm is done to others. For those with no religious opposition to euthanasia, the opposition has been principally concerned with practical questions of providing adequate safeguards against progress to non-voluntary euthanasia. Such concerns reflect fears that legal support for euthanasia might end in the compulsory killing of those considered to be disadvantageous to the state. In this context it may be well to remember that younger people, forgetting that they too must grow old, may sometimes believe that the rising proportion of old people in Western society is in itself a disadvantage to the state.

chapter twelve

Thoughts and Writings about Death

The scientific and clinical evidence for the belief that the final stages of dying are always easy is reviewed on pp. 209–10. This belief is borne out by the personal observations by numerous doctors of the deaths of their patients. There is also much support in the many recorded accounts of the deaths of celebrated people to strengthen this conviction.

Except for this final easy period, which is common to all, people's deaths are as variable as their lives. Some come to the last stage suffering pain from deadly disease, some remain in distress of mind until near the end. But all at the last come to death easily. Many drift imperceptibly into coma so that it is impossible to say exactly when awareness departed. Only a small minority – about 6 per cent – are conscious shortly before death. A great many die after falling asleep in the normal way. Studies have shown that at least one-third of dying people are unaware of their last day alive.

Montaigne (see p. 200) describes in an essay what happened to him when he believed that he was dying from injuries.

> My life seemed to me to be holding on at the point of my lips; I closed my eyes to help me, as I thought, to thrust it out, and took a pleasure in my listlessness and indifference. It was an idea that floated only on the surface of my soul, as weak and feeble as everything else; but in truth not only free from distress, but attended by that tranquil feeling we have when we are gently gliding into sleep.
>
> I believe that those whom we see faint with weakness in the agony of death are in the same state, and I think that we have no reason to pity them, and to imagine that they are tormented by grievous pangs and their minds weighed down by painful thoughts.

Francis Bacon's essay *On Death* is not based on personal experience but is so full of common sense and good comfort that it is worth including. This version is translated into more modern terms:

Men fear death, as children fear the dark. And just as that natural fear in children is increased with bogey tales, so is men's fear of death. It is right and proper for religious people to think of death as the passage to another world and as the penalty for their sins. But it is plain weakness of mind to fear death as a terrible demand nature makes on us.

People engaged in religious thought are often guilty of a mixture of vanity and superstition. In some of the holy books written to frighten you, you can read that, bearing in mind how painful it is to have just the end of your finger nipped in a door, you should imagine how dreadful the pains of death must be when the whole body is injured or putrefying. This, of course, is complete nonsense. Death doesn't happen this way and, in any case, the most vital parts are the least sensitive.

The philosopher Seneca – a very natural man if ever there was one – pointed out that all the fuss and pomp surrounding a deathbed has more terrors than death itself. When we see someone dying and observe all the groans and convulsions, and friends weeping and hanging up black curtains and engaging in funeral rites and so on, it's not surprising that we should consider death to be a terrible thing. But it is worth noting that there is no passion in the mind of man, however weak, that cannot master the fear of death. Why should we consider death to be such a terrible enemy, when a man has so many emotions that are stronger than death? The desire for revenge overcomes the fear of death; love slights it; honour aspires to it; grief flies to it; fear can exclude it.

We read that, after Otho the emperor had killed himself, the emotion of pity (which is the tenderest of affections) caused many of his followers to die out of mere compassion for their sovereign. To the list of emotions that can overcome the fear of death, Seneca adds satiety: 'Think', he says, 'how often you have come across the fact that a person may wish to die simply because he or she has had enough of life.' A person, who is neither brave nor particularly miserable, might wish to die simply from weariness of doing the same thing over and over again.

Consider also how little the approach of death appears to affect people's characters. In most cases, they appear to be quite unchanged right up to the last instant. Augustus Caesar died saying something nice: 'Livia, remember the good times we've had together. Live on and fare well.' Tiberius died being as dishonest as ever. As Tacitus said of him: 'His bodily strength and vitality were now departing, but not his hypocrisy and double-dealing.' Vespasian died on the toilet making a joke. Galba, about to be executed, died holding out his neck and saying: 'If it's for the advantage of the Roman people, strike.' Septimius Severus died in a hurry saying: 'Nothing remains to be done by me but to be gone.'

The Stoics, for all their claims to hardihood, made far too much of death and, by their great preparations, made it appear more fearful than it really is. Better is the person who says that the close of life is among the blessings of nature. It is as natural to die, as to be born; and to a little infant, perhaps, the one is as painful as the other. People who die while deeply concerned with something else are like men wounded in hot blood; at the time they scarcely feel the hurt. So a mind fixed upon something that is good averts the distress of death. But, above all, believe it, the sweetest canticle, when a man hath obtained worthy ends, and expectations, is *Nunc dimittis* – 'Now lettest thy servant depart in peace, according to thy word, for mine eyes have seen thy salvation.'

Finally, death has this to say for it: it opens the door to good fame, and extinguishes envy. However negatively we may have been regarded during life, we shall be loved after we are dead.

William Hunter, the surgical and obstetrical pioneer, a man of immense medical experience, said on his deathbed, 'If I had strength enough to hold a pen, I would write how easy and pleasant a thing it is to die.' Hunter, a successful and fashionable London doctor, world famous and rich, left behind a life full of satisfactions and pleasure apparently without regret.

In her biography of her husband Elie Metchnikoff, the Russian physiologist and immunologist, Olga Metchnikoff records how anxious he was that his serenity in the face of death should be known and should prove comforting to others. His example, he suggested, should show how at the end of their 'vital cycle' people fear death no longer. Death has then lost its sting for them. Shortly before he died Metchnikoff had been talking to his wife about the experience of dying and she tried to get him to stop. 'But, my child,' he said, 'why do you want to calm me? I am perfectly calm.'

Sir William Osler, the great Canadian physician and one of the fathers of modern medicine, wrote in his book *Science and Immortality*, that he could hardly remember a dying patient who, at the last, was afraid of death. Osler, in a study of 500 dying patients found that only 11 were afraid during their last illness. Osler was writing at the turn of the century and it may be that the widespread religious faith of the time was a factor in producing this low incidence of anxiety. More recent studies suggest that in the stage of acceptance, fear or deep anxiety are now much commoner than they used to be and that those with religious faith show least fear.

The difficulty about these figures is to be sure that like is being compared with like. It is true that at least a quarter of seriously ill people are deeply anxious about their condition. But most of these are, in fact, at an earlier stage and are anxious at the possibility that they might die. People who have accepted that they are dying and have come through the various stages of the process show a much lower incidence of anxiety, nearer to Osler's figures.

But the last word on this matter rests with Montaigne.

It is not without reason we are taught to take notice of our sleep for the resemblance it hath with death. How easily we pass from waking to sleeping; with how little interest we lose the knowledge of light and of ourselves. For, touching the instant or moment of the passage, it is not to be feared it should bring any travail or displeasure with it, forasmuch as we can have neither sense nor feeling . . .

Appendix

Achievements of the Elderly: Patterns for All

These brief biographies are of men and women whose achievements have extended well into the later years of life. This is not a collection of exceptional cases but a demonstration that, for people who do not accept an ageist stereotype, performance of this kind is normal. It is an inspiring example of how motivation can extend productive and satisfying life to an advanced age.

Adenauer, Konrad (1876-1967) The German statesman and president of the Prussian State Council, Adenauer was stripped of his appointments and imprisoned by the Nazis. At the age of 69, he was made Lord Mayor of Cologne for the second time and founded the Christian Democratic Union. He became Chancellor of Germany at the age of 73 and was re-elected at age 77 and 81. He played an important role in the re-establishment of Germany as a partner with other European nations in NATO, and was effective in promoting Franco–German friendship. At the age of 87 Adenauer finally agreed that he was getting a little old for the job and, reluctantly, resigned. He was 91 when he died. So much international business was conducted by world leaders at his funeral that Willy Brandt quipped: 'Konrad's was a working funeral.'

Arnauld, Antoine (1612-94) Known as 'the great Arnauld', the French philosopher, mathematician, lawyer and priest, devoted his life to many tasks including sustained and energetic attacks on the Jesuits. His opinions earned him official disapproval and he had to flee in disguise. As an old man he was hunted as if he had been a criminal and had to move frequently. Even so, he never ceased to work right up to the time of his death at 82. On being asked: 'Is it not now time for you to rest?' he replied: 'Rest! Have we not all eternity in which to rest?'

Ashby, Dame Margery Corbett (1882-1981) A devoted feminist, Liberal politician and enemy of sexual prejudice, Dame Margery stood for Parliament eight times without success in order to promote the rights of women. She lectured on liberalism all over the world and worked for many organizations promoting women's rights. She wrote extensively on the rights of women for various liberal journals and was editor of *International Women's News* from 1952 to 1961. A fluent and inspiring speaker who did much to promote gender equality in many parts of the world, she remained active and happy well into old age. At 96 she gave a notable speech at Westminster Hall in London, at a meeting on the 50th anniversary of the date on which women were first allowed to vote – an event for which she was, at least partly, responsible.

Bach, Johan Sebastian (1685–1750) Bach, one of the greatest musical composers of all time, did not live to a great age but was still composing works of sublime genius at 65. The quality of his work increased steadily throughout his life, reaching a peak at the time of his death. His output included a mass of compositions for the organ and harpsichord, about 300 church cantatas, the six *Brandenburg Concertos*, and two of the greatest choral works ever written – the *St Matthew Passion* and the *B minor Mass*. He fathered 20 children. Near to the end of his work on *The Art of Fugue* and halfway through one of the movements, the pen fell from his fingers. He was unable to continue and to complete this great work, not because of lack of will but because of blindness.

Baker, Josephine (1906–75) The American dancer and singer took Paris by storm in the 1920s and was for a time one of the most popular entertainers and a top star of the Folies Bergères. She is remembered for her then scandalous semi-nude dance in a skirt made from bananas. Baker was a heroine of the French Resistance during the war and entertained troops in Africa and the Middle East. She was awarded the Croix de Guerre and the Légion d'Honneur. She was a civil rights worker in the United States in the 1960s and continued to perform in public until her death at the age of 71.

Benedetti, Alfred (1893–) This American citizen continued to enjoy bowling twice a week at the age of 101 and had participated, for the previous 11 years, in javelin-throwing, shot-putting and free-throw basketball in the Senior Olympics.

Blixen, Karen (1885–1962) Less well known as Isak Dinesen, Blixen was a Danish writer who married her cousin, Baron Bror Blixen-Finecke, in 1914, and went with him to Africa to run a coffee plantation in Kenya and engage in big-game hunting. Her book *Out of Africa*, which made her famous, depicts her love of Africa and her sorrow at the demise of the simple African way of life she so admired. Blixen is notable for her demonstration of the fact that it is never too late to start on a successful career. Her first book was published when she was almost 50 and her last appeared when she was 76.

Boulanger, Nadia (1887-1979) The French keyboard musician, teacher, orchestral conductor and musical scholar, Boulanger studied composition under Fauré and Widor. She was the first woman to conduct the Boston Philharmonic, the New York Philharmonic and Philadelphia orchestras and the first woman to conduct an entire programme of the Royal Philharmonic Orchestra in London. Her recordings of keyboard works became legendary and her pupils included Lennox Berkeley, Elliott Carter, Aaron Copland, Jean Françaix, Roy Harris, Darius Milhaud, Walter Piston, and Virgil Thomson. Her influence as a teacher was enormous. At the age of 63 she was appointed Director of the American Conservatory of Music at Fontainebleu. She was still teaching at the age of 88 and travelling widely to judge music competitions.

Brian, Havergal (1876-1972) The English musician and self-taught composer Havergal Brian wrote five operas, including an enormous music drama called *Prometheus Unbound*, no fewer than 33 symphonies and two concertos. The composition of a single symphony is an enormous task calling for uncommon resolution and energy, but Brian actually wrote 20 of his symphonies between the ages of 83 and 92.

Burns, George (1896-1996) American comedian and star of vaudeville, radio, cinema and television Burns began his career at the age of 13 as a singer in the Pee Wee Quartet and later performed as a dancer, skater and comic. He married his showbusiness partner Gracie Allen in 1926 and the celebrated comedy team became an American institution that lasted for 40 years. They made 13 feature films together. The television series *The George Burns and Gracie Allen Show* ran from 1950 to 1958. Gracie Allen died in 1964 but Burns refused to retire and continued to work successfully, making many more films. At the age of 80 he co-starred in the film *The Sunshine Boys*, giving a performance for which he was awarded an Oscar. In the last 20 years of his life, he made many TV appearances. He was 100 years old when he died.

Calment, Jeanne (1875-) This Frenchwoman is included because of one notable achievement – having become, so far as is known, the oldest person in the world. No other person whose age can be confirmed is known to be older than this lady who turned 121 in February 1996 while still remaining lively and active.

Carr, Edward H. (1892–1982) The British political scientist and historian Edward Carr joined the Foreign Office in 1916 and was assistant editor of *The Times* from 1941 to 1946. He became fellow of Balliol College, Oxford, and of Trinity College, Cambridge. His best-known work was the 14-volume *History of Soviet Russia*, which he had started at the age of 53 and completed at the age of 86.

Cartland, Barbara (1901–) Cartland is an English romantic novelist and valetudinarian who, at the age of 95, is still turning out books at an undiminished rate. Currently, more than half a million of her titles are borrowed from public libraries every year. She has written over 600 books – more than any other author or authoress – and is officially acknowledged as the writer with the greatest numerical output of books in the world. She became a Dame of the British Empire in 1991. She has also published plays, poems, biography and autobiography.

Casals, Pablo (1876–1973) Spanish cellist and one of the most distinguished exponents of the instrument, Casals' career as a soloist and chamber music player dated from about 1898. He was still playing and organizing music festivals and continuing to exert a strong influence on the world's musical scene 70 years later. His recordings of piano trios with Cortot and Thibaud, and of the Bach unaccompanied cello suites, are prized by collectors. When he was 81 Casals married his 20-year-old pupil Maria Montanez and in 1961, at the age of 84, he gave a cello recital before President of the United States John F. Kennedy at the White House.

Cato, Marcus (234–149 BC) Also known as Cato the Elder, this Roman statesman and orator was the first important writer of Latin prose. Much of what he wrote has been lost but there remains a treatise on farming containing much information on ancient customs and superstitions. Cato became censor with Flaccus in 184 BC and at once set out to limit Greek influences which he thought were damaging Roman standards of morality. He taxed excess wealth and restricted access to the Senate. At the age of 81 he became ambassador to Carthage and what he learned there strengthened his conviction that the Greeks were the major enemies of Rome. 'Carthage', he repeatedly asserted, 'must be destroyed.' The year he died, Rome declared war on Carthage.

Cellini, Benvenuto (1500–71) The Florentine sculptor, goldsmith and writer whose autobiography is one of the half-dozen outstanding examples of the genre, Cellini was one of the most colourful characters of the Renaissance. He trained as a metalworker and produced superb work in silver and gold and in statuary, much of which was melted down. He was banished after a brawl, returned and was again indicted for fighting and condemned to death. He fled to Rome where he was found guilty of killing a rival goldsmith, but was absolved by Pope Paul III. After another fight he returned to Florence. Later in life he turned to sculpture and created a number of celebrated pieces. His frank and very human *Autobiography*, begun when he was 58 and completed four years later, gives a detailed picture of his life and times and has remained in print since it was first published. At the age of 65 he started work on an important treatise on sculpture and fine metalwork.

Chagall, Marc (1887–1985) Chagall was a Russian-born painter, printmaker and designer whose paintings, etchings, engravings, book illustrations, stained-glass windows and theatre, ballet and opera sets reflected the changing artistic values, changing political scene and his extensive travels over the course of a long and highly productive life. His work encompassed pre-surrealism, expressionism, cubism, impressionism, post-impressionism and Fauvism. In addition to innumerable paintings, he produced hundreds of book illustrations for such works as Gogol's novel *Dead Souls*, La Fontaine's *Fables* and the Bible. In 1952 he married and, at the age of 65, began a new career as a painter of Parisian scenes, a painter of murals and a creator of remarkable stained-glass windows. The most notable of these are the 12 windows in the Hadassah Medical Center in Jerusalem, which he began when he was 74, and those in the United Nations building in New York. In his old age he became one of the most popular innovators in the 20th-century school of Paris.

Chanel, Gabrielle (1883–1971) Universally known as 'Coco', Gabrielle Chanel was a French dress designer whose domination of Parisian *haute couture* lasted for almost 60 years. Her designs brought simplicity and comfort into women's fashion and changed it for ever. In 1913 she opened a small millinery shop to sell her creations and this expanded into an industry employing 3,500 people and producing textiles, costume jewellery and perfumes. Much of the financial backing for this came from the highly successful Chanel No. 5 perfume, first produced in 1922. Coco retired in 1938 but returned in 1954 at the age of 71 to introduce the Chanel suit and saw it widely copied by fashion designers. She retained control of her perfume and fashion empire until her death at the age of 87.

Chaucer, Geoffrey (c. 1340–1400) English poet, comptroller of Customs in the Port of London, expert on the astrolabe and author of the *Canterbury Tales*, Chaucer began to write this magnificent and extended work at the age of 54 and completed it seven years later. His status in English literature is reflected in the fact that he was buried in Westminster Abbey in the part that later came to be called Poet's Corner.

Chevalier, Maurice (1888–1972) French musical-comedy star noted for his debonair style, exaggerated French accent in English, and straw hat and cane, Chevalier began as a Parisian café singer in 1901 and was soon well known for his performances in French musical revues. His Hollywood début in *The Innocents of Paris* (1929) led to a series of highly popular musical films in which he co-starred with Jeanette MacDonald. At the age of 70 he starred in the film *Gigi*, at 72 in *Can-Can* and at 73 in *Fanny*.

Chevreul, Michel Eugène (1796–1889) Chevreul was a French organic chemist who pioneered the chemistry of fats, did much important work on dyes and studied the science and art of colour. After a distinguished career and many notable professional appointments, he became Director of the French Museum of Natural History at the age of 78. At 80 he published papers on the history of chemistry and when he was 92 wrote learnedly on the theory of matter.

Churchill, Winston (1874–1965) British politician, statesman, writer, painter, bricklayer, prime minister and wartime leader, Churchill, after an unpromising academic career, joined the army, read all the books he thought necessary for an education, and soon began to show remarkable capacity as a writer and indications of great enterprise, initiative and courage as a soldier. The success of his writing, his status as a military hero and the privilege of his position soon got him out of the army and into politics, and he entered Parliament in 1900. By the start of World War I he was in the Cabinet as First Lord of the Admiralty and successively Minister of Munitions and Secretary of State for War. Between the wars he was in and out of office but occupied himself with writing. In May 1940, at the age of 66, he became Prime Minister and war leader, and his speeches and uncompromising leadership in the face of seeming disaster almost certainly turned the outcome in the British favour. His role in many international conferences in Cairo, Casablanca, Potsdam, Quebec, Tehran and Yalta, and his close association with the US President Franklin D. Roosevelt profoundly influenced the shape of the postwar world. In 1951, at the age of 77, he again became Prime Minister and served in this capacity until he was 81. Thereafter, he retired to the back benches.

Colbert, Jean Baptiste (1619–83) Colbert was a French statesman who reorganized the French colonies, founded others, and provided France with a great navy and a large arsenal. His encouragement of science, technology, industry and commerce raised France to new powers. At the age of 60 he took up the study of Latin and the law.

Cooke, Alistair (1908-) A British journalist, author and broadcaster, Cooke has for many years, with quiet cultivation, charm and immense skill, masterfully interpreted the American scene to Britain in his weekly BBC feature *Letter from America*, a valued contribution to Anglo-American understanding. At 89, Cooke shows little sign of flagging or of losing his sharpness of mind or sense of humour.

Courtney, Cecily (1883-1980) Courtney was a British comic actress and star of stage and screen, whose career, starting at the age of eight, extended well into her 80s. Her partnership in light musical comedy with Jack Hulbert, whom she married, was one of the most successful and durable in the history of showbusiness. Her final appearance on the West End stage was in 1971, in *Move Over, Mrs Markham*, when she was 88.

Darwin, Charles (1809-82) Darwin was an English naturalist whose theory of evolution by natural selection, outlined in his book *On the Origin of Species* (1859) changed the whole of biological thinking and created a furore at the time because of its implicit rejection of fundamentalist religion. Darwin trained as a doctor, but anatomy disgusted him and he never practised. In spite of remarkably poor health and a seeming frail personality ('Anything which flurries me completely knocks me up afterward, and brings on a violent palpitation of the heart'), Darwin continued with observational and experimental biological work and to write books and innumerable scientific papers throughout the whole of his life. He also carried on a massive correspondence with many of the important scientists of his day. He wrote books on the voyage of the *Beagle*; the evolutionary descent of humans; volcanic islands; the geology of South America; fertilization of orchids; climbing plants; different forms of flowers; the power of movement in plants; and insectivorous plants.

de Gaulle, Charles (1890-1970) de Gaulle was a French general and statesman who rejected the French armistice with Germany in World War II and, in 1940, set up the Free French movement in England. He was head of the French provisional governments from 1944 to 1946 and became President of the Fifth Republic at the age of 69. De Gaulle was jealous of French independence in the European Economic Community and vetoed British entry when he was 77. He resigned his presidency at the age of 79, not through any concern over his ability to continue, but because of lack of popular support following the revolt of students and workers.

de Mille, Cecil B. (1881–1959) American film producer and director de Mille is best known for spectacular film productions with a biblical basis such as *The Ten Commandments* (1923 and 1956), *The King of Kings* (1927) and *Samson and Delilah* (1949). Other notable successes were *Cleopatra* (1934), *The Plainsman* (1938), *Union Pacific* (1939) and *The Greatest Show on Earth* (1952). He produced and directed the latter award-winning film when he was 71 and went on to bring out *The Ten Commandments* when he was 75.

de Valera, Eamon (1882–1975) American-born Irish politician who studied in Dublin and led men into action in the Easter Rising of 1916, de Valera was sentenced to death but survived to become president of Sinn Fein in 1917, and president of the Dáil in 1918. In 1927 he formed the Fianna Fáil party and was Prime Minister of Ireland three times – in 1937–48, 1951–54 and 1957–59. He was President of the Irish Republic from the age of 77 to the age of 91.

Desai, Morarji (1896–) Desai is an Indian ascetic who founded the Janata party in opposition to Indira Gandhi. He was successful against her in the 1977 election and became Prime Minister of India, serving until 1979 when he was 83.

Dryden, John (1631–1700) English poet laureate, whose complete works form the largest body of poetry by a single writer in the English language, Dryden wrote nothing of importance until he was nearly 30 but, thereafter, excelled in every branch of English literature – satire, essays, plays, comedies, heroic tragedy, translation and criticism. His enormous output included most of the works of Virgil including the *Georgics* and the whole of the *Aeneid* translated into rhyming couplets; at the age of 68, he proposed to translate the whole of Homer's *Iliad*, but died the following year.

Duggar, Benjamin (1872–1956) Duggar was an American plant pathologist who, at the age of 73, having been cast aside as too old by the University of Wisconsin where he had been Professor of Mycology, was offered a laboratory by the American Cyanamid Company. There, soon afterward, he isolated the fungus *Streptomyces aureofaciens*. After three years' work on this organism he was able to isolate and purify the antibiotic chlortetracycline which was marketed as Aureomycin and which proved highly successful in its own right and as the progenitor for a whole family of tetracycline antibiotics. Millions of lives, and an enormous amount of illness have been saved by the achievement of this man of 76.

Durant, Will (1885–1981) and Ariel (1898–1981) The Durants were popular American historians whose works were widely read. Will's most important works were *The Story of Philosophy* (1926) and, in collaboration with his wife Ariel, *The Story of Civilization* (1935–75). The latter is an enormous work, an 11-volume historical series that has won wide critical and popular acclaim and is now available on CD-ROM. The tenth volume of the work, *Rousseau and Revolution* (1967), won a Pulitzer Prize. Their last book, published when Will was 92 and Ariel 83, was *A Dual Autobiography* (1977).

Eddy, Mary Baker (1821–1910) Eddy was a prominent American religious figure who founded the Christian Science movement in 1866 and wrote the Christian Science textbook, *Science and Health with Key to the Scriptures.* She was a delicate child, unable to attend school regularly and privately taught. Her poor health persisted into adult life. Following a severe injury she was reading about Christ's miraculous healing when she came to believe that she understood how Christ performed his miracles. At once she was restored to health. This led her to the view that all disease was of mental or spiritual origin and started her on a long career of writing on the subject. In 1879 she founded the Church of Christ, Scientist and, at the age of 87 established the highly successful journal The *Christian Science Monitor.* She remained in close control of the Christian Science movement until her death at the age of 89.

Edison, Thomas Alva (1847–1931) The American inventor whose catalogue of new ideas and devices changed the face of society, Edison was the holder of patents for more than 1,000 inventions, including the incandescent electric lamp, the gramophone, the automatic telegraph, the ticker-tape machine for stock market prices, the carbon granule microphone, the thermionic diode, flexible celluloid film and a primitive system of moving pictures known as the kinetoscope. His discovery of the thermionic diode effect was the foundation of the science of electronics. At the age of 70, during World War I, he was actively engaged in naval warfare research. Edison made his last invention at the age of 81.

Einstein, Albert (1879–1955) Einstein was the German-born American physicist and mathematician whose special theory of relativity (1904), evolved to account for the seemingly anomalous results of the Mitchelson-Morley experiment on the speed of light, overturned ideas in physics and mathematics. Einstein's general theory of relativity (1916) further confounded the scientists by showing that gravitational mass must interact with the apparent mass of electromagnetic radiations such as light. This was triumphantly proved by astronomical observations in 1919 after which Einstein was lionized. He also made major contributions to quantum theory, for which he was awarded the Nobel Prize for Physics in 1921. The rise of the Nazi party caused Einstein to move to the United States when he was 54. Thereafter he abandoned his former pacifism. At the age of 60 he wrote to President Franklin D. Roosevelt urging the necessity for the United States to develop an atomic bomb before Germany did. In his 70s he boldly opposed the witch-hunting of the House Committee on Un-American Activities and continued until the time of his death to search for a theory that would cover both gravitation and electromagnetism – a unified field theory.

Ellington, Edward Kennedy ('Duke') (1899-1974) American bandleader, pianist and composer of highly organized and extremely popular jazz and swing music compositions, Ellington and his orchestra became famous as the stars of Harlem's Cotton Club where they played from 1927 to 1931. Subsequent radio broadcasts and European tours brought him international fame. Ellington wrote over 1,000 pieces including such celebrated numbers as *Mood Indigo, Black, Brown and Beige, Concerto for Cootie, Creole Love Call, Creole Rhapsody* and *Clarinet Lament.* He was still playing the piano brilliantly and made his last recording a few weeks before he died, at the age of 75.

Evans, Dame Edith (1888-1976) The British actress born Mary Booth made her London stage début in 1912 and subsequently appeared in numerous plays and films. She continued to act, both in modern drama and film, and was distinguished for her Shakespearean roles, notably as the nurse in *Romeo and Juliet.* She appeared in the film *The Whisperers* at the age of 78 and around this time is said to have asked that her dates should be omitted from books of reference because the truth might discourage producers from offering her work. She died ten years later.

Fiedler, Arthur (1894-1979) Fiedler was an American orchestral conductor best known for his brilliant work in interpreting light classical music with the Boston Pops Orchestra. He was also permanent conductor of the Boston Symphony Orchestra and a guest conductor of the San Francisco Symphony Orchestra, the New York Philharmonic Orchestra, and the NBC Symphony Orchestra. At the age of 85, in the year of his death, Fiedler celebrated his 50th anniversary as conductor of the Boston Pops Orchestra. He had, by then, become a household name in music and had produced many notable and commercially successful recordings.

Fields, W.C. (1880-1946) Born William Claude Dukenfield, this comic American film actor's potato nose, straw hat, rasping gravelly voice and unremitting put-down humour endeared him to millions. Fields' career began as a teenage juggler in stage reviews. He started in silent films at the age of 35 and appeared in many short comic items. By his 50s he was a highly popular and successful film personality and film writer. He made a brilliant Mr Micawber in the film *David Copperfield* (1935) and subsequently appeared in such films as *You Can't Cheat an Honest Man* (1939), *The Bank Dick* (1940), *My Little Chicadee* (1940) and, at the age of 61, in *Never Give a Sucker an Even Break* (1941). His last appearance was a year before his death at the age of 66. The misanthropy that was such a central feature of his work – he claimed to hate children, mothers-in-law, bank managers, wives, dogs, policemen and almost everything else – was probably bad for Fields. He acquired a reputation for being difficult, which prejudiced the latter part of his career and may have contributed to the illness that shortened his life.

Francis, Dick (1920–) Francis was a British champion jump jockey who embarked on a second career at the age of 42 and became one of the most popular and successful writers of thriller fiction of his day. He was in the RAF throughout the war and was a steeple-chase jockey from the age of 26 to 37. He was the first jockey to be retained by Her Majesty Queen Elizabeth the Queen Mother under National Hunt rules and remained a close friend thereafter. He was the racing correspondent of the *Sunday Express* from 1957 to 1973 but started to write novels in 1962. He has written over 30 novels that have delighted millions for their convincing characterization, well-researched and varied settings, suspense, tight plotting and an unusually convincing but unforced high moral tone. His work has been translated into many languages and has won several writers' awards in Britain and America. At 76, Francis is producing better books than ever.

Franco, Francisco (1892–1975) Spanish general and dictator who was commander-in-chief of the Falangists in the Civil War of 1936–39, Franco cooperated with Germany and Italy in keeping Spain out of World War II. With the assistance of his fellow dictators, Hitler and Mussolini, he defeated the Republican government and remained the autocratic head of state (*Caudillo*) from 1939 until his death at the age of 83 in 1975 when the monarchy was restored with the accession of Juan Carlos I.

Franklin, Benjamin (1706–90) Franklin was an American statesman, scientist, printer, newspaperman, essayist, moral philosopher, diplomat, Francophile, champion swimmer and inventor. Franklin assisted in the drafting of the American Declaration of Independence and, as ambassador to France from 1776 to 1785, negotiated an alliance between America and France and a peace settlement with Britain. By a rather dangerous experiment during a thunderstorm, Franklin proved that lightning was electrical in nature and went on to invent the lightning conductor. This made him world famous and he was elected to the British Royal Society in 1756 and to the French Academy of Sciences in 1772. He was responsible for the aphorism 'Early to bed and early to rise make a man healthy, wealthy, and wise'. His book *Poor Richard's Almanack*, written to show how a person might rise by hard work, thrift and honesty, sold widely and was translated into many languages. At the age of 42, Franklin had earned enough to retire comfortably but he then embarked on a long and distinguished career as an inventor, politician, public official, legislator, military leader and diplomat. He received honorary doctor's degrees from the University of St Andrews in 1759 and from Oxford in 1762. He reorganized the American postal system. At the age of 60 he became the principal defender of American rights in Britain. When the British Parliament passed the Tea Act of 1773 which was damaging to the colonies, Franklin wrote a series of satirical political essays detailing the injustices of British colonialism. At the age of 70 he became a revolutionary and was happy to sign the American Declaration of Independence. At the age of 72 Franklin became the first American minister to France and for seven years he worked tirelessly to raise money, arms and supplies for the new colony and to promote Franco-American relations. Eventually, he persuaded the British parliament that Britain could not win the war and he successfully carried out secret peace negotiations with officials sent to France from London. At 80 Franklin was appointed President of Pennsylvania.

Freud, Sigmund (1856–1939) The Austrian neurologist turned psychiatrist, Freud developed the technique of psychoanalysis into a major discipline. His ideas, formed on the basis of his experience of the 'talking cure' – the free association of ideas – and an imaginative analysis of dreams, were concerned largely with the nature and later consequences of infantile sexuality. Around the age of 64 Freud developed cancer of the upper jaw and suffered much pain and innumerable operations. In spite of this he remained highly active and productive, writing many books and papers, until he died from cancer at the age of 83.

Frost, Robert (1874–1963) American poet of country life in New England, Frost was four times winner of the Pulitzer Prize. At the age of 38, he sold his farm and with the money took his family to England to devote himself to writing. He was quickly successful. *A Boy's Will* was accepted by a London publisher in 1913 and favourably reviewed. In England he made friends with Ezra Pound, whose political confinement in a mental hospital he was later able to bring to an end, Rupert Brooke and Edward Thomas, whom he urged to turn from prose to poetry. Sales of his first two books, *A Boy's Will* and *North of Boston* financed further writing and when he was 42 he published *Mountain Interval* and took up teaching and lecturing. At 50 he received a Pulitzer Prize in poetry for *New Hampshire*, at 56 he published *Collected Poems*, at 62 *A Further Range*, and at 68 *A Witness Tree*. At the inauguration of President John F. Kennedy, Frost – then 86 – recited his poem *The Gift Outright* from memory. He died aged 89 having received a great number of literary, academic and other honours.

Gandhi, Mohandas (1869–1948) The Indian political and religious leader known as Mahatma Gandhi was largely responsible for bringing about India's independence from Britain by promoting a policy of passive resistance and civil disobedience. His activities, which included hunger strikes, were also concerned with the reform of social structures and especially the harsh treatment of people of the untouchable caste. He strove to promote amity between Muslims and Hindus and, at the age of 77 saw India achieve her independence. Gandhi strenuously opposed the partition of India into Muslim and Hindu states and was effective in promoting a mass movement against this. The following year he was murdered by a Hindu extremist who had misunderstood his intentions and thought him pro-Muslim.

Gladstone, William (1809–98) British statesman, leader of the Liberal Party, Prime Minister and master of political debate. Gladstone tried, but failed to achieve home rule for Ireland and abolition of income tax. He succeeded in getting rid of the secret ballot, in abolishing religious qualifications for university posts and achieved various important educational reforms. He was not assisted in office by Queen Victoria's obvious preference for his rival Disraeli. Gladstone was a highly sexed and morally tortured man who, although married, appeared to find the company of prostitutes irresistible: he even brought them to No 10. In his 70s he was regularly visiting brothels to try to 'save' the girls from their sin. This preoccupation was largely concealed from the public and he sought conscientiously to apply morality to politics. He was premier from age 59 to 65; from age 71 to 76; at age 77; and finally from age 83 to 85.

Goethe, Johann Wolfgang von (1749–1832) Goethe, the poet, dramatist, philosopher, scientist and courtier, is generally regarded as the greatest figure in German literature. His best-known works include *Faust* (1775–1832), in two parts, the second of which he completed when he was over 80, the dramas *Egmont* (1788) and *Tasso* (1790), and the series of *Wilhelm Meister* novels (1796–1829). Throughout his life Goethe was a great lover of women. At the age of 74 he fell madly in love with a 19-year-old girl called Ulrike Lentzow. He loved dancing with her and wanted to marry her but her mother objected and

Goethe's disappointment brought on a serious illness. Several years later he fell in love again. Even on the day he died he expressed admiration for an attractive woman.

Handel, George Frederick (1685–1759) Handel was an extraordinarily prolific composer who specialized in large-scale works. He wrote some 40 operas, 17 English oratorios and innumerable other works for keyboard and other instruments. In 1741, at the age of 56, Handel wrote the whole of the *Messiah* in just over three weeks. Without pausing for breath he started straight in on *Samson*, an equally large oratorio. Handel continued to write massive works including *Joseph, Semele, Judas Maccabeus* and *Solomon*. His last great work, *Jephthah*, appeared when he was aged 65. In his final years, like his contemporary J. S. Bach, he was restricted in composition by blindness.

Hardy, Thomas (1840–1928) Hardy was an English novelist and poet, most of whose novels are set in his native Dorset (fictionalized as Wessex). He wrote 15 novels, four collections of short stories, eight collections of poems, and a three-part epic drama. His best-known novels are *Far from the Madding Crowd* (1874), *The Return of the Native* (1878), *The Mayor of Casterbridge* (1886), *Tess of the d'Urbevilles* (1891) and *Jude the Obscure*, published when he was 55. After that he concentrated on poetry. *Wessex Poems* came out when he was 58, and a three-part blank-verse drama called *The Dynasts*, on which he had worked for many years, appeared in instalments between his 64th and 68th years. His last book of poems, *Winter Words* was published when he was 88.

Hearst, William Randolph (1863–1951) American newspaper publisher Hearst pioneered popular sensational journalism and, with the proceeds, founded a chain of newspapers, a major publishing enterprise and an enormous fortune. His long-running rivalry, as a promoter of 'yellow journalism', with his more conservative opponent Joseph Pulitzer was a source of sustained interest to millions and his support for the man in the street brought popularity that led him into high political ambition. He failed, however, to get the Democratic presidential nomination in 1904 or to become Governor of New York. In later years he turned conservative, built an impressive mansion at San Simeon, and eventually retired with his long-time actress mistress, Marion Davies, to Beverly Hills. Hearst's career inspired the remarkable film *Citizen Kane*, starring Orson Wells.

Hindenburg, Field Marshal Paul von Beneckendorff und von (1847–1934) German field marshal and statesman Hindenburg was responsible for German military strategy in World War I. He became president of Germany at the age of

78 and remained in office until his death at 87. Thinking that he could control him, Hindenburg appointed Hitler, whom he detested, as Chancellor in January 1933. By the time Hindenburg died, Hitler had ensured that all the reins of power were in his own hands.

Hobbes, Thomas (1588–1679) Hobbes was an English political philosopher, and author of an outstanding work of political theory, *Leviathan*, published when he was 63. This book promoted the principles of absolute sovereignty. At the age of 67 he produced the book *De Corpore* and at 69 *De Homine*. In his 80s he was still writing tirelessly. At 80 he finished *Behemoth*, an account of the causes of the civil war, at 84 he published an autobiography in Latin verse, at 87 a translation in verse of Homer's *Iliad*, and at 88 a translation of the *Odyssey*. Hobbes was an atheist whose writings aroused much opposition. He died aged 91: his last words were 'Death is a great leap in the dark.'

Hokusai, Katsushika (1760–1849) Hokusai was a Japanese artist and print-maker celebrated for his remarkable work *One Hundred Views of Mount Fuji*. He entered his great period at the age of 75. Although he had been studying his art throughout his life and started to publish at the age of 50, he believed that he had done nothing of much value before he was 70. According to his own account, he began to understand the structure of living things at the age of 73 and expected to achieve real depth at 90 and to be divinely inspired at 100. Actually, he died at 89, having achieved perpetual fame.

Hope, Bob (1903–) Hope is an English-born American comedian and comic actor of stage, radio, television and cinema whose immense popularity extends over 60 years. His long, joking, love-hate relationship with Bing Crosby was promoted in a series of *Road to . . .* films co-starring Dorothy Lamour. Among his best and funniest films are *The Cat and the Canary* (1939), *Road to Morocco* (1942) and *The Paleface* (1947). Hope's many worldwide tours to entertain American servicemen on duty in overseas stations greatly added to the respect and affection with which he was held. He was still appearing on stage and TV in his 80s.

Hugo, Victor (1802–85) The French novelist, dramatist and poet Hugo was one of the leaders of the romantic movement in French literature and author of *Notre-Dame de Paris* (1831, known in English as *The Hunchback of Notre Dame*) and *Les Misérables* (1862). His poetical works include the volumes of verse *Les Feuilles d'Automne* (1831) and *Les Contemplations* (1856). He wrote the plays *Hernani* (1830) and *Ruy Blas* (1838). Hugo's political views led to his exile, with his devoted mistress Juliette Drouet, to the Channel Islands, where he wrote *Les Misérables* and *Contemplations* as well as much bitter criticism of the French government. After 19 years he returned to Paris, a national hero, on the fall of the Second Empire. Soon afterward he was elected a member of the National Assembly and was then made a senator of the Third Republic. He remained active in politics and continued to write poetry right up to the time of his death at the age of 83.

Humboldt, Friedrich Heinrich, Alexander, Baron von (1769–1859) Humboldt was a German naturalist, explorer, chemist, mineralogist and thinker whose work of popular science, *Kosmos*, proved to be one of the most influential books of the time. This five-volume book, which provided a remarkably detailed account of the whole universe, was written by Humboldt between the ages of 76 and 89.

Ibsen, Henrik (1828–1906) The Norwegian dramatist and poet Ibsen was best known for his verse play *Peer Gynt* (1867) and his prose dramas on social questions, *A Doll's House* (1879), *Ghosts* (1881), *The Wild Duck* (1886), *Hedda Gabler* (1890) and *The Master Builder* (1892). He was considered deeply shocking in his day, but is now acknowledged as a writer of the first importance with great influence on modern drama. His last play, written when he was 71, concerns the importance of sexual love and defied conventional morality.

James, Henry (1843–1916) American-born novelist, short-story writer and literary critic, James was a devoted Anglophile and European who is said to have been so popular with London hostesses that he dined out every evening. He wrote 22 novels, 113 short stories, 15 plays, two biographies, seven travel books, three volumes of autobiography and an enormous amount of criticism, as well as a great deal of private correspondence, of which some 15,000 letters have survived. His novels include *The American* (1877), *Daisy Miller* (1878), *Washington Square* (1880), *The Portrait of a Lady* (1881), *The Bostonians* and *The Princess Casamassima* (1886), *The Wings of the Dove* (1902), *The Ambassadors* (1903) and *The Golden Bowl* (1904).

Jung, Gustav (1875–1961) Swiss psychologist and mystic Jung defected from Freud's school of psychoanalysis because of what he thought was an undue emphasis on sex. Jung deviated progressively from strictly scientific concepts and formulated concepts of a collective unconscious to account for many anthropological similarities. His ideas of archetypes were fruitful and he is well known for his personality classifications of extrovert and introvert. At the age of 85 he was still working and completed work on one of his best-known books *Man and His Symbols* (1961).

Karloff, Boris (1887-1969) Karloff was the English film actor who became famous for his many roles in horror films. He is best remembered for his portrayal of the monster in the film *Frankenstein* (1931). He was still working at the age of 80 and appeared in the film *Targets* (1967).

Kenyatta, Jomo (c. 1891-1978) Kenyan politician Kenyatta's involvement with the Mau Mau terrorist movement in the 1950s led to his imprisonment. He became President of the Kenya African National Union in 1961, Prime Minister of the newly independent Kenya in 1963, and President of Kenya in 1964. He remained in office until his death at the age of 87.

Kirk, Herbert (1896-) This 100-year-old American graduated with a bachelor's degree in art from Montana State University at the age of 97. Kirk continued to play tennis into his 80s and, at the age of 95, won gold medals for the 800 m and 5 km races and a silver medal for the 200 m at an International Seniors' Athletic meeting in Helsinki.

Landor, Walter Savage (1775-1864) English poet and essayist Landor is best known for his long prose work *Imaginary Conversations* (1824–29), consisting of 152 dialogues between outstanding men of the past. Landor pursued a writing career for no less than 68 years. He again took up *Imaginary Conversations* late in life and wrote conversations between Virgil and Horace and between Milton and Marvell when he was 82.

Liszt, Franz (1811-86) Hungarian composer, pianist, priest and ladies' man, Liszt's astonishing technique at the piano aroused enthusiasm wherever he played. His compositions are impressive and innovative with new harmonies, strong dramatic effects and sometimes a fine melodic line. Liszt originated the symphonic poem. His works include the symphonies *Faust* (1861) and *Dante* (1867), many piano compositions, transcriptions for the piano of orchestral and operatic pieces and organ works by J. S. Bach. His late music is often simple but surprisingly modern and influenced a number of later composers.

Macmillan, Harold (1894-1986) 1st Earl of Stockton, Macmillan was a British statesman and publisher who was Conservative Prime Minister from 1957 to 1963, assuming office on the resignation of Sir Anthony Eden over the Suez affair of 1956 and resigning after it was revealed that his friend John Profumo, whom he had supported in the House, had been misleading him over the sex scandal with Christine Keeler. His memoirs, in six volumes, were published between 1966 and 1973 and his *War Diaries* came out in 1984.

Mao Zedong (1893-1976) Mao was the Chinese Marxist leader and founder, in 1949, of the People's Republic of China of which he remained chairman until 1959. The son of a peasant farmer, he led a full and active life. He helped to found the Chinese Communist Party in Shanghai in 1921 and was leader of the Hunan branch. When, in 1927, Chiang Kai-Shek purged all communists Mao had to flee to the mountains of south China, where he established a guerrilla army. This led to Mao becoming Chairman of the Chinese Communist Party, a position he held until he died at the age of 81. He opposed the Japanese in World War II, and afterwards defeated the Kuomintang regime in a civil war. He instigated the Cultural Revolution in 1966. Mao is ranked with Marx and Lenin as one of the three great theorists of Marxian communism.

Marx, Groucho (1890-1977) Marx was the American surrealist comic actor whose painted moustache, loping walk and astonishing wisecracks became known throughout the world. With his somewhat less extrovert brothers Harpo, Gummo and Zeppo, Marx made a number of comic films that were to reach cult status. These include *Animal Crackers* (1930), *Monkey Business* (1931), *Horse Feathers* (1932), *Duck Soup* (1933), *A Night at the Opera* (1935), *A Day at the Races* (1937), *Room Service* (1938) and *A Night in Casablanca* (1946). The team then split up but Groucho continued his career as a solo performer, most importantly as the aggressive, hilariously funny, double-talking host of the radio and television quiz show *You Bet Your Life*. This ran from 1947 to 1961 when Groucho was over 70.

Meir, Golda (1898-1978) Meir was the Russian-born Israeli politician and stateswoman, who, after Israel declared its independence in 1948, became ambassador to the USSR, Minister of Labour from 1949 to 1956, Minister of Foreign Affairs and head of the Israeli delegation to the United States from 1956 to 1966 and, in 1968, Prime Minister of Israel. She served until 1974 by which time she was 76 years old. She resigned because of her inability to form a government after her party suffered criticism that they had been unprepared for the Egyptian and Syrian attack on Israel in 1973.

Metchnikoff, Elie (1845-1916) The Russian bacteriologist Metchnikoff worked in the Pasteur Institute in Paris where he may be said to have founded the modern science of immunology. His original work in which he showed that the immune system operated by the action of cells called phagocytes which attacked and destroyed germs earned him the Nobel prize for physiology or medicine for 1908. Metchnikoff was a great believer in the health-giving powers of yoghurt which, he thought, countered dangerous putrefaction of food residues in the large intestine.

Michaelangelo Buonarroti (1475-1564) Michaelangelo was an Italian painter, sculptor, scholar and poet and one of the finest draftsmen of all time. His sculptures *Pietá* and *David* and painting of the ceiling of the Sistine chapel and of the *Last Judgement* are known all over the world. Michaelangelo preserved his creative genius until extreme old age. One of his creations represents an old man in a go-cart with an hour-glass on it and the inscription *Ancora imparo!* (I'm still learning!).

Monet, Claude (1840-1926) The French landscape painter and leading exponent of the Impressionist movement, Monet was fascinated by the varying effect of different light on colour and painted a series of pictures of the same subject at different times of day. He was extremely poor until the 1880s when he began to be recognized. His best-known works are *Haystacks* (1889–93), *Rouen Cathedral* (1892–94), *The Thames* (1899–1904) and *Water Lilies* (1899–1906). Monet was a close associate of Renoir and knew Bazille and Sisley.

Moore, Henry (1898-1986) British sculptor now acknowledged as one of the greatest of the 20th century, Moore was noted for his distortions of the human figure by means of which he conveyed his deep sense of the power and invincibility of humankind. He continued to be creative into his 80s, producing graphics as well as sculpture. Moore's works include the *Madonna and Child* (1943) at St Matthew's Church, Northampton.

Moses, Anna Mary ('Grandma') (1860-1961) This self-taught American primitive painter began to paint seriously at the age of 75 after many years as a farmer's wife. Working mainly from memory, she produced large numbers of colourful paintings of scenes from American rural life and built up a substantial reputation as America's most renowned primitive painter. When she was 81 Grandma Moses received the New York State Prize for the painting *The Old Oaken Bucket*, and when she was 89 President Harry S. Truman presented her with the Women's National Press Club Award for outstanding accomplishment in art. At the age of 92 she published her autobiography, entitled *My Life's History*.

Mumford, Lewis (1895-1990) American sociologist, cultural historian, social philosopher and authority on architecture and urban planning, Mumford studied the development of human communities. He wrote books on American art and architecture, wrote a regular column on architecture for *The New Yorker*, and eventually made his reputation with the book *The Culture of Cities*, published when he was 43. This was the start of his great period and he wrote many more books as a critic of technology and of the mechanization and materialism of society. At the age of 59 he published a condemnation of nuclear warfare called *In the Name of Sanity* and at 67 he published *The City in History*, which won a National Book Award in 1962. When he was 72 and 75 he published the two volumes of *Myth of the Machine*. At 82 he published his 28th book, and at the age of 87 he published his autobiography *Sketches from Life*.

Nash, John (1752–1835) Nash was an English town planner and one of the leading British architects of the early 19th century. After various early vicissitudes including the loss of his fortune, his luck changed when he acquired the patronage of the Prince Regent, later King George IV. At the age of 54 he was appointed architect to the Commission of Woods and Forests, and two years later commissioned to begin the great design of Regent's Park in London and a processional route from the park to Buckingham Palace. This led to his designing Regent Street, Oxford Circus, Piccadilly Circus, Trafalgar Square, Carlton House Terrace and the Marble Arch. He was responsible for the enlargement of Buckingham Palace. Nash also rebuilt the prince's seaside retreat, the Royal Pavilion at Brighton, turning it into into an Oriental pleasure palace and completing this work when he was 71. He was 78 when the king died and he lost his job, but retired to a Gothic castle of his own design on the Isle of Wight.

Nicklaus, Jack (1940–) This American professional golfer won the British Open Championship in 1966, 1970 and 1978, and the US Open Championship in 1967, 1972 and 1980. In his late 50s Nicklaus is still turning in impressive performances in many of the world-class golf championships: in the 1996 British Open Championship, he played magnificent golf and was at one stage in third place at seven under par.

Niemöller, Pastor Martin (1892–1984) A German Protestant theologian, Niemöller was imprisoned from 1938 to 1945 for preaching against the pagan tendencies of Hitler's regime and openly declaring his church's opposition to the Nazis. Niemöller had served as a submarine commander during World War I but became a priest in 1924 and was appointed pastor at the fashionable Berlin-Dahlem church in 1931. After his arrest he was confined at Sachsenhausen and then at Dachau concentration camp, but survived to become president of the World Council of Churches at the age of 68. He continued in this appointment until he was 76 and, at the age of 79 he was awarded West Germany's highest honour, the Grand Cross of Merit.

Nightingale, Florence (1820–1910) Known as the 'Lady with the Lamp' and famous for her work during the Crimean War and for her unremitting battles with military medical bureaucracy in the interests of the sick and wounded, Nightingale did much to raise the status, quality and reputation of the nursing profession and founded a training school for nurses in London. Later in life she was heaped with honours and was so famous that, at the age of 87 she was given a proclamation signed by thousands of women who had been named after her. She died at the age of 90.

Ogilby, John (1600–76) Scottish mapmaker, printer and dancing teacher Ogilby lost everything in the Civil War but after the Restoration was favoured by the court and became a publisher in London. He built up a thriving business but his whole stock was destroyed in the Great Fire of London. He managed, however, to get the job of surveying the destroyed city and with the proceeds of this employment set up a successful printing firm. Perhaps his most remarkable feat was to take up the study of Latin and Greek after the age of 50 and then to produce translations of Homer and Virgil.

Pannell, Dr W. L. (c. 1878–1980) Pannell was an American physician who, at the age of 101, was still practising medicine in East Orange, New Jersey. Along with nine other people aged 100 or over, he addressed a committee set up by the House of Representatives to study ageing. Pannell's prescription for long life was hard work for both body and mind.

Pertini, Alessandro (1896–1990) The Italian journalist and politician Pertini joined the Socialist party in 1918 and vigorously opposed the Fascist policies of Benito Mussolini. Between the years 1926 and 1943 he spent most of his time in prison, but at the age of 50 he was elected to the Italian parliament. When he was 72 he became president of its lower house, the Chamber of Deputies. He was appointed President of the Republic of Italy at the age of 81 and served in that capacity until he was 89.

Picasso, Pablo (1881–1973) Spanish painter and sculptor, resident in France. Picasso was one of the most highly influential figures in 20th-century art and produced an enormous amount of work – some 20,000 paintings, drawings, sculptures, ceramics and other artefacts. Among the best-known of his works are *The Dwarf Dancer* (1901), belonging to his blue period; the first cubist painting *Les Demoiselles d'Avignon* (1907); *Woman's Head* (1909), *Ambroise Vollard* (1909–10), *Three Dancers* (1925) which appeared in the first surrealist exhibition, *La Joie de Vivre* (1946) and, perhaps best known of all, *Guernica* (1937), inspired by an event in the Spanish Civil War. Picasso never stopped working. At the time of his death at the age of 92, he was universally recognized as the foremost artist of his era.

Rockefeller, John D. (1839–1937) American industrialist and philanthropist Rockefeller, with others, set up an oil business in Cleveland that took over most of the many Cleveland oil refineries and expanded to become the largest refining operation in the world. In 1870 Rockefeller founded the Standard Oil Company of Ohio and amassed enormous personal wealth, much of which he gave away in philanthropic enterprises. He created the Rockefeller Foundation, the General Education Board, the Rockefeller Institute for Medical Research and the University of Chicago, remaining active in business and philanthropy up to the time of his death at the age of 98.

Rockwell, Norman (1894–1978) A highly realistic and humorous American illustrator, Rockwell was noted especially for magazine covers, especially those used for the *Saturday Evening Post.* He is also highly regarded for the series entitled *The Four Freedoms,* painted when he was 47 and used as posters during World War II. Rockwell's original artwork for the magazine covers now commands high prices. His autobiography, *My Adventures as an Illustrator,* was published when he was 66. At the age of 82 Rockwell was the guest of honour at a Norman Rockwell parade in which living tableaux reproducing some of his best-known covers were displayed.

Rodin, Auguste (1840–1917) Rodin was a French sculptor and painter, noted for his portrayal of the human form. His best-known works include *The Kiss* (1886), *The Burghers of Calais* (1896) and *The Thinker* completed when he was 65. At the age of 40 he was commissioned by the French government to design doors for a proposed museum. This he based on Dante's Inferno, but the work, which went on for most of his life, inspired the production of some of his best-known figure sculptures. He was ahead of his time and some of his finest works were condemned as botched and unfinished. Rodin was greatly in demand as a portrait sculptor and produced magnificent busts of many of the most celebrated people of his time. He was still producing small studies of ballet dancers in his 70s but he suffered greatly during World War I and died, broken in health of body and mind, at the age of 77. A few months before his death, he married Rose Beuret with whom he had lived for more than 50 years.

Routh, Martin Joseph (1755–1854) This persistent, scholarly and painstaking man of learning became a Fellow of Magdalen College, Oxford at the age of 20 and President of Magdalen at the age of 36. He was still President at the age of 99 when he died, having held this office for 63 years. In old age his mental powers remained unimpaired and in his 94th year he could walk six miles.

Rubinstein, Artur (1886–1982) This Polish-born American pianist enjoyed one of the longest active performing careers in the history of music. His first public performance was at the age of seven and at 13 he played a Mozart piano concerto in Berlin. He continued to enchant audiences with his sensitive interpretations of Chopin, Brahms, Schubert, Schumann and Spanish music almost right up to the time of his death at the age of 96; at 90 he played the long athletic left-hand octave section in Chopin's *Polonaise in A flat* with power, control and delicacy. Rubinstein published two volumes of autobiography, *My Young Years* in 1973 and *My Many Years* in 1980.

Russell, Bertrand (1872–1970) British philosopher and mathematician, Russell was awarded the Nobel Prize for literature in 1950 when he was 78. In the political sphere he is best remembered for his active campaigning against nuclear warfare. At the age of 83 he organized a manifesto against nuclear weapons which was signed by Einstein and other scientists. At 85 he took part in the first Pugwash conference and at 86 became the first president of the Campaign for Nuclear Disarmament. Two years later he formed the more militant Committee of 100, dedicated to civil disobedience in pursuit of its aims. At the age of 89 he took part in a mass sit-down on the steps of the War Office in Whitehall and participated in a demonstration six months later, as a result of which he and his wife were sentenced to two months in prison. He insisted that President John F. Kennedy and Prime Minister Harold Macmillan were more wicked than Hitler. He died within three months of his 98th birthday. His many books include *Principles of Mathematics* (1903); *Principia Mathematica* (1910–13) written in collaboration with A. N. Whitehead; *Introduction to Mathematical Philosophy* (1919); *The Problems of Philosophy* (1912); *The Analysis of Mind* (1921); *An Enquiry into Meaning and Truth* (1940); *Human Knowledge: Its Scope and Limits*, published when he was 76; *Portraits from Memory*, published when he was 84; *My Philosophical Development*, published when he was 87; his three-volume *Autobiography* (1967, 1968, 1969), the last volume of which was published when he was 97; *Common Sense and Nuclear Warfare* (1959); *Has Man a Future?* (1961); and *Unarmed Victory* published when he was 91.

Schweitzer, Albert (1875–1965) Franco-German medical missionary, philosopher, theologian and organist, born in Alsace, Schweitzer had doctorates in philosophy, theology, music and medicine, which he took up at the age of 30. At the age of 38 he became a medical missionary and devoted most of the rest of his life to a mission hospital at Lambaréné, Gabon which he built and where he died at the age of 90. Schweitzer was awarded the Nobel peace prize at the age of 77.

Segovia, Andres (1894-1987) Segovia was a self-taught Spanish guitarist who, almost alone, raised the status of the instrument to that of an exponent of classical music. Previously considered to be an instrument suitable only for accompanying songs and playing flamenco music, the guitar took on a new importance in 1924 when the 30-year old Segovia began to give concerts in Paris. Four years later his concerts in the USA consolidated his status as a master musician. Segovia devoted the rest of his life to revolutionizing the fingernail and thumbnail technique of the guitar, transcribing numerous works for the instrument, making many classic recordings and giving concerts. In his 80s, Segovia was still delighting audiences with recitals of music written and arranged for the instrument. His technique and artistry were an inspiration to a generation of classical guitarists.

Shaw, George Bernard (1856-1950) Irish music critic, dramatist and polemic writer who lived and worked in England from 1876, Shaw was an opinionated man who could support his often paradoxical opinions with great force and conviction. He was active in socialism and was a founding member of the Fabian Society but his major works are social satires rather than political tracts. His early works, a number of novels, failed and at first he had difficulty in getting his plays performed. So he wrote long prefaces for them and published them as books. They include *Arms and the Man* (1894), *Candida* (1894), *Man and Superman* (1903), *Major Barbara* (1905) and *Pygmalion* (1913), the basis of the successful musical comedy and film *My Fair Lady*. When he was 60 he wrote *Heartbreak House* – a new departure concerned with the collapse of civilization. At 65 he produced *Back to Methuselah* (1921) and, at 67, *St Joan* (1923). In 1925 at 69 Shaw was awarded the Nobel prize for literature. At 72 he published *The Intelligent Woman's Guide to Socialism*, and at 76 *The Adventures of the Black Girl in Search of God*. At 82 he produced the play *Geneva*. Shaw was a man of immense vitality who remained active and productive well into his 90s. He expected to live for well over 100 years, and there are suggestions in his later writings that he may have considered himself a member of a new, longer-lived, evolutionary subspecies.

Stokowski, Leopold (1882-1977) This British-born American conductor did much to popularize classical music and the image of the flamboyant orchestral conductor. Stokowski became an American citizen in 1915. His orchestral transcriptions and film appearances, especially in the Walt Disney film *Fantasia* (1940) brought the symphony orchestra to the notice of millions who had previously ignored it and made Stokowski famous. The light classical, orchestral music content of this film and its revealing graphic accompaniments taught many that classical music could be greatly enjoyed. Throughout his career he continued to scandalize the music establishment by his transparent bids to popularize both himself and the symphony orchestra. He would, for instance, have a spotlight playing on himself when conducting. Stokowski conducted the Philadelphia orchestra from the age of 25 until he was 51. He then took up film music and conducted the scores for a number of films. He was co-conductor of the NBC Orchestra, with Toscanini, from the age of 59 to 61, and then, sequentially, of the New York City Symphony Orchestra, the New York Philharmonic, the Houston Symphony Orchestra (age 73 to 78) and, from the age of 80 to 90, of the American Symphony Orchestra.

Stradivari, Antonio (c. 1644–1737) The Italian violin-maker of Cremona, Stradivari was probably the most celebrated maker of all time, who made over 1,000 violins, violas and cellos and who was still working and producing superb instruments at the age of 94. Some of the instruments he made after the age of 90 show subtle indications of loss of his highest abilities – there is, for instance, perceptible irregularity in the inlaying of the purfling strip near the edges of the plates – but even these instruments stand high in comparison with those of the best other makers in their prime.

Stravinski, Igor Fedorovich (1882–1971) This Russian-born American composer was noted for his radical break with classicism. His work, especially the ballet suite *The Rite of Spring* (1913), created a scandal as much for its content as for the, to many incomprehensible, quality of the music. Stravinski, now regarded by many as the most important composer of the 20th century, also wrote the ballet scores *The Firebird* (1910) and *Petrushka* (1911). He then produced the neoclassical works *Oedipus Rex* (1927) and the *Symphony of Psalms* (1930). In the 1950s he embraced serial techniques, which he used in the *Canticum Sacrum*, produced when he was 73, the ballet *Agon*, produced when he was 75 and *Requiem Canticles*, first performed when Stravinski was 84.

Tennyson, Alfred Lord (1809–92) Tennyson was an English poet who was Poet Laureate from the age of 41 to the time of his death. His best-known poems include *The Lady of Shalott* (1832), *Morte d'Arthur* (1842), the collection *In Memoriam* (1850) and *Idylls of the King* (1859). Tennyson continued to publish poetry right up to the time of his death at the age of 83.

Theophrastus (c. 372–c. 287 BC) This Greek philosopher from Lesbos studied under Aristotle and wrote extensively. Most of his work has been lost but his book *Characters of Men*, containing 30 studies of different personality types, remains in print to this day. Theophrastus began this brilliant work at the age of 90 and was interrupted only by his death.

Titian (Tiziano Vecellio) (c. 1487–1576) Titian was an Italian painter of the Venetian school, one of the greatest painters of the Renaissance and one of the most influential masters in the history of European art. At least 400 surviving paintings are reliably attributed to Titian, and he certainly painted many more during his long and active career. Titian is especially noted for his religious and mythological works, such as *Bacchus and Ariadne, The Entombment, Venus of Urbino* and *The Crown of Thorns.* He was greatly in demand, also, as a portrait painter and these, too, are highly notable. He painted *Shepherd and Nymph* when well into his 80s.

Tito, Josip Broz (1892–1980) This Yugoslav statesman led the communist guerrilla resistance to German occupation during World War II. Tito was leader of Yugoslavia from the age of 53 until his death at 88. He was Prime Minister from 1945 to 1953 and President from 1953 to 1980. Under his rule Yugoslavia enjoyed a long period of peace, prosperity and absence of ethnic conflict.

Tolstoy, Leo (1828–1910) Count Lev Nikolayevich Tolstoy was a Russian novelist, short-story writer and philosopher. He is acknowledged as Russia's greatest novelist. He started writing seriously in his 20s during military service, but his first notable work, *The Cossacks,* appeared when he was 35, some seven years after leaving the army. He then wrote his two best-known novels *War and Peace* (1865–69) and *Anna Karenina* (1875–77). After these books were published he entered a crisis period, detailed in his books *Confessions* (1879) and *Memoirs of a Madman* (1884). These describe how he conceived a philosophy of life based on poverty, non-violence, rejection of militarism, hard work and self-improvement. His doctrines became widely influential and, together with his novels, made him famous. He continued to write, producing *The Death of Ivan Ilych* (1886), *The Devil* (1889), *The Kreutzer Sonata* (1890), *Master and Man* (1895), *What Is Art?* (1897), *Father Sergius* (1898), *Resurrection* (1899) and *Hadji Murad* (1904), when he was 76.

Toscanini, Arturo (1867–1959) Italian musician who became one of the world's best-known and most popular orchestral conductors, Toscanini's career started as a cellist in an opera orchestra in Rio where, at the age of 19, when the conductor abruptly left, he took over and conducted the whole of Verdi's *Aida* without a score. He was involved in the premier performances of Verdi's *Otello,* Leoncavallo's *I Pagliacci* and Puccini's *La Bohème.* In 1898 he became chief conductor at La Scala, Milan and in 1908 was appointed conductor at the New York Metropolitan Opera. Later, he was principal conductor of the New York Philharmonic Orchestra and of the NBC Symphony Orchestra. He travelled extensively as a visiting conductor and made numerous recordings. Toscanini continued to conduct until the age of 87.

Travers, Ben (1886-1980) Travers was a British dramatist, best known for his successful stage farces. After studying the plays of Pinero, Travers went to work in the office of John Lane of the Bodley Head. Lane published his first novel, *The Dippers*, in 1922. Travers then rewrote this book as a stage farce which ran for 173 performances. He followed this with *A Cuckoo in the Nest* which was also turned into a farce and was produced at the Aldwych theatre with cast including Yvonne Arnaud, Mary Brough, Ralph Lynn, J. Robertson Hare and himself. This was a great success and in the next seven years Travers wrote eight more farces: *Rookery Nook* (1926), *Thark* (1927), *Plunder* (1928), *A Cup of Kindness* (1929), *A Night Like This* (1930), *Turkey Time* (1931), *Dirty Work* (1932) and *A Bit of a Test* (1933). These earned a great deal of money. Travers continued to write plays, film scripts and short stories. He gave distinguished service during the war and afterwards continued to write. Most remarkably, at the age of 89 his sophisticated, sex-centred play *The Bed Before Yesterday* was produced at the Lyric. With Joan Plowright in the lead it was immensely successful. Travers remained enthusiastic, amusing and of lively wit right up to the time of his death at the age of 94.

Verdi, Giuseppe (1813-1901) Verdi was an Italian composer of operas, including *Nabucco* (1842), *Macbeth* (1847), *Rigoletto* (1851), *Il Trovatore* (1853), *La Traviata* (1853), *Simon Boccanegra* (1857), *La Forza del Destino* (*The Force of Destiny*) (1862), *Don Carlos* (1867) and *Aïda* (1871). He appeared to give up the writing of operas at the age of 58 and produced little music until, at the age of 75, he wrote *Otello* (1887) and then, at the age of 80, produced his greatest masterpiece *Falstaff* (1893). These two operas, based on Shakespearean plots, were his finest achievements.

Victoria Regina (1819-1901) Queen of the United Kingdom from the age of 18 until her death at the age of 82, Victoria reigned for longer than any other British monarch. She married Prince Albert of Saxe-Coburg-Gotha in 1840 when she was 21 and remained a mourning widow after his early death 21 years later. She had borne him nine children and her many descendants helped to fill most of the thrones of Europe. Among her grandchildren were Emperor William II of Germany and Alexandra, consort of Tsar Nicholas II of Russia. Victoria tried to rule as an autocrat during the most expansive phase of the British Empire, working mainly through the two Prime Ministers Gladstone and Disraeli. The latter, however, whom she greatly admired, was clever enough to flatter her into cooperating with his own purposes. Victoria's popularity

264 Guide to Health in Later Life

declined for a time as a result of her withdrawal after Albert's death but later recovered and she became a widely approved symbol of British imperialism. Disraeli made her Empress of India in 1876. At her death she was mourned by millions.

Wallis, Barnes (1887-1979) This English aeronautical engineer and inventor was best known for his idea of the bouncing bomb which was used in 1943 to destroy Ruhr dams during World War II. Wallis started as a marine engineer and then moved to the airship department of Vickers Ltd. There, in the late 1920s he designed the airship R100 which successfully flew across the Atlantic. Established as an aircraft structural engineer Wallis went on to design the Wellesley and Wellington bombers, which proved important during the war. When well into his 60s Wallis perfected the 'swing-wing' principle which made the Tornado fighter-bomber possible. Wallis lived to be 92.

Walton, Izaak (1593-1683) Walton was an English writer, best known for *The Compleat Angler*, one of the most popular and successful books on fishing ever written. Subtitled *The Contemplative Man's Recreation*, this book is a description of English rivers and fishponds and their fish, and of fishing equipment, interspersed with short philosophical essays, moral reflections, verses and scraps of dialogue. Walton published this book when he was 60 but greatly enlarged and improved it and the fifth edition came out when he was 83. He wrote many other works including a number of excellent biographies of his near contemporaries, such as Donne, Wooton and Hooker. The last of his 'Lives' – that of George Sanderson – was published when Walton was 85.

Wayne, John (1907-79) The American film actor, born Marion Michael Morrison, Wayne appeared in more than 150 films, usually as the star. He was noted especially for his many Westerns, which include *Stagecoach* (1939), *The Long Voyage Home* (1940), *Red River* (1948), *She Wore a Yellow Ribbon* (1949), *They Were Expendable* (1952), *The Quiet Man* (1952), *The Searchers* (1956), *Rio Bravo* (1959), *The Alamo* (1960) and *The Green Berets* (1968). At the age of 57 he was discovered to be suffering from cancer, but at 62 won an Oscar for the film *True Grit* (1969).

Wellington, Duke of (1769-1852) Arthur Wellesley was a British soldier and statesman and victor over Napoleon in 1815. After Waterloo Wellington, known as The Great Duke, went into politics and served in several Tory ministries. He became Prime Minister of Britain at the age of 59 and served for two years. He was again Army Commander-in-Chief from the age of 73 until he died at the age of 83. Still a national hero, his funeral was a major national event.

Wells, H.G. (1866–1946) Wells, a British writer, came to fame when he wrote some of the earliest high-quality science fiction. These stories include *The Time Machine* (1895), *The Island of Dr Moreau* (1896) and *The War of the Worlds* (1898). Wells was a prolific writer of novels and non-fiction works, including much political writing. He produced well over 100 books, including *The Outline of History* (1920), and an enormous amount of journalism. Like many other people of great energy, he was highly sexed. His 10-year love affair with Rebecca West has been extensively documented. At the age of 60, having broken with Rebecca when he was 57, Wells had a passionate love affair with another woman and discovered in himself unsuspected sexual powers.

West, Mae (1892–1980) West was an American film actress who, largely because of her preoccupation with sexiness and sexual innuendo remained a legend, both in the United States and elsewhere for more than 50 years. Occasionally she went too far; in 1926 she was jailed for ten days after being convicted of obscenity. Immensely quick-witted and humorous and enormously energetic, she started in burlesque and went on to become a successful playwright and screen scriptwriter. Mae 'Come up and see me sometime' West starred in her own plays *Sex* (1926), *Drag* (1927) and *Diamond Lil* (1928) and in her films *She Done Him Wrong* (1933), *I'm No Angel* (1933), *Going to Town* (1934) and *My Little Chickadee* (1940). At the age of 77 she made a successful appearance in Gore Vidal's *Myra Breckinridge* and, at 84 she starred in the film *Sextette*.

Wodehouse, Pelham Grenville (1881–1975) This English-born American author was renowned for his comic novels of the socially unenlightened aristocracy of England, their trivial preoccupations and their relationship with their intellectual superiors in the lower classes. Characters such as the hair-brained clubman Bertie Wooster, with his total dependence on the ingenious, infinitely respectful but fundamentally contemptuous Jeeves, have taken their place in the pantheon of English comic literature. Wodehouse was a master of witty prose, transferred epithet and bizarre quotation and won high praise from critics as a notable stylist. He wrote 96 novels, all of which continued to sell well for many years. In addition to the novels, Wodehouse wrote 18 plays and the lyrics for 33 musical shows, including *Oh, Boy!* (1917), *Show Boat* (1927) and *Anything Goes* (1934). Wodehouse published his final Jeeves book at the age of 90, having published no less than 13 books in his 80s. He became an American citizen in 1955 but was knighted at the age of 94 shortly before he died.

Woolworth, F.W. (1852–1919) This American entrepreneur, after several years as a farm worker and shop assistant, founded what became an international chain of department stores selling inexpensive goods. The original Woolworth shops were known as the 'five and ten' stores because goods on sale were available at two prices only – five cents and ten cents. The formula was an immense success and when translated to Britian in 1910 was equally successful for many years before being overtaken by rival chain establishments. By the time of his death at 66 Woolworth was in control of over 1,000 branches and had opened his business headquarters in what was, at the time the tallest building in the world – the Woolworth Building in New York City.

Wright, Frank Lloyd (1869–1959) Wright was an American architect and writer – his designs included the Imperial Hotel, Tokyo, when he was 47, Fallingwater (Kaufmann House) when he was 67, the Guggenheim Museum, New York when he was 74 and many private houses. His philosophy of 'organic architecture' sought to achieve a close relationship between buildings and their natural surroundings. Wright's influence on modern house design was enormous and is largely responsible for current 'open-plan' patterns, enormous windows, terraces and low sweeping roof lines. He believed that buildings should use reinforced concrete in the same way as natural objects such as sea shells and snail shells used calcium. He also came to believe that very tall buildings could be built like trees with a deeply rooted central trunk from which floors were cantilevered like branches. Wright worked right up to the time of his death at the age of 89 and his largest-ever design, completed just before he died, was built afterward.

Useful Addresses

Age Concern England
(National Council on Ageing)
Astral House
1268 London Road
London SW16
Tel: 0181 679 8000

Age Concern London
54 Knatchbull Road
London SE5
Tel: 0171 737 3456

Age Well Project
Leisure Activities for Elders
St John's Community Centre
Albert Road
London E16
Tel: 0171 511 3692

Alzheimer's Disease Society
National Office
10 Greencoat Place
London SE1
Tel: 0171 306 0833
Recorded information: 0800 318771

Arthritis and Rheumatism Council
25 Bradiston Road
London W9
Tel: 0181 964 5590

Arthritis Care
5 Grosvenor Crescent
London SW1
LinkLine: 0800 289170

Association for Disabled and
Elderly Persons
375 High Street
London E15
Tel: 0181 519 3267

British Council for Prevention of
Blindness
12 Harcourt Street
London W1
Tel: 0171 724 3716

British Council of Ballroom
Dancing
240 Merton Road
London SW19
Tel: 0181 545 0085

British Deaf Association
25 Cockspur Street
London SW1
Tel: 0171 839 5566

British Diabetic Association
10 Queen Anne Street
London W1
Tel: 0171 323 1531

British Geriatrics Society
1 St Andrews Place
London NW1
Tel: 0171 935 4004

British Heart Foundation
14 Fitzhardinge Street
London W1
Tel: 0171 935 0185

British Nursing Association
24-hour Nursing and Home Care
21 Widmore Road
Bromley
Kent
Tel: 0181 464 7426

British Society of Rehabilitation
Medicine
Royal College of Physicians
St Andrews Place
London NW1
Tel: 0181 550 0114

British Society of Rheumatology
41 Eagle Street
London WC1
Tel: 0171 242 3313

CancerLink Ltd
Support and Information
17 Britannia Street
London WC1
Tel: 0171 833 2451

Cancer Relief Macmillan Fund
15 Britten Street
London SW3
Tel: 0171 351 7811

Cancer You Are Not Alone
31 Church Road
London E12
Tel: 0181 553 0333

Carers National Association
20–25 Glasshouse Yard
London EC1A
Tel: 0171 490 8818

Centre for Policy on Ageing
25 Ironmonger Road
London EC1
Tel: 0171 253 1787

Cruse–Bereavement Care
Cruse Bereavement Line
Tel: 0181 332 7227

Disabled Advice Service
305 Garrett Lane
London SW18
Tel: 0181 870 7437

Disabled Living Foundation
380 Harrow Road
London W9
Tel: 0171 289 6111

Elderly Accommodation Council
46 Chiswick High Road
London W4
Tel: 0181 995 8320

Help the Aged
St James Walk
London EC1
Tel: 0171 253 0253

National Alcohol Help Line
Tel: 0345 320202
Dial and listen: Mercury freeCall
0500 801802

National Association of
Bereavement Services
20 Norton Folgate
London E1
Tel: 0171 247 1080

National Care Homes Association
5 Bloomsbury Place
London WC1
Tel: 0171 436 1871

National Council for Hospice and
Palliative Care Services
59 Bryanston Street
London W1
Tel: 0171 611 1153

National Nursing Agency
44 Lewisham High Street
London SE13
Tel: 0181 297 2744

RNIB Talking Book Service
Nuffield Library
Mount Pleasant
Wembley
Tel: 0181 903 6666

Royal Association in Aid of Deaf
People
27 Old Oak Road
London W3
Tel: 0181 743 6187

Royal London Hospitals
Bancroft Unit, Care for the Elderly
Tel: 0171 377 7000

Royal National Institute for the
Blind
224 Great Portland Street
London W1
Tel: 0171 388 1266

Royal Society for the Prevention of
Accidents
Canon House
Priory Queensway
Birmingham
Tel: 0121 200 2461

The Samaritans
LinkLine: 0345 909090

Bibliography and References

'Age, ageing and intensive care' *Lancet*, 26 January 1991, p. 209.
'Ageing' Alex Comfort Lecture, *Journal of the Royal Society of Medicine*, December 1995, p. 698.
'Ageing biology' *Scientific American*, May 1989, p. 8.
'Ageing, amyloid and Alzheimer's' *New England Journal of Medicine*, 1 June 1989, p. 1484.
'Ageing and cell division, new enzyme found' *New Scientist* 7 October 1995, p. 19.
'Ageing and growing younger' *New Scientist*, 19 February 1994, p. 22.
Ageing and the Human Condition Gari Lesnoff-Caravaglia, Human Sciences Press, New York, 1982.
'Ageing at work' *Lancet*, 9 January 1993, p. 87.
'Ageing brain, ageing mind' *Scientific American* book *Mind and Brain*, 1993.
'Ageing brain and mind' *Scientific American*, special issue September 1992.
'Ageing drivers' *Journal of the Royal Society of Medicine*, April 1992 pp. 188, 199.
'Ageing population' *Lancet*, 3 June 1995, pp. 1386, 1409.
'Ageing skin treatment with retinoids' *Dermatology in Practice*, February 1990, p. 5.
A Good Age, Alex Comfort, Mitchell Beazley, London, 1977.
A Green Old Age A. Lacassagne, John Bale, Sons and Danielsson Ltd, London, 1923.
A Handbook of Psychogeriatric Care K. L. K. Trick and R. A. Daisley, Pitman Medical, Tunbridge Wells, 1980.
'Brain in ageing and in Alzheimer's disease' *Lancet*, 17 September 1994, p. 769.
Caring for Someone at Home, Gail Elkington and Jill Harrison, Hodder and Stoughton, 1996.
'Calorie restriction and aging' *Scientific American*, January 1996, p. 32.
Caring in a Crisis seven handbooks published by Age Concern.
Completing the Circle: New Ways of Life After Fifty, Margaret Torrie, Turnstone Press, Wellingborough, 1982.
'Dementia, ageing and stress' *Lancet*, 18 March 1995, p. 666.
Dictionary of National Biography, Oxford University Press, Oxford, 1992.
Directory of Aids for Disabled and Elderly People, Anne Darnborough and Derek Kinrade, Woodhead-Faulkener, Cambridge, 1986.
Directory for Disabled People, Anne Darnborough and Derek Kinrade, Woodhead-Faulkener, Cambridge, 1985.
Endurance of Life, Macfarlane Burnet, Cambridge University Press, Cambridge, 1978.

Evolutionary Biology of Ageing, Michael R. Rose, Oxford University Press, 1991.
'Factors in ageing, free radicals, radiation etc' *Journal of the Royal Society of Medicine*, 3 September 1994, p. 540.
'Fractals and chaos in ageing' *Journal of the American Medical Association*, 1 April 1992, p. 1806.
'Free radicals and ageing, protein oxidation' *Science*, 28 August 1992, p. 1220.
'Genes and ageing book review' *Lancet*, 9 July 1994, p. 115.
'Glutathione and ageing' *Lancet*, 19 November 1994, p. 1379.
Health Care of the Elderly, Gari Lesnoff-Caravaglia, Human Sciences Press, New York, 1980.
'Human ageing' *Scientific American*, April 1993, p. 18.
'Human telomeres' *Scientific American*, August 1991, p. 34.
'Is senile dementia age-related or ageing-related?' *Lancet*, 7 October 1995, p. 931.
Longevity, Senescence and the Genome, Caleb E. Finch, University of Chicago Press, 1990.
Man Against Ageing, Robert S. de Ropp, Victor Gollancz Ltd, London, 1961.
Memory Thomas Butler, Blackwell, Oxford, 1989.
Modern Biological Theories of Ageing, H. R. Warner *et al*, Raven Press, 1987.
Neuroimmunomodulation: Interventions in Ageing and Cancer, Ed. Walter Pierpaoli and Novera Herbert Spector, New York Academy of Sciences, 1988.
Offices, Essays and Selected Letters, Marcus Cicero, Everyman's Library, J M Dent & Co, London.
Old Age Simone de Beauvoir, Penguin, London, 1977.
Ourselves Growing Older, Paula Brown Doress and Diana Laskin Siegal, Simon & Schuster, New York 1987.
Pensioners and Carers, Paul Brown, Anne Mountfield and Alka Patel, Directory of Social Change, London, 1995.
Retirement, A Guide to Good Living, Renee Myers, Crowood Press, 1990.
'Telomeres, cancer, culture and immortality' *New Scientist*, 27 November 1993, p. 18.
'Telomeres, cancer and immortality' *New England Journal of Medicine*, 6 April 1995 p. 955.
'Telomeres and telomerase' *Lancet*, 15 April 1995, p. 935.
'Telomere repair, telomerase for immortality?' *New Scientist*, 9 September 1995 p. 16.
The Biology of Human Ageing, Ed. A. H. Bittles and K. J. Collins, Cambridge University Press, Cambridge, 1986.
The Carer's Companion, Richard Corney, Winslow Press, Bicester, 1994.
The Neurobiology of Memory, Yadin Dudai, Oxford University Press, 1989.
The MsTaken Body, Jeanette Kupfermann, Robson Books, London, 1979.

The New Old: Struggling for Decent Ageing, Ed. Ronald and Beatrice Gross and Sylvia Seidman, Doubleday, New York, 1978.

'The oldest old' *Scientific American*, January 1995, p. 50.

The Silent Passage: Menopause, Gail Sheehy, HarperCollins, Glasgow, 1993.

The Social Challenge of Ageing, Ed. David Hobman, Croom Helm, London, 1978.

Tolstoy's Bicycle, Jeremy Baker, Helicon, Oxford, 1995.

To the Good Long Life, Morton Puner, Macmillan Press for the Open University, London, 1974.

Vitality and Ageing: Implications of the Rectangular Curve, James F. Fries and Lawrence M. Crapo, W. H. Freeman and Co, 1981.

'Why do we age? ageing' *Scientific American*, December 1992, p. 86.

Your Brain Is Younger Than You Think, Richard M. Torack, Nelson-Hall, Chicago, 1981.

Euthanasia

'American vote on euthanasia' *Lancet*, 24 October 1992, p. 1028.

'Assisted suicide euthanasia' *British Medical Journal*, 24 August 1991 p. 431.

'Assisted death euthanasia' *Lancet*, 8 September 1990, p. 610.

'Assisted death euthanasia' *New England Journal of Medicine*, 5 November 1992, p. 1384.

'Australia's euthanasia law' *British Medical Journal*, 3 June 1995, p. 1427.

'California rejects euthanasia' *British Medical Journal*, 14 November 1992, p. 1175.

'Canadian euthanasia debate' *British Medical Journal*, 26 February 1994, p. 554.

'China considers voluntary euthanasia' *British Medical Journal*, 25 March 1995, p. 761.

'Doctor euthanasia accused of murder' *British Medical Journal*, 26 September 1992, p. 731.

'Dutch euthanasia' *British Medical Journal*, 13 February 1993, p. 415.

'Euthanasia in Holland' *British Medical Journal*, 12 February 1994, p. 431.

'Euthanasia in Holland' *Lancet*, 10 March 1990, p. 591.

'Euthanasia in Netherlands' *British Medical Journal*, 21 May 1994, p. 1346.

'Euthanasia dying rites' *New Scientist*, 20 June 1992, p. 25.

'Euthanasia editorial' *British Medical Journal*, 26 September 1992, p. 727.

'Euthanasia in Germany' *British Medical Journal*, 6 February 1993, p. 351.

'Euthanasia new issues' *British Medical Journal*, 7 December 1991, p. 1422.

'Euthanasia widening gap public-profession' *Lancet* 29 July 1995 p. 259.

'Euthanasia debate' *British Medical Journal*, 3 June 1995, p. 1466.

'Euthanasia safeguards' *New England Journal of Medicine*, 16 July 1992, p. 201.

'Euthanasia in dementia' *British Medical Journal*, 22 May 1993, p. 1364.

'Euthanasia in Oregon' *Lancet*, 18 December 1993, p. 1543.

'Euthanasia doctor convicted of murder' *Lancet*, 26 September 1992, p. 782.

'Euthanasia Dutch way of death' *New Scientist*, 20 June 1992, p. 28.

'Euthanasia Dutch view' *British Medical Journal*, 25 June 1994, p. 1656.

'Euthanasia Dutch prosecutors get tough' *British Medical Journal*, 30 April 1994, p. 1119.

'Euthanasia Lords judgement' *Lancet*, 19 February 1994, p. 430.

'Euthanasia book review' *British Medical Journal*, 29 May 1993, p. 1487.

'Euthanasia around the world' *British Medical Journal*, 4 January 1992, p. 7.

'Euthanasia, debate in Canada' *Lancet*, 26 February 1994, p. 534.

'Euthanasia' *British Journal of Hospital Medicine*, July 1990, p. 11.

'Euthanasia' *British Journal of Hospital Medicine*, October 1990, p. 242.

'Euthanasia' *British Medical Journal*, 17 December 1988, p. 1593.

'Euthanasia' *Lancet*, 10 May 1986, p. 1085.

'Euthanasia' *Lancet*, 14 September 1991, p. 669.

'Euthanasia' *Lancet*, 2 December 1989, p. 1321.

'Euthanasia' *Lancet*, 8 May 1993, p. 1196.

'Gee whiz Dutch euthanasia on TV' *British Medical Journal*, 29 October 1994, p. 1107.

'GMC decision on euthanasia, case' *British Medical Journal*, 28 November 1992, p. 1311.

'Holland euthanasia legislation' *Lancet*, 13 February 1993, p. 426.

'Lords reject euthanasia' *British Medical Journal*, 26 February 1994, p. 553.

'Mercy killing euthanasia' *Journal of the American Medical Association*, 16 January 1991, p. 326.

'NHS doctors' attitudes to euthanasia' *British Medical Journal*, 21 May 1994, p. 1332.

'No to euthanasia in UK' *Lancet*, 14 May 1994, p. 1219.

'Right to die euthanasia' *British Medical Journal*, 21 March 1992, p. 765.

'Slow euthanasia' *British Medical Journal*, 19 May 1990, p. 1321.

'Will the Chinese legalize euthanasia?' *Lancet*, 25 March 1995, p. 783.

Index

accidents 84, 88, 89; *see also* falls
accommodation 84
  residential 98–9
  sheltered 84, 89–90
acne 160
acromegaly 34
acyclovir 79
adrenal glands 34
adrenaline 86
aerobics 92
aflatoxins 62
ageing
  philosophies 183–205
  processes 1–2, 9–14, 15–17, 151–2
ageist stereotype 166–7, 237
AIDS 9
alarm systems 89, 90, 96
alcohol consumption 13, 18, 27, 94, 101
alcohol toxicity 162
alendronate 33
allergy 86
alopecia 56, 57
Alzheimer's disease 102, 105, 109, 116, 117–21
  causes 119–21
  and Down's syndrome 119
  hereditary forms 118, 119
  and HRT 33
amino acids 2
aminoglycocides 100
amyloid precursor protein (APP) 119, 120
anabolic steroids 33
anaemia 57, 83
  pernicious 83, 116
  sickle cell 3, 148
anaesthetics 82
angina pectoris 18–19, 152–4
antibiotics 100, 116
anti-cancer drugs 57, 162

anticholinergic drugs 75–6
anti-depressant drugs 113–14, 121, 129
antimalarial drugs 57
antioxidants 143–52
  and Alzheimer's 120
vitamin sources 12, 18; *see also* vitamin A; vitamin C
anxiety 111, 117, 130, 169, 235
aortic aneurism 137
appetite 51–2
  loss 101, 116
apples 150, 151
aquarobics 92
arteries 17
  and free radicals 136–42
  vertebral 72–3
arthritis 86, 93, 101, 128; *see also* osteoarthritis; rheumatoid arthritis
artistic pursuits 179–80
asbestos workers 150
ascorbic acid *see* vitamin C
Aspergillus flavus 62
aspirin 20, 70, 101
atherosclerosis 17–28, 83, 87, 94
  and free radicals 136–42, 150–51, 153
  and mental functioning 141–2
  and post-menopausal women 32
  and telomeres 10
  and vertigo 72–3
athlete's foot 57

Bacon, Francis
  Essay on Youth and Age 199–200
  On death 233–5
bad breath 80
balance problems 71–3; *see also* falls

baldness 56
Balzac, Honoré de 124
basal cell carcinoma 53–4
Beauvoir, Simone de 204–5
bed rest, dangers of 73, 91
bed sores *see* pressure sores
Bell's palsy 79
bendrofluazide 100
benzodiazepam 100
bereavement 85, 113, 223
beta-amyloid protein 119–20
beta-blocker drugs 27, 57, 100
beta-carotene (provitamin A) 149, 152, 156, 158
biographies 237–66
Blackburn, Elizabeth H. 7, 8
bladder 37–40
  cancer 66
  see also urinary incontinence
Bland, Tony 226
blindness *see* eyesight
blood
  pressure 18, 20
    high (hypertension) 22, 25–8, 87, 129, 139
      drugs for 27–8, 129
  red blood cells 148, 162
  in stools 64
  tests before surgery 81
body heat regulation (hypothermia) 83, 88, 95
body weight 13, 18, 21; *see also* overweight
bones 34, 37, 144; *see also* osteoporosis
bowel cancer 63–5
brain
  and atherosclerosis 21–3
  cell loss 105
  damage
    and Alzheimer's 117–21
    and memory loss 109–10, 115–6

276 Guide to Health in Later Life

and the experience of dying
208, 209–10, 211
haemorrhage 22
mental processes 105–21
and Parkinsonism 77–8
tumour/blood clot 121
breast cancer 11, 31–2, 58, 61,
63, 66; *see also*
mastectomy
bronchitis 94
La Bruyère, *Characters*, 198–9
butyl-alpha-phenylnitrone
(BPN) 151
butylated hydroxyanisole
(BHA) 144
butylated hydroxytoluene
(BHT) 139

calcitonin 33
calcium 33–4
in foods 35
supplements 33, 37
cancer 6, 8, 9, 12, 58–69, 83,
87
danger signs 65
and diet 62–3
and free radicals 156–7, 162
and pain 66–8
and quality of life 68–9
and radiation 134
carbon disulphide poisoning
77
carbon monoxide poisoning
77
cardiac arrest 20
caring for elderly people
102–3, 121
carotenoids 149, 150
catalase 152
cataract 25, 46–9, 83
and free radicals 158–9
and vitamins 158, 159
catheterization 39–40, 76
cats 88
cell biology 2–12
censoriousness 171–2
cerebral artery thrombosis
137
cerebral haemorrhage 22; *see
also* stroke
ceruloplasmin 144
cervical cancer 35, 58
Chateaubriand, François 124
cheerfulness 172
chemical poisoning 77, 135,
162, 208
chest infections 88, 96
chicken pox 78
cholesterol 17–18, 23, 137,
138–9
chromosomes 4–8, 119, 120

Cicero, *De senectute*, 183–97
cimetidine 129
cirrhosis of the liver 85, 94
claudication 24
cognitive function, and
atherosclerosis 141–2
cold, effects of (hypothermia)
83, 88, 95
colitis 76
colon, cancer of 63–5
colostomy 64–5, 128
compulsions 111
computers 176–9
confusion 117, 118
constipation 77, 101
coronary arteries 18–21, 137
coronary thrombosis 17,
19–21, 31, 32, 137, 151
and free radicals 135, 138,
139–40, 154–6
and sexual expression 126,
129
corticosteroids 70
cortisol 86–7
cortisone 86–7
Cox, Nigel 225–6
Creutzfeldt–Jacob disease 116
criticism 171–2
crutches 96–7
Cushing's syndrome 34
cysteine 144

dance classes 92
day centres 84
deafness 42–4, 72, 79, 100,
114; *see also* hearing
death and dying
acceptance 218–19
denial 219–22
dignity 211
experiences of 207–10
fear 213–14
and the medical profession
210–11, 214–15
telling the patient 214–18
thoughts and writings 192–7,
233–6
defence mechanisms 110–11
dehydration 83, 88
delirium 115
delusions 114–15, 169
dementia 84, 102, 103, 115–17
causes 115–16, 121
and faecal incontinence 76
progressive 22
and propantheline 76
simple (pseudodementia)
112–14, 121
see also Alzheimer's disease
depression 30, 77, 83, 91, 112–14,
169

reactive 221–2
recognizing 113, 121
dermatitis 57
diabetes 34, 83, 87, 129, 162
diarrhoea 76, 101
diet 90
and ageing 11–12, 13
and atherosclerosis 21, 150
and cancer 62–3
and high blood pressure 27
and longevity 151–2
see also fat in diet
dietary fibre 63, 64, 77
digoxin 100
dilatation and curettage
(D & C) 35
disability
physical aids 179–81; *see
also* mobility; walking
and sexuality 126–9
disorientation 116, 117, 118
d'Israeli, Isaac 203
Curiosities of Literature 203
diuretic drugs 27, 100
diverticulitis 76
dizziness (vertigo) 71–2, 76,
79, 96
DNA 2–5, 7–9
and cancer 58–9, 157
and free radicals 133, 134,
135, 142–3, 157
mitochondrial DNA 142
dogs 88, 92
domestic help 84, 103
dopamine 77
replacement 78
Down's syndrome 119
D-penicillamine 144
drinking (alcohol) 13, 18, 27, 94
drug abuse 115
drugs
and instability/falls 72
and nail changes 57
over-the-counter 101
prescription 27, 57, 99–102
and sexual potency 129–30
side-effects 99–101
*see also specific drugs and
types of drug*
duodenal ulcers 70–71, 101, 120

ear, inner 42, 43, 71, 72, 100
and shingles 79
see also hearing
electro-convulsive therapy
(ECT) 114
embolism 23
emphysema 94
encephalitis 78
endometrial cancer 31, 33, 35–6
endorphins 209